D0371625

0   1000   2000

Scale of miles at the Equator

INTERNATIONAL
POLITICAL
ANALYSIS

David V. Edwards

The University of Texas

HOLT, RINEHART AND WINSTON, INC.
*New York   Chicago   San Francisco   Atlanta
Dallas   Montreal   Toronto   London   Sydney*

INTERNATIONAL POLITICAL ANALYSIS

To my teachers: professors and students

International Political Analysis by David V. Edwards
Copyright © 1969 by Holt, Rinehart and Winston, Inc.
Library of Congress Catalog Card Number: 69–17651
SBN: 03–074545–4
Printed in the United States of America
1 2 3 4 5 6 7 8 9

Preface

In these times, a concern for international politics needs no justification. However, with many introductory books on the subject available, the offering of another may. Most teachers of international politics, like most students of the subject, probably disagree in some measure with the approaches found in present texts, and could easily write a book based on their disagreements. But a minor disagreement hardly justifies yet another book.

My disagreement is, however, substantial. My experience as a teacher of international politics has led me to develop the approach I present in this book in an attempt to meet the two problems that I have found all available texts unable to surmount. The first of these problems results from what can fairly be termed the underdeveloped state of international relations as an academic discipline. It is clear that, while progress has been made, we have much to do before we can have high confidence in our findings and especially in our application of them to policy problems. As I attempt not just to state but to demonstrate in the text, this weakness seems to call for more carefully designed approaches to the major problems that confront us. I have chosen to concentrate here on war, crisis, alliance, and cooperative arms control. My approach is directed toward developing general theoretical explanations of the occurrence of these phenomena, not by concentrating on postulations of the motives and capabilities of states, but by concentrating on the behavior of decisionmakers and states and on the circumstances they find themselves in when wars, crises, and so on break out, develop, and terminate.

The second problem I have attempted to meet is pedagogical. It has gradually become clear to me that, to be profitable, an approach such as mine to the teaching of international politics requires an explicit consideration of general theory, and further — and most important — that effective learning can best be achieved if the student is encouraged to confront the challenge of theorizing himself, rather than simply told to learn the theories of others. This approach, based on my experience in experimenting with the design of my courses, is confirmed by the findings of educational psychologists. Learning is most efficient and generates the most enthusiasm when it is learning by *doing*, rather than by merely receiving. In a field where the generally accepted knowledge is as small as it still is in international politics, the emphasis on students engaging in their own theory-building is not only pedagogically sound but should lead to substantive improvement of the field itself. This is the rationale for my approach.

The book itself falls between the traditional approach, which emphasizes historical analysis of individual cases and of topics like war, and the emergent approaches, which emphasize the careful development and manipulation of data in an effort to create and test theoretical propositions that generalize about why things happen as they do. It does not employ the quantitative approaches that some on the frontiers of the discipline are now using, because these are not yet developed well enough and remain obstacles to the progress and enthusiasm of the student. However, those wishing to use these approaches will find that the essential conceptual and analytical groundwork for them is presented and developed here. Similarly, those who prefer a more traditional approach should find this volume quite compatible with their teaching methods. Indeed, the book benefits greatly from employing studies of the Cuban missile crisis, the Berlin blockade, and other interesting materials found in some present books. Teachers of nearly all persuasions should find that the text helps to encourage the student along profitable lines of analysis by contending that a study of individual cases will contribute toward the advancement of our understanding of the things that happen in international relations. At this time, when the old battles between realist and idealist and the newer battles between traditionalist and behavioralist seem to be dying down, this book attempts to uncover and employ the best from these schools, and concludes that their better elements are quite compatible—indeed, helpfully complementary.

Most authors are dependent on others for assistance in assessing and improving their manuscript, and here I have been particularly fortunate. Those who have read one or another version of the manuscript have come to it from rather different perspectives, and many have taken strong issue with major portions of it. The final book reflects many of their recommendations. Each would very likely have written a different book and perhaps none will easily recognize his effects on this one. Special credit belongs to Paul Y. Hammond and Charles A. McClelland for their painstaking and imaginatively comprehensive assessments and suggestions. Ernest L. May and I. William Zartman also read the entire manuscript and were both critical and encouraging. My colleague Francis A. Beer, and Sven Groennings, also helped by reading the entire manuscript and making encouraging comments. Eugene J. Meehan and Kenneth N. Waltz read parts of it, and, with their divergent views, made helpful contributions. Harrison Wagner over the years has debated with me most of the content of the book and my pedagogical approach and deserves much of the credit for it whether he is willing to accept it or not. Perhaps the greatest responsibility, however, lies with the hundreds of students who have read various versions of the manuscript and have kindly yet firmly criticized my efforts from the perspective that matters most—that of the student. Foremost in this category are Sharon Weldon and Susan Saegert. Further, Peter van Leuven's occasional research assistance was particularly helpful, and Billy Pope assisted with page proofs and indexing.

It is pleasant to enumerate my underlying intellectual debts in the creation of this work. I began my study of international relations under Kenneth N. Waltz as an undergraduate at Swarthmore College. Our views about politics differed drastically, and his pessimism about my radical solutions to problems spurred me to greater realism (with a lowercase *r*). At Harvard I studied primarily under Stanley Hoffmann, who continually insisted that I cope with history and respect theory; Morton H. Halperin and Henry A. Kissinger, both of whom encouraged my interest in military affairs; and Thomas Schelling, who opened multitudes of doors to me by demonstrating that fresh approaches to political analysis drawn from the study of everything from family life to the economy can often illuminate problems that conventional political science cannot. I also studied social thought with Barrington Moore, Jr., in a way that I often felt at the time had limited promise, but that ultimately enabled me to begin the effort to develop and test manageable explanatory propositions about society and politics.

I recount these stages in my education partly out of gratitude and partly because they have had a crucial impact on the nature of this book, for my approach, whatever else may be said of it, is an eclectic evolution of divergent influences.

But by far my greatest debt, and my greatest pleasure, has been my students at the University of Texas. They have not only stimulated me—which is important and inevitable if one takes teaching seriously—but much more importantly, they have demonstrated conclusively, in every course I have taught, that they can cope effectively with, learn impressively from, and improve imaginatively upon the departures from conventional teaching that I increasingly attempt and that this book reflects.

My students and I together have developed the approach in this book. Some may feel that it demands too much of the student; and some may think that it does not teach because it does not convey all the facts that may be required by the student and found in most textbooks. Our experience undermines these reservations. It is my hope that increasing adoption of this kind of approach—not just in international politics but in all the social sciences—will enable students to join scholars quickly and effectively as active minds and constructive contributors to the knowledge we so desperately require to reform our societies and mend our relations.

Austin, Texas   *D.V.E.*
March 1969

Contents

List of Illustrations

[1]Except for the Cuba-centric map, all maps are Mercator projections, which means that distances are greater the farther the distance from the equator.

PART I
INTRODUCTION

chapter 1

International Politics

A Crisis Develops Just after 8 o'clock Tuesday morning, October 16, 1962, McGeorge Bundy, United States Special Assistant for National Security Affairs, reported to President Kennedy that "there is now hard photographic evidence, which you will see a little later, that the Russians have offensive missiles in Cuba." After making certain that the information was accurate beyond challenge, Kennedy called an emergency meeting of his top advisers for later that morning.[1] The next six days were filled with continuous intensive policymaking in the highest echelons of the American government. Everyone involved attempted to pursue his regular activities in order to avoid arousing suspicion until the American response to the Soviet initiative had been determined and the President could announce it publicly. By Sunday, decisions had been made and plans formulated. At a final meet-

[1]See the fascinating account of the development of the crisis and American policymaking in Elie Abel, *The Missile Crisis* (Philadelphia: Lippincott, 1966).

ing to check preparations, Secretary of State Dean Rusk advised participants to get as much rest as possible before Monday evening's address by the President, because "by this time tomorrow, gentlemen, we will be in a flaming crisis."[2]

When confronted suddenly with a situation perceived to be a serious threat to a nation's security, policymakers immediately ask two things: What can we do about it? and If we do such-and-such, what will they do? But depending of course on the amount of time available for deliberation and decision, these reactions are likely to be based on answers (sometimes only semiconscious) to several more basic questions.

In the case of the missile crisis, for example, where there was a period of careful deliberation, American policymakers first established precisely what it was the Soviet Union had done —how many and what kinds of missiles and other threatening weapons were introduced into Cuba—and then began to analyze the motives behind the Soviet Union's action. Later they might delve more deeply into the causes of the event, particularly if the action seemed to be irrational or based on poor information rather than on sound or promising expectations. But for the present their job was to figure out, at least roughly, what had led the Soviets to make such a provocative move.

The next major question for American policymakers to attempt to answer was, What effects was the Soviet action likely to have on the U.S.; more specifically, What impact would it have on American interests in the Western Hemisphere and on Soviet-American relations in general?

Their third immediate problem, arising out of the previous questions, was to evaluate the Soviet move and the new international situation thus created; to decide whether the United States could accept the action, and if it could not, how far it should go in opposing it.

The fourth question concerned what steps the United States should take in response. But to answer this, the American policymakers had first to answer the previous ones, and then to consider possible responses from the standpoint of both the strategic situation and American capabilities, assessing the likely costs and benefits in that light.

Once they had answered these four basic questions, U.S.

[2]Roger Hilsman, *To Move a Nation* (New York: Doubleday, 1967), p. 207.

officials could then decide on their policy and begin to implement it. At that point they were "in a flaming crisis" and the
strategists of both nations were attempting to "manage" it so
as to gain whatever advantage each side could.

These questions are similar to the ones that concern us in
this book. We study international politics for various reasons,
the main one being merely to understand more fully why events
such as a missile crisis or a Vietnam war come about. We may
also wish to be better informed so that we can be more responsible
citizens, not just as voters but also as participants in efforts to
affect government policy. Some of us are interested in advancing
the academic discipline of international politics for whatever
ends that may serve. But however varied our objectives, we do
have in common an innate curiosity about the nature and causes
of events, and that is what leads us to study international politics.
Because we are not directly involved in decisionmaking we have
the time and leisure for careful study and perhaps the possibility
of being somewhat more objective than the government decisionmakers. These advantages, if we can attain them, will be
particularly important, for the study is unquestionably a difficult
one.

We shall need to acquire a general knowledge of the nature, causes, and patterns of international relations, which we
can then apply to particular instances or cases to increase our
understanding of them. Hopefully, we can then make more
relevant and useful recommendations on foreign policy to those
who must make quick decisions in surprise events such as the
missile crisis or extremely complicated determinations in such
extended affairs as the Vietnam war.

Some of the knowledge we need is basically descriptive.
We need to know the nature of the situation that the policymaker
finds himself in. More generally, we must know what actually
happens in the world and the process by which various types
of events develop. By this we mean, in the terminology we
will use, a theory of international politics that reveals what
causes or factors have what effects under what conditions. Whenever a nation chooses a policy or carries out an action, the decision is a result of, or is based on, its theory of international
politics. This theory is usually tacit or implicit or perhaps even
unconscious, but it is there. The same is true of scholars or citizens who analyze or recommend policies. They usually begin

with a brief description of an international political situation —
generally a crisis, a war, or another such challenge to the country's interests — and then recommend a course of action in response to the challenge. Sometimes such recommendations include a statement of the objectives which they believe the nation
should pursue. But rarely do such statements include an *explicit
connection* between these objectives and the policy recommended. The *implicit connection* must indicate, given the objectives and the situation described, that the recommended action
will achieve the objectives because the world operates in a certain
specified way. In other words, when a nation undertakes a particular course of action, it brings about a particular change in
the political situation, and that change is supposed to include
or result in the attainment of the objective sought.

Thus if the United States faces a crisis over Berlin in which
the Soviet Union attempts to cut off Western access to West Berlin
(as happened in the Berlin crisis of 1948–1949), a recommendation that the United States begin an airlift to the city (as was
done) or a recommendation that the United States threaten to
bomb or begin bombing targets in the Soviet Union (as was not
done, of course) should indicate what effects the action recommended is expected to have. And it should also indicate how
these effects will result in the attainment of the American objective (in this case, regaining regular access to the city) without
unacceptable costs (such as a major ground war in Europe or,
a nuclear war between the United States and the Soviet Union).

If the policy recommendation is not based upon an understanding of the dynamics of world politics shared by government
officials and by advisers, the former may not be able to compre-
hend the recommendation of the latter, much less be able to accept or reject the recommendation on its merits.

For our analyses to be beneficial then, they must include
(at least tacitly) valid general propositions about the way international politics works. In other words, our knowledge must include statements that are applicable not just to a single case but
to any similar case, and these statements must be as accurate as
possible. To develop such statements we must carefully study
what actually happens in international politics. To be sure that
they are valid, we must test the statements we develop against
each other for consistency and against the historical record in

order to insure that they apply to cases other than those from which they were developed.

This difficult task is of great import if we are to increase our ability to understand world politics in this age of continuing revolutions in communication, transportation, nationalism, and of other novel developments. It is especially important if we are to develop the ability to criticize national policies and to suggest improvements in them. In short, the attainment of both these objectives is crucial to the development of a satisfactory theory of international politics.

The Nature of International Politics
International politics is made up of many different types of happenings: war, crisis, alliance, diplomatic nego-tiation, arms race, arms control agree-ment, and so on. If we listed everything that has international political implications, we would probably decide to include not only these obviously political occurrences but also events like the Olympic Games, which contribute to national prestige and thus at times raise political disputes over which nations should be invited to compete in them. Similarly, we would probably include international organizations such as the United Nations, as well as international individuals such as the Secretary-General of the United Nations or the Pope.

The easy way of deciding what to include and exclude in our study is to rely on a definition of "international politics." A definition of the sort found in dictionaries is basically a his-torical record of the ways in which a word has been used.[3] We rely on dictionaries, and on past usage in general, in order to understand what others have meant when they used these words and how we ourselves will probably be understood when we speak and write. Words have no *intrinsic* meaning (although they do generally have root meanings from which they were con-structed and from which their present usages have developed), and so we can define a word in any way we please or in any way we find useful. But if we choose to define a word in a way sig-

[3]The most comprehensive such record is the *Oxford English Dictionary* (Oxford: Oxford University Press, 1933), which gives representative uses of each term from its first to its most recent use.

nificantly different from the way others have defined it, we must preface our use of it with a reminder of our different meaning for it, a task which will prove to be quite tedious.

Popular usage is no help either. People tend to use words carelessly, and as scholars we wish to attach more precise meanings to our terms so that they clearly refer to the phenomena we are describing and *only* to them. Thus in coming chapters we shall attempt to define "war" basically by describing in specific terms those happenings people have generally called war, focusing on features common to all wars (such as physical force employed by several parties against each other) and paying particular attention to those features that vary from war to war (such as the countries fighting it, the weapons they employ, and whether or not it is declared in accordance with international law). We shall do the same for the other phenomena we study, such as crisis, alliance, and cooperative control.

"International"

For the moment, our concern is with the concept "international politics" and more particularly with the two words that constitute it. According to the *Oxford English Dictionary*, the word "international" was first used by the British philosopher Jeremy Bentham in 1780. He spoke of "international jurisprudence" (today we would say "international law"), adding: "The word *international*, it must be acknowledged, is a new one; though, it is hoped sufficiently analogous and intelligible. It is calculated to express, in a more significant way, the branch of law which goes commonly under the name of the *law of nations*."[4] The term has since come to refer to those relations carried on or otherwise existing between different nations.

"Politics"

The term "politics" derives from the Greek word *polis*, or "city," and more directly from *politikos*, "of a citizen." This suggestion that politics concerns affairs of the city or of the citizen is not particularly helpful to us here, but neither are most present dictionary definitions of politics, which suggest either

[4]Jeremy Bentham, *Principles of Legislation*, XVII, Sec. 25, quoted in OED, Vol. 5, page 410.

the science and art of government or factional scheming within a group.[5]

"International Politics"

Do these words as we generally use them adequately describe what we would want to call international political events? The chief problem with the term "international" is that it suggests happenings exclusively among *nations.* One drawback of this is that our traditional concept of a nation as a territorially based group of people sharing a common language and culture as well as a government ceased to be satisfactory — if indeed it ever was — with the breakup of dynastic empires, and became highly misleading with the granting of independence to many states composed of very dissimilar tribes. The term "interstate" may be more accurate, but even this is somewhat misleading for much of the political action in which we are interested increasingly takes place in nonstate units such as interstate organizations (The North Atlantic Treaty Organization) and transnational or multinational organizations (The United Nations). Even nonstate organizations such as professional groupings (scientists, laborers, businessmen) may play significant political roles, and even individuals (the Pope, humanitarians like the late Albert Schweitzer) may have some effect on international affairs. Thus there is no term that satisfactorily incorporates all these different units or actors in "international politics." The best approach seems to be to continue using the term "international" with the clear understanding that we do not intend to limit our meaning solely to "nations" or "states."

The term "politics" causes even more difficulty. Political scientists have long disputed the nature of the political happening or of what is political in general. There seems little point in discussing that debate here, but it might be useful to examine briefly the definition that continues to be most popular today: "the authoritative allocation of values for a society."[6]

[5]For an interesting and amusing brief review of uses of the term, see Charles Burton Marshall, "Waiting for the Curtain," in *SAIS Review* Vol. 10. No. 4 (Summer 1966), pp. 21–27, esp. pp. 21–22.
[6]See David Easton, *The Political System* (New York: Knopf, 1953) and his more recent *Framework for Political Analysis* (Englewood Cliffs, N.J.: Prentice-Hall, 1965) and *A Systems Analysis of Political Life* (New York: Wiley, 1965).

For several reasons this definition, although quite useful in the study of politics *within* a nation, is less helpful in the study of international politics. The first reason is that it is not clear that there is an international "society" in a meaningful sense. (We shall return to this point later.) Second, in international politics, "authority" is derived from power or capability plus other characteristics (also to be discussed below), and the high degree of force evident in international allocations does not always appear to be authoritative. Finally, what is valued varies significantly among the parties to international relations — resources, capabilities, status, prestige, and the like — so much so, in fact, that there is nothing like the pure competition that seems to be implied by this characterization of politics. This is not to argue that this characterization is highly inaccurate, but rather that its implications are misleading and that a less specific characterization might therefore be more useful at this stage of our inquiry.

International Politics

What seems clearly to characterize those phenomena we wish to term "international political" is that there exists among the parties some difference in objective or in acceptable means and that efforts are being made to resolve it.

Our usual concept of politics is formed in a highly civilized, constrained, and routinized society. International politics lacks much of this, and so tends to have a much higher violence content, a higher change rate, and other distinctive features. One consequence of these differences is that international politics is more dependent on the nonpolitical aspects of international relations — economics (such as development, trade, and aid) in modern times; social (such as blood ties among ruling families) in the past and on those semi-political aspects of international relations, especially the military. Again we want a definition of international politics broad enough to cover not only war and diplomacy, but also international trade and even, as mentioned earlier, the Olympic Games.

For these reasons we shall view international politics as made up of incidents in which the *units* or *actors*, generally nations or combinations of nations, differ over power, resources,

status, or other desired ends, and attempt to resolve their difference by whatever means available and acceptable.

Our   We want, eventually, not only to know
Interests   what happens when nations interact
in these ways and to understand why,
but also to improve our ability to control them. This in its turn
depends on our understanding of the way the world works—
our "theoretical knowledge"—as well as on our ability to predict likely developments. Even from ordinary experience, we
can predict that the sun will appear on the horizon tomorrow
morning and be very confident of our prediction because we have
detected regularity. Similarly, we would like to find enough
regularity in politics that we could predict something as specific as war tomorrow in the Middle East or in Asia, or at least
know that if one nation does a certain thing to another nation
under certain conditions, war will very likely break out. Prediction, then, depends on observing regularity in events. Furthermore, the credibility of the prediction depends on our understanding why the regularity exists or holds. We are confident
of the sun appearing daily not just because we have seen it do
so daily in the past, but because we are able to *explain* in a
rational, scientific way, its appearance in terms of the motions
of the earth and the heavenly bodies. Similarly, our confidence
in our prediction about the likelihood of war will be markedly
increased if we can explain why one nation's doing something
to another is likely to stimulate the other to war.

As we attempt such explanation, prediction, and control,
we will have to make a number of decisions about what sorts of
factors to consider. One problem will be deciding whether to
look for immediate causes alone (what incident led to the outbreak of hostilities or to the creation of a crisis) or whether to look
for the roots of those causes—in other words, whether to move
backward in time to the stages in the development of the war or
the crisis. Similarly, we shall have to decide what levels to concentrate on in our study. One level is interaction among nations.
This involves such actions as the hurling of weapons by the forces
of one state at those of another, or the exchange of diplomatic
messages. Another level is the decisionmaking by the leadership

of the various states. This involves supposedly rational calculation of the expected costs and benefits of various possible actions.
Further, we could look to the level of the factors that tend to produce certain decisions, such as domestic politics and the international situation.

The phenomena we first think of when we contemplate
international politics—war, crisis, alliance, and the others—
come about through interaction among nations, and that interaction has its bases in the policies and actions of the nations involved. Thus one nation will adopt a policy and implement it
(that is, put its bureaucracy and political and military instruments
to work) through taking action either outside its boundaries or
directed at other nations. If this action is perceived by another
nation to be seriously detrimental to its interests, that nation
will react. At this point what has been national action becomes
multinational interaction—the stuff of international politics.
This interaction may continue as the first nation perceives and
reacts to the second nation's reaction, and so on. The outcome,
perhaps ongoing rather than static, will be a change in the international political situation.

As students of international politics, our interest is in describing these actions and reactions, or this interaction and its
outcome (such as continuing peace or an expanding war), and
the interaction that eventually follows. Among the questions that
will concern us are, What is war really like? What are the conditions of peace? What is the nature of cooperation among adversaries? But we are further interested in learning why these phenomena occur when and as they do, and so we are likely to find
ourselves inquiring backward in time into the policies of nations
and even into the factors that determined those policies.

All these considerations, however, only bring us once again
to the first question that generally confronts a policymaker in a
crisis: What caused this to happen? As previously stated, an answer to this requires information on the ways these circumstances
were related, the ways in which certain conditions caused others.
This knowledge might be referred to as principles of cause and
effect in international politics or, in the language we shall use,
as a theory of international politics. But because scholars have
not yet developed a theory of international politics, we must
settle for less. We may begin with little more than an ability to
reason about the occurrence of the crisis, by making inferences

from what evidence we have, and by employing partial theories and causal propositions in an effort to make sense out of what might otherwise be an incomprehensible happening.

Actually, we must have this same knowledge and theory to answer the other three questions of the policymaker. Employing our knowledge of the situation and our theory or propositions to develop a picture of the likely future, we predict the effects of the instigator's action. Moreover, in order to evaluate the adversary's action we must be able to predict the consequences of the act. And to select a response, we must know the effects of our own various alternatives.

In seeking an answer to the questions posed in this chapter, we must first consider how to go about studying international politics in a systematic fashion. The importance of this pursuit is as obvious to scholars as its success is important to presidents. As John F. Kennedy is said to have declared on the eve of the Cuban missile crisis, "This is the week when I earn my salary."

chapter 2

Social Science

The Scientific Method Until very recently the methods by which the subject of international relations was studied had little in common with those used in the traditional social sciences of economics, sociology, political science, and perhaps anthropology and social psychology. There were several major reasons for this difference. One was the fact that the products of these other social sciences were not very impressive when compared with those of the "harder," or physical sciences, and few were interested in devoting their efforts to an approach that did not promise fruitful applications. Even more fundamental was a pervasive general skepticism about the possibility of applying scientific approaches to the study of international politics due to the recalcitrance of the data—a consideration still raised and one we shall examine shortly. Related to this was the underdeveloped state of social science methods and techniques in general. A social scientific approach to international politics, perhaps even more than to other subjects less complex, would require highly developed methods and techniques from which the student could select. Furthermore, many people studying international politics were very much policy-oriented. They were concerned with averting another world war, and believed that there was not sufficient time to spend developing methods and techniques. Finally, few who were particularly interested in international politics had the training (or access to those who did) to attempt a social scientific-oriented study of international politics.

All these conditions, however, have changed somewhat over the years since World War II, and the other social sciences — particularly economics, psychology, and, increasingly, sociology — have progressed to points where the student of politics, and in our case international politics, can envy their capabilities. Increased rigor of thought among analysts of the social sciences[1] has led many to conclude that what have long been considered fundamental logical and practical obstacles to the social scientific study of disciplines such as international politics are not insurmountable. Coupled with this development have been both an increase in the available data[2] and a development of improved analytical concepts and devices for processing them. There has arisen, too, a disillusionment with the efforts of those who are untrained in social science methods but interested in policy questions to cope satisfactorily with these issues. And finally, many colleges and universities are offering students many more opportunities to do some of their academic work in the other social sciences and to attempt to apply the methods and techniques of the sciences to political studies. International relations has been one of the last disciplines in political science to fall to such infiltration. This book reflects that change, and will further develop those methods and techniques. We shall find it instructive, however, first to look briefly at the ways in which

[1]For a good if difficult introduction, see Richard S. Rudner, *The Philosophy of Social Science* (Englewood Cliffs, N.J.: Prentice-Hall, 1966). See also Maurice Natanson, ed., *Philosophy of the Social Sciences* (New York: Random House, 1963); and Fred Frohock, *Nature of Political Inquiry* (Homewood, Ill.: Dorsey, 1967), and the many works to which these books refer.

[2]See, for example, Bruce M. Russett *et al.*, *World Handbook of Political and Social Indicators* (New Haven, Conn.: Yale University Press, 1964); Arthur Banks and Robert Textor, *A Cross-Polity Survey* (Cambridge, Mass.: M.I.T. Press, 1963); and Richard L. Merritt and Stein Rokkan, eds., *Comparing Nations* (New Haven, Conn.: Yale University Press, 1966).

international politics has been studied in the past in order to see what sorts of changes the social scientific approach is bringing about.

Approaches to the Study of International Politics

Political science arose out of the disciplines of history, philosophy, and law, passing through a stage where it was studied as political economy.[3]
The discipline of international relations in particular has developed out of the study of diplomatic history and international law. Both general studies of relations among nations over long periods of time and specific studies of war, alliance, crisis, and other happenings have long been undertaken by scholars. But in the past, when historians studied political events they primarily attempted to reconstruct chronologically exactly what occurred. And although there is a developing interest in social scientific approaches among some historians, they still, especially when moving beyond reconstruction of the past, generally attempt to explain why the particular event occurred in terms of notions of how individuals, collectivities, and nations tend to behave.[4] Rarely do they attempt to develop general explanations of how and why individuals, collectivities, and nations do behave. This is the realm of the social scientist.

The Policy Orientation

Disillusionment with the state of international relations before and after World War I led many to become interested not only in finding ways of making international politics more pacific, but also in finding means of *guaranteeing* the peace of the world. Students of international politics, generally trained in diplomatic history or law, or occasionally economics, attempted

[3]For an interesting account of its development, see Albert Somit and Joseph Tanenhaus, *The Development of American Political Science* (Boston: Allyn and Bacon, 1967).

[4]For a presentation of the issues underlying historical study, see William Dray, *The Philosophy of History* (Englewood Cliffs, N.J.: Prentice-Hall, 1965). See also the useful essays in William Dray, ed., *Philosophical Analysis and History* (New York: Harper & Row, 1966), and in George Nadel, ed., *Studies in the Philosophy of History* (New York: Harper & Row, 1965); and the many other studies to which these works direct the reader.

to apply their knowledge and speculations to specific policy problems, such as creation of promising international organizations and the removal of the material causes of war. Students of international politics have been interested in policy questions ever since and have attempted to contribute to the attainment of such objectives as peace and justice. Most people would agree that this is to their credit, but recently many have sensed that this immediate policy orientation has had several unfortunate limiting effects. One limitation has been that our knowledge of the workings of international relations is still inadequate to the tasks of policy, and has not been sufficiently improved by a continuing study of diplomatic history as such. Thus these policy-oriented scholars, despite noble efforts, have on the whole been unable to make the convincing and successful contributions that are called for by the precarious state of the modern world and by the interests of the countries they serve — security, liberty, justice, welfare, stability. Furthermore, the understandable commitment to the attainment of such objectives has sometimes colored or distorted the study of the nature and dynamics of relations among nations on the basis of which those with strong policy orientations make their recommendations. All of us continually face this danger; objectivity in the social sciences is obviously a greater problem than that in the physical sciences, where humans are not so directly involved.[5] But the danger is much compounded if the immediate objective is not just to understand why the world works the way it does, but how to make it work quite differently.

Thus, in terms of orientation and objective, it has seemed to many that the best attitude is to divorce themselves temporarily from the policy objectives and instead attempt to improve their own understanding of the how and why of international politics. The issue of how this is to be done continues to be disputed by the "traditionalists" and the "scientists."

The Traditional Approach

Many of the most prominent students of international politics in the postwar years have continued the traditional approach, which one of its advocates has summarized as

[5]See Karl Mannheim, *Ideology and Utopia* (New York: Harcourt, Brace & World, 1936); and Richard Rudner, *Philosophy of Social Science* (Englewood Cliffs, N.J.: Prentice-Hall, 1966), for analyses of these problems and citations of further discussions of them.

the approach to theorizing that derives from philosophy, history, and law, and that is characterized above all by explicit reliance upon the exercise of judgment and by the assumptions that if we confine ourselves to strict standards of verification and proof there is very little of significance that can be said about international relations, that general propositions about this subject must therefore derive from a scientifically imperfect process of perception or intuition, and that these general propositions cannot be accorded anything more than the tentative and inconclusive status appropriate to their doubtful origin.[6]

The key elements here are the reliance on *judgment* and *intuition* and the *assumption* that a more scientific approach produces little of significance.

The traditional approach has produced much that is significant. Until very recently almost all study of international politics has been of this sort, and we certainly have made progress in this period. Yet that traditional approach has also produced, or at least has nourished, the long-dominant schools of international political thought — "idealism" and "realism." In the years in which they successively dominated the discipline, these two schools have inhibited its progress toward a more comprehensive and sophisticated understanding of the nature and determinants of international relations by focusing attention on the question whether man and his states are basically good or evil rather than on the patterns of international relations as they actually occur.[7]

The Social Scientific Approach

In a sense, the scientist in the study of international relations will hold that these approaches have been too underdeveloped and too limiting, that the conceptual frameworks they employed

[6]Hedley Bull, "International Theory: The Case for a Classical Approach," in *World Politics*, 18 (1966) 361–377 at 361. See also the subsequent "response" by a "scientist": Morton A. Kaplan, "The New Great Debate: Traditionalism vs. Science in International Relations," in *World Politics*, 19 (1966) 1–20. See also the "response" to these two by a "moderate": David Vital, "On Approaches to the Study of International Relations", in *World Politics*, 19 (1967) 551–562. And, finally, see James N. Rosenau, "Games International Relations Scholars Play," in *Journal of International Affairs*, 21 (1967) 293–303.

[7]They may also, in their impact on policy, have been contributors to many of the major difficulties in international politics and foreign policy in this century, as has been alleged frequently by one school against the other. We shall examine these theories again in Chapter 13.

have narrowed inquiry so much that reality has been overly distorted. To be sure, any effort to do more than simply describe reality with abstraction and categorizations will distort that reality somewhat. But this is the necessary price we pay for being able to relate one event to another in various ways — such as classifying the two as similar or linking the two as cause and effect. Although such activities of description, classification, and explanation are the fundamental activities of all students of human affairs, the more important question is whether they have been undertaken systematically enough, with conceptual tools developed well, and through modes of study sophisticated enough, to offer or promise satisfactory results. The "traditionalists," though, will generally admit that their results, whether they are explanations of particular events (such as the Cuban missile crisis), propositions about groups of events (such as wars), or theories about categories of happenings (such as international politics), have not been satisfactory — either because they have not seemed wholly accurate or because they have not been sufficiently credible or reliable. But, they argue, we cannot do better. The recent upsurge of interest in the social scientific study of politics is based on the belief that indeed we can do better.

It is, of course, possible that scholars will fail. Certainly no one expects exact and comprehensive general theories of politics like the theories in physics. No one expects perfectly accurate and reliable mathematically expressible equations that, linked together, would offer us a comprehensive model of human behavior, not to mention multinational behavior. Rather, the objective is to increase our understanding of — and particularly our ability to explain — political events. And our criterion for satisfaction is only to do better than those efforts that are based fundamentally on intuition and individual judgment.

Social Scientific Study   But what is the nature of social scientific study? In past years it was often contended that the student of society should adopt the approach that the student of physical phenomena employed, that the social scientist should adopt the "scientific method" of the physical scientist. This method is generally described as a succession of deliberate, intellectual activities: observation, then statement of the problem, then formulation of a hypothesis to solve the problem, then a test of that hypothesis, and finally validation or rejection of the hypothesis on the basis of that test. This general outline of aspects of the scientific method assumed that the scientist was in some important sense open-minded and constantly seeking the truth, even if that truth contradicted his own previous work. But when students of the history of science studied what scientists actually did and how they justified it, they came generally to the conclusion that, on the contrary, neither of these contentions was satisfactory. Often they found that after the scientists had settled on a hypothesis or a theory they clung to it for dear life, and attempted to dismiss every challenge to it, or any improvement on it by others. They also found that because it is very difficult to prove that a statement is true, most scientists simply attempt to prove that some other statement is not true, or at least is not sufficient. The point is that the orthodox view of science as highly objective and as possessing a regular, rigorous method was, in many respects, inaccurate.[8]

The Crucial Emphases

What, then, are those features of the "scientific" approach or method that might be relevant to the study of international politics? There are several key characteristics. One is the emphasis on analysis and the other is the emphasis on theory. As we have seen, much of the previous study of international politics has been highly speculative. Students have asked themselves what has happened and have attempted "common sense" explanations of why it has happened, without always doing enough careful research about the event itself and without always fully understanding what must be done in order to satisfactorily explain its causes.

The social scientist emphasizes the importance of careful research into what actually happens as well as the attempt to

[8]The literature in this area is now immense. Among the studies most interesting and useful in presenting a variety of views are Thomas Kuhn, *The Structure of Scientific Revolutions* (Chicago: University of Chicago Press, 1962); Karl Popper, *The Logic of Scientific Discovery* (New York: Basic Books, 1959); Mario Bunge, *Intuition and Science* (Englewood Cliffs, N.J.: Prentice-Hall, 1962); W. I. B. Beveridge, *The Art of Scientific Discovery* (New York: Norton, 1950); N. R. Hanson, *Patterns of Discovery* (New York: Cambridge University Press, 1958).

generalize about these events both in terms of the conditions under which they happen and the reasons why they happen. Rather than settle for describing and explaining a particular war —which is typically the activity of the historian—the social scientist is interested in gathering descriptions of a number of wars so that he can develop a comprehensive concept of war in its general and specific manifestations, from which he can then consolidate explanations of various wars into propositions that explain why wars occur and develop as they do. When he generalizes his explanations like this he is developing a theory—a collection of related propositions that explain why in general a phenomenon happens—which can then be applied to a particular case to explain it.

International Politics and Social Science

Because international politics obviously deals with individuals in interaction, or collectivities, it must be "social" in its nature or concern. But must it be a science? There are, as we have already seen, many different aspects of this term. It became increasingly clear that science is not characterized at all times and in all cases by employment of one particular method, and some suggested that science might be characterized by employment of standard techniques. Yet some scientists use telescopes, others use microscopes and others use the naked eye. So there are no particular techniques or instruments necessarily characteristic of scientific investigation and discovery. Perhaps, then, the significant feature of science is not in its "context of discovery," but rather in its "context of validation." Scientific discoveries can often be replicated or reproduced by experiment in order to be tested. But because we cannot make international politics happen even once just for our benefit, let alone repeat itself, one might argue that we cannot engage in scientific study of international politics. However, the key issue here is not simply the possibility of controlled experiment, but its purpose. The purpose of experimentation for the physical scientist is to enable him to validate or confirm his conclusions about what is happening and why. If this is so we too must develop a satisfactory method of validation. The question of whether our strategies of inquiry can be coupled with the tactic of drawing tentative conclusions which can lead to satisfactory progress in understanding international politics is what we will attempt to answer by our study.

Before we proceed any further, it would be prudent to consider the arguments of those who object to such an approach. They usually focus on two problems—that of discovery and that of validation. In terms of discovery, those who maintain that a social *science* in general is impossible have held that because social science is clearly a self-study—that is, a study of people by people—one cannot observe himself and others objectively and hence cannot satisfactorily discover what is happening and why. This important objection has several aspects we must consider. The first is the difficulty of perceiving the world accurately; the second is the difficulty of recognizing and coping with the possible impact of our values on our conclusions.

The Problem
of Perception

Man reacts, of course, to how he *perceives* reality rather than to reality as such. The sum of what we think we know, rather than what is really true, determines what plan or policy we adopt and what actions we then attempt.[9] We may think we know and understand reality, and perhaps we usually do. But there will be instances in which we do not; at those times, our plans and actions will likely be at odds with reality, and our actions will probably have unanticipated consequences. The policymakers of a nation may believe that the nation has the capability to win a war and therefore may be willing to undertake it; but if they are mistaken, if their image of their capabilities relative to those of the adversary is inflated or otherwise distorted, they are likely to be greatly surprised by what happens in the war they undertake—when, in other words, reality inter-

[9]This idea is developed by Kenneth Boulding in *The Image: Knowledge in Life and Society* (Ann Arbor: University of Michigan Press, 1956), and applied to international politics in his article, "National Images and International Systems," in *Journal of Conflict Resolution*, 3 (1959) 120–131. Its conceptual basis seems to be the contention by W. I. Thomas, often termed the dean of American sociologists, that "if men define situations as real, they are real in their consequences." See Robert Merton's discussion of the "self-fulfilling prophecy" in chap. 11 of *Social Theory and Social Structure* (New York: Free Press, rev. ed., 1957).

venes. This point seems rather obvious to us now, for the recent emphasis of scholars on human behavior rather than on institutions and their structure has increased its acceptance.

Scholars have much the same problem of accurate perception of reality as policymakers have, for all things must be in some sense "perceived" to be dealt with in studies and deliberations, and whenever these phenomena are perceived by human beings they may actually be misperceived just because perception depends heavily on the perceiver. Scholars attempt to be accurate, or at least to discover the nature of perceptual distortions, by checking their observations with those of others, in much the same way that the physical scientist will engage in replication (exact repetition) of another scientist's work to assure himself and others that the work done first was accurate.

The Problem of Values   One major possible interference with accurate perception—one factor that may distort perception—is values. Throughout history those who have been concerned with human action have often contended that one or another action or institution was the "best" or the "correct" one. Such contentions have often resulted in arguments and even wars because debaters thought they were arguing about objective facts rather than about preferred values. To avoid this, scholars in recent decades attempted to be particularly careful to separate their own individual preferences from their work. Instead of arguing simply that war is bad, they have sought to understand what war is and why it occurs, leaving to the policymakers the efforts to abolish war. Instead of arguing that democracy is the best form of government, they have sought to describe the way in which a democracy works and the effects a democratic form of government is likely to have on the people it rules and the policies it adopts. To those who must decide what form of government to adopt or whether or not to change the existing form of government they have left the conclusions as to whether or not these effects and these policies are desirable.

Basically, this shift on the part of the student of society and its institutions from a "value" orientation to a "value-free" orientation (as the two positions have often been called) has been a constructive one, for it has enabled scholars better to understand the ways in which institutions operate and the reasons for their operation. But it would be a mistake to believe, as some have suggested, that it is possible for the scholar to divorce himself fully from his own values and to eliminate value considerations from his scholarly work, for values will influence his work at many stages.

The Impact of Values

The first stage in which values will play a determinant role is the selection of the objectives of study. Why do we study international politics? Some would argue that the subject is inherently interesting; others would say that it is puzzling and that they value solving puzzles. Perhaps more would suggest that international politics affects their lives and, because they hope those lives will be long and happy, they want to see if they can contribute to the creation and maintenance of lasting peace or to the better attainment of their own nation's interests in the world. Each of the reasons an individual gives for studying international politics arises out of that individual's own value system. It is important for us to understand why the world works as it does, whether in order to increase our knowledge, to decrease our perplexity, or to enable us to change the world or our own nation's success in the world. There are probably many other reasons for the study of international politics (as of any other subject), but each is built on some particular personal value.

This personal value is likely to determine, or contribute to the determination of, not only the selection of problems to be studied, but also the objective of study. Someone who wants to help bring about lasting peace is more likely to study problems of war than the Olympic Games. And someone who seeks the answers to questions about international politics that puzzle him will tend to study those particular problems rather than others.

These goals are not likely to meet any considerable objection. Somewhat more objectionable, however, is the role values will play in determining when we believe we are operating acceptably in studying our subject. In ordinary conversation we often say that someone is being illogical, and everyone understands what is meant when we make such a statement. We were brought up on what is often referred to as Aristotelian logic, which is a system of rules about acceptable ways of thinking in which one contention will follow from other contentions. To use an example that philosophers often employ, if we accept the general proposition that "all men are mortal" and are given the specific proposition that "Socrates is a man" we can conclude logically that "Socrates is mortal." Karl Marx, however, rejected Aristotelian logic in favor of the Hegel's *dialectical logic* which sees every phenomenon or every argument (a thesis) giving birth to its opposite (antithesis), which in turn combines to produce a synthesis, and so forth. Although it is difficult for us to understand dialectical logic if we have been brought up as Aristotelians, and although this is not the place for an ambitious comparative study of the two, it should be clear that whichever of these logics we accept as a criterion for determining whether or not our study is logical, will be likely to have a significant effect on our conclusions.

On another plane, deciding whether to be "scientific" or "intuitional" in our study will probably affect our results. This decision of which approach or which criteria of acceptability to select is also based on our values.

Coping with the Impact of Values

It should be clear, then, that it is particularly important first of all to realize that values will influence our study at many stages, and then to "allow" for this influence where possible. But how might we "allow" for it? Perhaps the best way to answer this question is to look at a more obvious way in which values may affect our study or color our results. Values are shaped considerably by cultural and historical environments and hence vary within a nation over time and across nations at any given time. When we study international politics we must be able to describe and understand the actions of nations very different from our own, and then we must attempt to explain why they act as they do. "Understanding the other side" is likely to be particularly difficult because most of us are brought up believing that our country is somehow right and our adversaries are somehow wrong in instances where the two conflict, and from this belief it is but a short distance to the conclusion that what our adversary does is a product of evil intentions and dangerous capabilities. Although such factors may be part of the explanation, there are likely to be other factors as well and we may tend to overlook them. Thus, explaining the Soviet placement of missiles in Cuba in 1962 simply in terms of a Soviet desire to outmaneuver the United States may neglect the possibility that Khrushchev was having difficulties with militant members of his ruling group as well as with Castro. On the other hand, merely describing and explaining the American involvement in Vietnam and her efforts to bring about a settlement there solely in terms of America's conflict with China, while neglecting the impact of U.S. congressional and presidential elections and of America's relations with her allies in Europe and Asia, may also be misleading. The point is that we may be unable to see the wide range of possible determinants of policy and action—out of which we will eventually select the one or more that seem to be most significant—unless we are conscious of our inbred biases and inclinations. Thus we wish to be continually conscious of such biases as we should be of other value considerations, such as reasons why we are studying this particular problem, the objectives of our study, and the criteria for verification and acceptance of it.

This is not to say that it is necessarily wrong or even unfortunate that values will influence our work. It is only to say that we must be conscious of the impact they have. For who would really care to argue in favor of the senseless, purposeless inquiry that would have to result if values were not important? And indeed some values *must* inform or influence any inquiry— even if they are nothing but the desire to pursue a senseless study!

The important question, then, is how can we cope with the impact of our values on our study? One obvious way, some have suggested, is to anticipate the effects whenever possible and to inject a correction factor whenever desirable (as we might do in studying the behavior of our nation's adversary). Another is to check our views and conclusions with those of other students —perhaps, if possible, with those of people working in or coming out of different backgrounds and influenced by different values.

Clearly it is difficult to speak of such compensation in these abstract terms, but it will be important to consider the problem specifically whenever we undertake studies where our values may markedly affect our conclusions. In the meantime, these brief inquiries suggest that the first necessity is to be conscious of what we are doing and of the possibility that our study may differ significantly from reality. Such consciousness is clearly a prerequisite for social scientific study. This is not to say that the non-social scientific students are always unconscious of these matters. But they are more pessimistic about the possibility of successfully coping with the impact of values by being conscious of them, and some have neglected being conscious of such effects.

The Prospects for a Scientific Study of International Politics

There seems, however, some reason for optimism about the possibility of social scientific study despite the problems of perception and values interfering with scientific analysis. The more general objection, that the student cannot objectively observe himself, much less others, and hence cannot objectively discover what is happening and why, must be examined in the context of its effect on *any* scientific endeavor as well as its impact on international political scientific endeavor.

Scientists have discovered that even in studying nuclear physics, which is about as far removed from human interference as a science can be, the actual observation of phenomena sometimes changes those phenomena. This effect cannot be examined here nor satisfactorily understood without considerable scientific knowledge, but it is interesting to note that although this effect (called the Heisenberg principle) has influenced scientific inquiry it has not debilitated it. Perhaps in a similar way, the effects of observation upon the observed (or more generally the impact of the fact that we are people in some sense studying ourselves) need not weaken our study too greatly. Only time and our efforts to study ourselves accurately will tell. But another thing to remember in our study of international politics is that we generally study large collectivities and not individuals; hence the effects of individual variations at low levels may not distort our work as much as it might distort, say, psychological inquiry.

The other major obstacle proposed is that of validation. As has already been mentioned, most natural scientific experiments (with exceptions, such as the astronomical) can be both undertaken and replicated, whereas international political experiments (and most other social science experiments) cannot be undertaken even once, let alone repeated. Often all the social scientist can do is observe actual happenings. If the student of international politics wishes to study the causes of war, he cannot put together some "causes" to see whether war "occurs." All he can do is study why particular wars occurred in the past. The question then is how we can come to have confidence in our conclusions even though we will never be able to have the same confidence we have in natural scientific conclusions. Indeed, unless alternative methods of validation are devised, this doubt seems inevitable. Perhaps we will be able to make enough significant progress in *partial* validation to enable the student to reach *tentative* conclusions. For the present, these tentative conclusions may well — indeed, should — prove to be better than no conclusions at all or conclusions based on nonscientific inquiry.

Thus, as we attempt a social scientific study of international politics, our concern must be with the strategy of inquiry and the tactics if drawing tentative conclusion. Hence the basic questions will be whether we can deal satisfactorily with the problems of discovery and validation which underlie any effort to undertake social scientific study. At this point we must ask more specifically how we might study international politics as a social science.

Social Scientific Study of International Politics The social sciences attempt to analyze and explain human occurrences. They do so through the application of those methods and even those techniques used by physical scientists, where those methods and techniques are appropriate and promising; and, when not appropriate, through the development and application of new methods and techniques beyond those of the natural sciences. *International political science,* as we shall call our approach, is that area of the social sciences which attempts to analyze and explain multi-state happenings through the application of those methods and techniques of the social sciences that are appropriate in terms of our data, and promising in terms of our desires, and through the development and application of new methods and techniques where those of the social sciences are not suitable.

Generally, our data will be events perceived or inferred among nations. Our tools will be definitions, classifications, and analytical concepts. Our methods will be operations on the data undertaken to explain their occurrence. Our objective: propositions and theories explaining international politics. We must now examine each of these further.

The Data

The nature of the data distinguishes international politics from other types of politics, for we are basically interested in occurrences among two or more states, such as diplomatic communication, war, crisis, peace making, treaty making, trade and aid, alliance, arms control, peace keeping, and other happenings. All these arise in a world where no superpower or sovereign even exists, much less is recognized as supreme. Moreover, states tend to have divergent or conflicting interests and objectives, and as a consequence tend to pursue divergent or conflicting courses. Because our basic interest is in describing these phenomena and explaining why they occur as they do, we are concerned with the constituents of the phenomena—basically national policies and actions that combine, or "interact," to produce various "outcomes." Thus, diplomatic communication (warnings, threats, promises, arguments, and so on) will consist of a statement by one party and a response by another based on how it perceives that communication. The source of each of these statements will be the nation's policymaking and implementation mechanisms (in the United States, the President and the State Department's communications facilities). But in asking why the statement was made, we shall be interested in the factors or considerations that led the policymaker to make a particular decision. Consequently, our interest and our data may well include, not only the foreign, but the domestic politics of a nation, the characteristics of its leaders, its economic situation, and other possible determinants of national policy.

Similarly, when we study the interaction in such phenomena as crisis and war, we shall be interested not only in why they come about, but also in how and why they develop as they do. We shall want to know the factors that enabled one combatant to win and the other to lose. Thus we shall pay much attention to the nature of multistate interaction and the determinants of the outcomes of such interaction.

Our data will come from history, but our approach will be different from that which historians use. They tend to study only happenings that are distant enough to allow them historical perspective, while we tend to be particularly interested in *recent* happenings because the conditions under which they took place and the actors which brought them about are the most similar to present conditions and actors. Because historians tend to study materials less helpful to us and because they seldom engage in sufficiently rigorous causal analysis, we must often conduct such basically historical studies ourselves rather than immediately employing the products of historical study in generalizing about international political phenomena.

As historians are perhaps better aware than are political scientists, the data from studies of the past are not always reliable and complete. There are problems of perception and of interpretation, and much of what we deal with we must be inferred from our discoveries. For example, when we study a crisis, we may have access to considerable data about one side's policymaking and action, but very little about the other's, and so we must make educated guesses about those things we do not know with confidence. We must always guess to some degree, because even official documents are apt to be misleading (deliberately or accidentally). This means that our reconstructions and our conclusions are subject to considerable error, and since this is so, we must be ready to correct this by qualifying our conclusions and comparing them with as many similar instances as possible, if necessary.

Tools

In order to compare in a satisfactory manner instances that differ from one another in complexity and quality, we must have well-developed tools of analysis. These tools will be discussed at greater length in coming chapters, but for now it is important to realize that our interest at all times will be to analyze or break down happenings into their component parts, to move backward in time from effect to cause and from cause to origins. In addition, we shall wish to examine phenomena on various levels, such as the level of individuals, the level of the group, and the level of a group of groups. International relations can be studied in terms of the actions of individuals: chief executives making decisions or diplomats and soldiers carrying out those decisions; or as the interplay of individuals in a group: policymakers within a government, executors of policies within a state, diplomats at a conference; or as the interplay of groups (particularly nations) in the international arena or, as it is often termed, "the international system." Each of these approaches and levels is useful for some kinds of study, and we shall employ each at various times.

When we break up an international political happening like a crisis into its various *stages* (outbreak, development, and termination), or when we break up an event into its various *levels* (individual, group, society of groups), we shall want to reassemble the parts once the nature of the crisis has been determined, so as not to lose track of the fact that we are actually studying crises and nations. With this in mind, we can undertake further study to attain our basic objective: again, to understand why things happen as they do.

Methods

We attain this objective by performing certain operations on our data. First, we are interested in describing or collecting the conditions that preceded an occurrence—in a war, the conditions just before its outbreak (tension, economic depression, military instability, political turmoil, or whatever). When we discover the same precedents to the same phenomenon, we begin to suspect that they in some sense *caused* that phenomenon. Generally, we reach conclusions about causes by relating such instances of "correlation" (that is, repeated occurrence before the phenomenon) to our more general knowledge of the way things operate. Thus, we may know (or believe very strongly) that if a nation considers its vital interests gravely threatened by another it will attack. If we find that the massing of troops on a nation's border has preceded war in all or most cases, we may conclude that this troop massing causes war and explain it in terms of this general principle. If we then seek to determine why one nation massed troops on another's border, we may find that this massing was preceded by economic or political unrest, or both, within the nation. Believing, on the other hand, that a nation may undertake military movements to distract attention from economic or political problems at home, we may then say that the cause of the troop massing was the presence of political unrest, and further say that political or economic unrest was indirectly the cause of the war. However, such attempts at general explanation of the occurrence of war can be undertaken only after careful thought about the nature of explanation and careful study of specific instances and their relations. For the moment this example (admittedly neither very well developed nor particularly stimulating) is used only to suggest the kinds of operations on data that are undertaken in social scientific study of international politics.

Objectives

The object of our study is to produce general statements that will explain international political happenings. These general statements will fall into several categories. The more specific will be propositions or hypotheses about the conditions under which a given event may be anticipated (if a nation masses troops on another's border, war will occur or tend to occur), or in reverse, the event that may be anticipated under given conditions (war will occur, or will tend to occur, if there is political or economic unrest in a country). When these propositions are collected or unified, theories may be produced (such as the theory that wars are to be explained by the existence of certain internal economic conditions in the participant nations).

Again it must be stressed that the propositions and theories cited here have all been suggested before by scholars at various times, and that the theories are neither well developed nor confirmed by careful study in this chapter. Indeed, at this stage in our inquiry, it would be as impossible to produce promising propositions and theories as it would be to test them. Our approach has been designed merely to improve our abilities to develop and test such propositions and the broader theories they constitute.

chapter 3

Analysis
and Theory

Our Operations Improvement of our understanding of international politics will depend basically on two intellectual operations: analysis and theory-building. Analysis, in the sense in which we shall use it, consists essentially of decomposing or breaking down into its component parts the subject matter we wish to understand. Theory-building, in our sense, involves taking those components and developing from them general statements about regularities or patterns which can then be applied to particular instances or cases. We do this not only to understand why events occur, but ultimately, to be able to predict and control these events. We must now examine closely each of the operations as they are done in international political analysis.

Analysis There are various ways one could break down international politics into smaller units for study. Perhaps the most obvious is to decompose it into the actions of individual states. But the actions of individual states are so multitudinous and complex that it would be quite difficult to make sense of international politics in this way.

Phenomena

Thus our first analytical simplification is to speak of various smaller phenomena such as a crisis, a war, an alliance, an international agreement, or an Olympic contest. Each of these is also a very complex combination of foreign actions by states in interaction, and each is a combination that recurs quite frequently among various groups of nations. It is easy to tell a crisis from the Olympics, but not so easy to differentiate a crisis from a war. To improve our ability to distinguish between such similar phenomena, we must develop clear definitions or concepts of various types of international political phenomena. We break down international politics into various phenomena to make the study more manageable; we choose the phenomena we do because they are the most interesting and important aspects of relations among states. We must be rigorous and consistent in doing so to avoid ambiguity.

Stages

But even these categories are too general for much of what we hope to achieve. Crises will contain a great many different types of interactions. We will be interested not only in why crises occur, but also in why they then develop as they do and why they terminate in a certain way. When we begin to break a crisis down into different stages—outbreak, development, termination—we are actually creating a descriptive model of the parts or stages of the crisis over a period of time. Such decomposition makes it possible for us to be much more specific about what makes crises occur when and as they do. It also makes it possible for us to specify just what factors we believe may prove significant at these different stages so that we can look for that specific information when we study each given crisis, and ultimately can begin to generalize about what factors determine the nature of each stage of a crisis. Thus we might find that an aggressive threat to the status quo by one nation is the most important factor in creating a crisis, that the relative military strengths of the two parties will most likely determine how it develops, and that whether the crisis ends in war or in negotiated settlement will depend on how willing the states are to compromise. We cannot be much more specific than this until we have examined a number of crises to see what actually occurred. But we cannot engage in such specific examination until we have broken the crisis down into stages and have attempted to decide which are the key factors. This will be our first concern in the coming chapters, not just for the study of crisis, but for the study of war, alliance, and other international political phenomena as well.

Levels

Once we have broken up the phenomena into their various stages, we must then examine them in terms of various levels. In studying the outbreak of a crisis, we shall concentrate on the decision of one nation to initiate it and the decision of the other to respond to that initiation. When examining a nation's decisions, we are actually concentrating on the calculations that we believe enter the minds of that nation's policymakers. But if we ask what factors enter their minds, we encounter a great variety of possibilities—ranging from their thinking about the available military forces and political objectives, through the apparent military strength of their friends and adversaries and the objectives these other states appear to seek. In some cases—and especially in phenomena like war and foreign trade or aid—other factors will be considered, such as the nation's economic strength and its social unity. As we shall see later, some scholars argue that there are the various unconscious factors in the calculations of policymakers to consider, such as resentment over past humiliation or personal aggressiveness. Hence it may prove desirable to examine such unconscious factors, too, if possible. When we consider these various elements we are looking at what we call various *levels:* from the unconscious mind of the decisionmaker to the national economy and military establishment to the international environment in which the nation finds itself. Any one or any combination of these levels might be the significant determinant of the decision in which we are interested.

But we might want to look even further in our effort to understand the behavior of states in their foreign relations. Rather than end with an analysis of the calculations of the decisionmakers, we might want to ask why *those* particular men were making decisions in the crisis. The answer to this might reside in the type of political system the nation has. Thus in a democracy the decisions are generally made by officials who are elected by the people and by the assistants whom they appoint, whereas in a nondemocratic system decisions are often made by those men with direct control over the police and the military forces of the country. But, whatever the system, in a crisis it must produce decisions under tension and in a shortened time span. In a crisis, decisions are generally *not* made by the officials who would ordinarily make foreign policy. In the early stages of the Cuban missile crisis, for example, only a very small group of American officials even knew the missiles had been discovered. The number was kept small to unduly avoid upsetting the public and to avoid warning the Russians. Those who knew were the ones deeply involved in the decisionmaking. If we go on in our study of crisis to ask not just why a given decision was made but why certain people rather than others made that decision, we may find that who makes decisions is a result not only of the type of government in the country but of the pressure under which the decision is made. In such a case, we are looking at another possible level of determination: the political system of the state.

We could also, of source, go even farther back in time in our effort to understand why things happened as they did. We could examine such possible influences as national character or culture. These, again, are other levels of analysis, and we may find ourselves drawn to them in our study.

But whether or not we find that any of these levels actually determines or helps to determine what happens, we can still describe what is happening at any given time on various levels. Thus, for example, we can describe a war in terms of the decisions governments make, or we can describe it in terms of the movements of a nation's military and diplomatic forces, or in terms of the actions of individual soldiers and diplomats, or in terms of the interaction of the forces (the soldiers and the diplomats) of the states involved. When we do this, we are saying nothing about what is actually causing things to happen as they do. Indeed, we are engaging in analysis that is basically static (a description of what is happening at a given time) rather than dynamic (an account of what event or factor at one time causes an event that follows it). We may find it desirable to engage in such description at various levels because this procedure enables us to marshal all our facts carefully, suggesting to us causes we might have overlooked had we used only one level of description (say the movements of military forces or the decision level). It is clear, however, that merely describing what is happening can be very complex, and thus making distinctions among levels for description and for explanation can help us to be both careful and imaginative. We will try to bring some order to this complex chaos when we examine the problem of levels in detail in Chapter 5.

Of course, we can no more understand international politics by studying one nation alone than we can by studying decision alone. International politics is composed of the interaction of states — action, reaction, and reaction in a chain that is virtually unending. Any of our decompositions is necessarily somewhat arbitrary. We break into this continuing chain in order to focus on some particular segment of relations. What will distinguish one such segment from the ongoing fabric of relations is the fact that it has a pattern to it — perhaps a beginning with a sudden change in the status quo coupled with a rise in tensions, a middle or development, and a return to more normal relations. Moreover, that particular segment, and the pattern to it, will be similar to another. We are interested not just in the pattern that we call crisis, but also in the patterns that make up crisis — from the smallest action and reaction up to the more complex collections of such action-reaction patterns, such as those termed threat-response. By breaking a phenomenon down into its major stages and then into the smaller interaction patterns of threats and promises, and even further sometimes into actions and their reactive perceptions by other parties, we hope to be able to single out those parts or patterns that are crucial in determining why things occur as they do. We shall be doing just that in Chapter 6 and then in our more specific study of crises and other phenomena.

All these analytical activities are only desirable if they help us move from the examination of any given happening toward an explanation of *why* it happened as it did and more generally toward a *theory* that would help us to understand why such things in general occur. As we shall see, any explanation depends on or implies a theory, whether articulated or not. Frequently, because we do not state that theory outwardly we do not examine it carefully, and we thereby settle for a theory that is inadequate or even inaccurate. In order to understand why we must engage in all this analysis and why we must be particularly careful that we do our analysis well, we must examine the nature and function of theory in the study of international politics.

The Term "Theory" We use the term "theory" in many different ways. When we distinguish between "theory" and "practice" we are indicating that things are one way in our minds and another way in our actions. When we differentiate "theory" from "reality" we suggest that things are not going as we envisaged them. Similarly, we may apply the term "theory" to beliefs about what ought to be as against what actually is. And more generally we may refer to any abstraction or generalization as a "theory." Thus "theory" is like other key words that are used variously and often ambiguously by the ordinary man as well as by the scholar. Words like "theory," however, are so central to the consideration of international politics that despite their ambiguity we shall continue using them, but only after determining precisely what we mean by them.

Even careful scholars sometimes use the term "theory" in the sense of a generalization, or, more accurately, a classificatory description. Thus, a catalogue of the various forms of government (such as democracy, autocracy, oligarchy, plutocracy, aristocracy, and others) in terms of the number and nature of rulers might be referred to as a *theory* of types of government. But this would not be a particularly helpful use of the term unless this were the beginning of a quest for an explanatory theory that would tell us under what conditions and why various types of government arise.

In our particular use of the term, "theory" is a generalization that tells us the conditions under which something occurs and if possible explains why it occurs under these conditions. Thus by "theory" we shall mean a collection of propositions about the occurrence of phenomena — in our case, propositions about the conditions (and, if possible, causes) of international political phenomena such as wars, crises, and alliances. This definition does not tell us much, but before we get more specific, it will be helpful to consider the reasons why we are interested in finding or developing international political theory.

The Functions of Theory

Theory in the study of international relations may serve a half dozen important functions:

1. It will enable us to organize data so that we can handle them in our later work and make sense out of them. Particularly, it enables us to perceive regularities and irregularities in data which we can then attempt to explain.

2. It will help us toward understanding events by ordering them causally, thereby explaining their occurrence. Thus it will provide a set of answers to some of the questions that led us to engage in our study: why wars occur, why alliances disintegrate, which party will prevail in a crisis, and so on.[1]

3. Developed theory simplifies the data of the world, and our explanations of them, by subsuming individual cases under general categories. Thus, if we have a theory that tells us why wars occur, we can subsume the outbreak of the Korean conflict under it and need not be troubled to remember why it and all the other explicable wars occurred, for we need only remember our theory to know why wars occur.

4. It provides a guide for further research. As we develop theory about international political happenings, we shall sense what factors are most significant and what factors are unknown or not fully understood. Our theory provides a framework in which we can locate those needed data and those undetermined casual relations. Thus, even if it is quite underdeveloped, theory may provide a set of questions for us to answer with our research.

---

[1]As we shall see in our discussion of explanation in Chapter 7, there is some disagreement as to how theory makes events understandable. In the words of one analyst, "One school argues that explanation consists in showing the particular event to be subsumed under more general laws. The other school holds that explanation is accomplished by showing that the unfamiliar comports with familiar experiences. Obviously if the more general laws are a part of our *familiar* experience the problem is resolved . . . However, the argument of the anti-general-law explanation school is that the true explanation consists in accounting for the more general laws, and that this is done by analogy, or in the case of mathematics by mathematical neatness." — Arthur S. Goldberg, "Political Science as a Science," *Yale Political Science Research Library*, Publication no. 1, reprinted in N. W. Poslby, R. A. Dentler, and P. A. Smith, eds., *Politics and Social Life* (Boston: Houghton Mifflin, 1963), pp. 26-36, at pp. 29-30.

5. It offers its material in an organized form that may be useful to other disciplines. Thus the study of international economics or of diplomatic history may be able to profit from our international political hypotheses and the theories into which they are combined. Further, because theory is generalized rather than specific, study of international politics may provide useful suggestions about the operation of politics in general that might contribute to a general theory of politics. Such contributions can follow only from a theory that is general enough to have such applications; they cannot arise directly from specific studies of individual instances. Thus integration of disciplines and of studies may benefit considerably from theory.

6. It may prove useful in several major applications. The first of these is prediction, which we shall examine in some detail in Chapter 14. For the moment we should realize that the easiest and most reliable way to predict the future is to employ a theory that tells us how international politics develops, and what consequences follow that development. Admittedly, satisfactory predictability will require comprehensive confirmed theory of a kind not now available, but partial theories may well prove useful in prediction today and tomorrow. As we shall discover later, all prediction is based on some sort of theory, and the clearer we are about this and about our own theories, the more likely we are to be accurate in predicting.

The other major application of theory is control — affecting to some degree the future course of events. We shall examine this application in detail in Chapter 15. For the present we should realize that the basis for the ability to achieve given objectives must be an understanding of what makes things happen as they do, and this is precisely what a developed theory of international politics is intended to tell us. Some scholars claim either that they are not interested in affecting the world through their knowledge, or that exerting such an influence is not the appropriate activity for scholars. But whether they want to control events or not, it is clear that theory may contribute considerably to such activity.

These, then, are the contributions theory can make, as well as the objectives we may hope to achieve by developing a theory about international politics. At this point several key questions arise. One concerns the shape and content of international political theory; the other concerns the strategy and tactics of its achievement. This latter, called "theory building," or the development of theory, will be examined in Chapter 8. The rest of this chapter will examine in more detail the nature, form, shape, and content of international political theory.

The Nature of Theory

Theory in the physical sciences has traditionally been viewed as a collection of theorems. These theorems are propositions that are strict logical consequences of a combination of certain definitions and of other propositions that are assumptions. The theorems must be translatable into assertions about the tangible world that are in some way verifiable.[2] A fully developed scientific theory consists of definitions and assumptions from which theorems are deduced. Other theorems are then deduced from these, and so on, down to the level of the particular events or situations with which the science is concerned. Thus from certain definitions and assumptions including the laws of motion, one might deduce theorems that would explain why apples fall from trees the way they do, or why missiles fall from the sky as they do. We know in fact that no such falling bodies follow these laws precisely because of the effects of other factors such as air friction; hence we must build these factors into our assumptions in order to be able to deduce a proposition that accurately describes what happens when a missile plummets from the sky. The physical scientist can do this quite satisfactorily — even if in very complex terms — and he thereby explains such events.

Of course, this account of what the physical scientist does misrepresents his actual activity. For he, like us, begins by observing some occurrence he wishes to explain. He in effect asks himself what would have to be true for this to happen. His answer provides him with his theory. He then asks himself what else would follow from this theory, and attempts to discover whether these other derived consequences do indeed hold. Consider again the missile falling to earth. If the missile's descent can be explained by, or subsumed under, a complex theory that includes the laws of motion, then the fall of an apple ought also to be explainable by this theory. He checks it to see how an apple would be expected to fall, and then studies falling apples and

[2]For a discussion and examples of this concept of theory, see Anatol Rapoport, "Various Meanings of 'Theory'," *American Political Science Review*, 52 (1958), pp. 972–988.

finds that indeed the theory seems to apply. But this does not complete his task, for he must then see if his general theory will also explain other sorts of motion, such as automobile crashes. He probably finds that other refinements incorporating the principles of inertia are required, and builds them into his theory through additional assumptions. Eventually, his theory includes theorems deduced from these assumptions which will apply to all such instances of motion in the real world. He then concludes—at least until an exception occurs or is discovered—that his theory is satisfactory.

The Forms of Theory

But this concept of a developed theory in the physical sciences does not apply accurately to our theories in the social sciences such as international politics—at least not yet. We, too, have our definitions and assumptions and we, too, have our propositions or theorems (we generally call them propositions or hypotheses), but our collections of theorems or propositions are not generally linked deductively in a comprehensive and logically satisfactory way.

Indeed, the forms of our theories today vary immensely—all the way from efforts that are highly systematic and begin with assumptions and deduce propositions explicitly, to fragmentary works offering contentions that can be called propositions but that do not state explicitly the assumptions they imply. Most work in international politics, like that in diplomatic history, simply assumes without articulating, and at best offers only propositions that *may* explain given happenings, while at worst offers only statements linking events causally without enunciating the general proposition that links the two. We need only pick up and study an average history book or a typical study of international relations, let alone a speech by a public official on foreign policy, to discover the vast array of *implicit* theory that underlies what explicitly looks like a wholly nontheoretical discussion of international politics.

As social scientists, we notice, like the physical scientists, occurrences we wish to explain, and we ask ourselves what propositions might serve to do this. These are generally called hypotheses and take some version of the form, "If X is the case, then Y will be the case (or can be expected to be the case, or may be the case)." As we test our hypothesis against various cases and find that it survives, we generally refer to it as a tested proposition. If we should develop a proposition that seemed to survive intensive testing, we might refer to it as a "law," but because that term suggests certainty, we would not be inclined to bestow it on our propositions at this underdeveloped stage of international political theory.

The Shape of Theory

Theory in the physical sciences is a deductively related set of laws. This does not mean that such laws and their organizing theory are always perfectly correct. Rather, it means that they are believed to be as accurate as presently possible, and they are always subject to revision.

Theory in the social sciences is perhaps not so different as might be expected. Rare is the time when theory is a deductively related set of laws, although certain economic theories, generally discredited for failing to correspond adequately to the real world, would so qualify. Indeed, most social scientific theories have not even been deductively related propositions, let alone laws. Our deficiencies have been due to a lack of comprehensiveness and rigor in testing, as well as weaknesses in logical organization. But although our theories have tended to be loosely knit collections of propositions, this is decreasingly so, as we shall see later when we examine a number of recent theories of international politics. Furthermore, we can be encouraged by the fact that, although the propositions of some theories could not be related deductively due to logical contradictions in their assumptions, other theories, with better organization and elaboration, could be made more rigorous and logical. In Chapter 8 we shall discuss procedures for such development of theory.

The Content of Theory

The key general features of the content of international political theory are its generality and its substance. The generality of a theory may vary in two different senses. On the one hand, a theory, in its application to individual instances, may be so general as to include many such instances through the elimination of specific referents. Thus at one extreme, our propositions about the outbreak of wars might include even the names of specific nations, or at least specific types of nations, whereas at the other extreme they might include merely the terms "nations" or "states" or even "political units." We do not generally consider it legitimate to include the names of states in our propositions — mainly because such propositions are not usually very useful. On the other hand, propositions so general as to apply to all political units or even to all states are not likely to be as substantively interesting as those somewhat less general. Consequently we tend to strike a compromise between specificity and generality, in ways and on grounds which we shall consider in Chapter 8.

Another way our theories may vary in generality is in the quantity of phenomena they explain or include. Thus we shall be working toward developing what might be termed "partial" theories which are centered around particular phenomena such as war, crisis, and alliance. Each of these partial theories may contain any degree of inclusiveness that we desire or find possible. Eventually, we shall wish to combine them into a general theory of international politics. But for now we may find it useful to limit this type of generality and limit the variety of phenomena included in our theory.

The other important feature of the content of a theory is its substance. In our international political investigations we are concerned, as was suggested above, with both the focus of attention and the locus of causation. We may analyze or describe our phenomena at any one level or some combination of many levels — from the minds of the leaders, through the governments and domestic political systems of states, to the international system. And, similarly, we may state the propositions in our theory at various levels of description. In addition, we may find the locus of causation at any one level or some combination of such levels, and of course we would then specify that locus in our propositions. Even this latter determination of the locus of causation is, to a certain extent, a matter of preference rather than something compelled by our data and our conclusions, for we may move backward in time in such a way as to settle on what might actually be the cause of the cause of a war as the significant or useful locus of causation.

Criteria for a Successful Theory

This possibility raises the final consideration in our analysis of the nature of international political theory: its success. One measure of a theory's success can be its accuracy or confirmation. We may wish to distinguish even among these, applying accuracy to the correctness of the theory, whether that correctness is realized or not, and applying confirmation to the realization through successful testing of the correctness. In either event, we may conclude that we are satisfied if our theory or even our discrete propositions are accurate and confirmed. We shall examine possible criteria for satisfaction with confirmation in Chapter 8.

But if we desire more than accurate theory, we shall have other tests for success. These will include the strength of the theory in organizing data and in simplifying the explanation of the phenomena. They will probably also include some sense of understanding. And if we are scholars in the field we shall likely be interested in the research suggestiveness or usefulness of our theory as discussed above. Finally, particularly if we are policymakers or their advisers, we shall be interested in prediction and contribution to controllability as measures of usefulness of our theories. Such interest in control may lead us to move to certain manipulable levels in our quest for the loci of causation, as was suggested above.

We have noticed, in our brief examination of the nature of international political theory, that such theory is likely to differ significantly from the comprehensive, deductive, quantitative theory of the physical sciences — at least for the time being. We have noted also that its forms will vary, and we have concluded that its substance and usefulness will vary, partly as functions of each other and partly as functions of our imagination and competence in theory building. Such imagination and competence will depend heavily on our ability to analyze in the ways that were briefly considered at the outset of this chapter; hence it is to the methods of such analysis that we now turn.

PART II
ANALYSIS

chapter 4

International Political Phenomena

Types The interaction between the United
of Phenomena States and the Soviet Union following
Soviet introduction of missiles into
Cuba is referred to as a *crisis*. The interaction between Israel and
her neighbors in June 1967 is called a *war*. The North Atlantic
Treaty Organization is regarded as an *alliance*, and the nuclear
testban treaty an international arms control *agreement*. Not all
political interactions are as clear cut as these, but there are enough
clear cases to provide adequate material to begin our analysis of
international politics in terms of phenomena like crisis, war,
alliance, and international agreement.

Generally speaking, we make such distinctions among various phenomena for several reasons. First, without clear concepts or ideas of the various types of phenomena we can neither
recognize instances of them nor discuss them with others. Thus
we generally try to define our terms and describe the instances
we wish to recognize. But in the academic study of such phenomena as international political occurrences, it is not enough

to have common terminology and concepts of events. To be able to analyze these happenings carefully in terms of the conditions under which they occur and in terms of their causes, we must be able to distinguish among types. It seems likely that the conditions and causes of international agreement will be different from the conditions and causes of war. Furthermore, the conditions and causes of a world war will probably be different from those of a civil war. We must first examine and distinguish among these types of occurrence before we can inquire into their causes.

The Nature of War

If our only concern were being able to understand each other's reference to war and to recognize a war when we encountered one, we would probably not have to give much attention to war. About a century ago the French writer Pierre Proudhom wrote: "There is not a reader who has to be told what war is, either physically or empirically. Everyone has some idea of it, whether through having witnessed it, through having had extensive connections with it, or, as in the case of a great number, through having taken part in it."[1]

Whether we have experienced war or not, we all have a good idea of its nature. No one would doubt that World Wars I and II qualify for inclusion in that category, nor would there be much dispute about the conflict in Korea, even though it was in many ways different from the previous two. Similarly, few would object to terming the struggle in Vietnam a war, even though some call it merely a liberation movement. There have also been major civil wars, such as the Chinese, and minor civil wars, such as the Dominican, that share many characteristics with the previous wars. Even further, we still often refer to the U.S.-Soviet conflict as "the Cold War." But it is at this point that the term "war" becomes ambiguous, and for this reason alone we should examine the concept somewhat before attempting to explain why wars occur. But in addition, to understand how they originate, how they develop, how they terminate, and how they affect other aspects of international politics, we must pay close attention to the nature of wars both as continuing happenings and as collections of stages occurring over time.

[1]Quoted in Gaston Bouthoul, *War* (New York: Walker, 1962), p. 11.

Most dictionary definitions of war describe it as "armed conflict between countries or between factions within a country." Although this definition clearly excludes the Cold War, it applies to the others we have thus far mentioned, and it certainly describes a fundamental feature of war. But this definition only tells us that it occurs between countries or between factions and that it is armed conflict; it does not tell us about the phenomenon itself. Obviously, we shall be interested in whether or not there are significant differences between those wars involving countries and those involving only factions within a country, and what accounts for those differences.

Even more important, we shall be interested in the stages of war. The first of these is its outbreak in which a nation adopts a policy and implements it by taking action that is in some sense "aggressive" or "provocative." This of course results in a response to it by the party affected. There will then follow a continuing interaction of indeterminate duration, finally terminating in one party's absolute defeat (unconditional surrender), or marginal defeat (acceptance of offered terms), or in a stalemate where both parties agree to a compromise settlement.

These distinctions among the stages of a war will be of considerable importance when we attempt to discover and state the conditions and causes of war, for we shall then be concerned not just with why one nation attacks and another resists, but also with why the attack continues, and finally with why it terminates as it does. In such study we would seek to specify the conditions under which each of these "stages" of a war takes place and the reasons why it takes place as it does.

But before engaging in causal analysis we must extend our descriptive analysis. The actions nations take in war will have as their immediate objectives either destruction of the adversary's capabilities or denial of success to those capabilities should they be employed—as well as continuing efforts to increase their own capabilities and maintain them against the adversary's efforts to destroy them. Thus in war, nations are likely to bomb to destroy, blockade to deny, and arm and defend to maintain capabilities. In the long run, their objective is to change either the minds or the regime of the adversary in order to prevail against his aggression or resistance.

While these brief descriptions concentrate on war as a series of stages and interactions within them, we can also view war as a "state," whether legal or actual, persisting over time. Indeed, most of the prevalent definitions seek to describe a *state* of war, and it is such definitions that raise the major problems in distinguishing among the various types of conflicts manifest in World War I, World War II, the Korean conflict, the Vietnam action, the American Civil War, and the Cold War. The world wars were declared by nations; the Korean War was "declared" by the United Nations; the Vietnam war was not declared by anybody and much of it was "unconventional," involving guerrilla actions rather than pitched battles on clear lines of confrontation; the Civil War involved parties within a nation rather than nations as wholes (which might also be said of some of the fighting in World War II and much of that in Vietnam); and the Cold War involved generally nonmilitary conflict between the superpowers, plus a reciprocal tendency to assume animosity in the attitudes and actions of the adversary. It is possible, and sometimes helpful for increasing our understanding of the nature of war, to develop definitions of war which would include various combinations of these five different wars so that we can see more clearly the differences among them and become more aware of the effect that our definition of a term will have on its inclusiveness or exclusiveness in the analysis of international politics.[2]

When we select which definition to employ, we may refer to various criteria. Generally, we shall have a notion of which types of phenomena we wish to study and we shall want a definition that will allow us to include them. But we shall also want to make our study easier rather than harder. And although our understanding of a phenomenon such as war may increase markedly if we are able to cope with a wide variety of instances (say, for war, everything from the Cold War through World War II), it may be much easier to develop propositions that satisfactorily explain the occurrence and outcome of war if we (at least temporarily) eliminate widely divergent cases (such as civil wars and nonviolent wars like the Cold War). Thus we might be inclined to settle on a definition of war as "purposive armed conflict among nations or their would-be governments" (a rather inclusive defi-

[2]In the literature of international politics there are many different definitions of "war." Among the more interesting are those offered or discussed in the following works: Karl von Clausewitz, *On War* [many editions]; Gaston Bouthoul, *War* (New York: Walker, 1962); Thomas Hobbes, *Leviathan* [many editions]; Quincy Wright, *A Study of War*, 2 vols. (Chicago: University of Chicago Press, 1942).

nition, but one which eliminates the Cold War) or, alternately, "a legal condition in which two or more hostile nations carry out conflict by armed force" (a narrower definition excluding undeclared war and civil war). Selection among such definitions will vary with our objectives—and perhaps with our patience as we attempt to develop general propositions and theories that will explain the broad ranges of phenomena usefully. We shall return to these considerations when we examine the explanation of war in Chapter 10.

The Nature   Another political phenomenon, quite
of Crisis   similar to war in many of its aspects,
  is crisis.[3] We are interested in crises
for several reasons. Obviously their consequences—wars or quick changes in relations among parties to the crisis—are significant. Furthermore, they seem likely to combine the features of both wars and diplomatic negotiations, all compressed into a very short time period. Indeed, it is probably this condensation of the time dimension for decisions that is the most distinguishing characteristic of a crisis.

Crises may, of course, occur within wars or apart from them. There have been many since the end of World War II, including the Berlin Blockade (1948–1949), the march of United Nations' troops to the Yalu River and the Chinese entry into the Korean

---

[3]The best—indeed, almost the only—general analytical study of crisis is Charles A. McClelland, "The Acute International Crisis," in *World Politics*, 41, (1961) 182–204. See also the studies of crisis in J. David Singer, ed., *Quantitative International Politics: Insights and Evidence* (New York: Free Press, 1968). See also Oran R. Young, *The Intermediaries: Third Parties in International Crisis* (Princeton, N.J.: Princeton University Press, 1967).

For recent literature on crisis management, see esp. Harlan Cleveland, "Crisis Diplomacy" in *Foreign Affairs*, 41 (1963), pp. 638–649; Edward Weintal and Charles Bartlett, *Facing the Brink* (New York: Scribner, 1967); Alastair Buchan, "Crisis Management" (Boulogne-sur-Seine: Atlantic Institute, 1966); Herman Kahn and Anthony Wiener, *Crises and Arms Control* (Harmon-on-Hudson, N.Y.: Hudson Institute, 1962), much of which was incorporated in Kahn's *On Escalation* (N.Y.: Praeger, 1965).

Studies of specific crisis include Elie Abel, *The Missile Crisis* (Philadelphia: Lippincott, 1966); Terence Robertson, *Crisis: The Inside Story of the Suez Conspiracy* (New York: Atheneum, 1964); and Hugh Thomas, *Suez* (New York: Harper & Row, 1967). See also the analyses of Thomas Schelling, esp. in *Arms and Influence* (New Haven, Conn.: Yale University Press, 1966).

conflict, the attacks on Quemoy and Matsu, the Hungarian revolt, the Sinai-Suez conflict of 1956, the Middle East crisis of 967, the building of the Berlin wall, the Bay of Pigs invasion, the Cuban missile crisis, the *Pueblo* crisis, the Congo collapse, the Laotian conflict, and perhaps certain instances in the Vietnam situation. But such acute crises have seldom been studied carefully as international political phenomena.

One recent comprehensive study of crises developed a list of characteristics that tend to be present in a crisis:

> turning points are perceived
> decisions and actions are required
> threats, warnings, or promises are seen
> the outcome will shape the future
> events converge
> uncertainties increase
> control of events is decreased
> urgency increases
> information may become more inadequate
> time pressures increase
> interrelations among actors are changed
> international tensions increase[4]

The authors of this study recognized that these features tend to overlap and that not all will characterize a crisis. But on the basis of this list, which they derived from studying those instances generally considered crises, they defined an international crisis as "a situation involving significant actual or potential international conflict in either a novel form or at an abruptly changing level." They added that they wished "to exclude all chronic, static, stabilized, or routinized forms of conflict, which nations have learned to control. This exclusion extends to wars themselves if they are being fought in a routine manner. But the outbreaks of wars, battles involving turning points, major strategic decisions, and terminations of wars constitute crises in the sense of this report."[5]

These authors suggested that the most important characteristics of a crisis include the main points in dispute, the participants, the geographical area in which they develop, the degree

[4]Wiener and Kahn, *Crises and Arms Control*, p. 12.
[5]Wiener and Kahn, *Crises and Arms Control*.

of intensity at the maximum point, historical similarities, initiating incidents, techniques employed by the various participants, the way in which military force is used, and points of reference (government, subgovernmental organizations, international organization, and so on).

But whether we focus our attention on these or other aspects of crisis, we shall be examining the policies and actions of the participants as they constitute interaction. We shall be concerned not simply to outline such interaction in various crises, but to discern recurrent forms and patterns in this interaction. In this way we can delineate differing types of crisis and then develop propositions explaining their occurrence and resolution in terms of what we know or expect of the behavior of interacting units.

Cooperation in International Politics Our preliminary analyses of war and crisis have suggested the presence of cooperation in international politics. There has never been a war in which there was not some agreed upon limitation — whether involving territory not invaded or attacked, types of weapons (such as gas and germs) not employed, targets (such as civilians) not hit, or other such limitations.[6] Much of this "limitation" in wartime may derive from continued acceptance of the "rules of war" in international law (rules that generally concern such subjects as treatment of prisoners and protection for civilians) or it may develop out of discovery of a mutual interest in keeping the war within certain boundaries.

Similarly, crises, although distinguished by the inability of nations to respond in a wholly routine way, are still characterized by acceptance of diplomatic channels for interaction and frequently by continuing appeals to international law, prudence, and other possible common grounds of interest that might encourage cooperation within the conflict situation.

Other types of interaction often thought of as conflictual also contain cooperative elements. The debate that takes place in the United Nations may be harsh, but it is limited to that forum

[6]See Robert Osgood, *Limited War* (Chicago: University of Chicago Press, 1957); and Morton Halperin, *Limited War in the Nuclear Age* (New York: Wiley, 1963), for major studies of the limitation of war.

rather than extending to the battlefield, and it is further limited by acceptance of the forum and its parliamentary procedures — for all parties have found it in their interests to cooperate in maintaining and observing these institutions and restraints. International negotiation and agreement, too, have strong cooperative elements, as well as those conflictual elements that have led the nations to bargain and negotiate.

Other international political phenomena are also generally thought of as instances of cooperation. Among them are peacemaking, alliance, and cooperation with adversaries to limit armaments, warfare, or other manifestations of competition and conflict.

Peace

People generally conceive of peace as the absence of war. If the Cold War falls within our definition of war, the world has not had peace since 1939. On the other hand, if our definition of war excludes the Cold War and civil wars, there have been major periods of peace in this century. Indeed, unless we say that any war anywhere in the world precludes all nations from being at peace, we would conclude that peace existed among the major powers at all times except during the two world wars.

On the other hand, since World War II there have been many conflicts — wars of aggression, frontier disputes, colonial wars, civil wars, frontier claims, civil wars involving internal minorities, international disputes concerning minorities, and ideological civil wars. One study lists sixty six such conflicts in the first fifteen years following World War II.[7]

For our purposes, however, we are particularly interested in relations between two countries (or larger groups) that are not characterized by war. For we shall want to develop propositions that will help us to explain how relations come to be peaceable and how they may eventually degenerate into relations in which conflictual elements predominate over peaceful relations. Of course, we shall also be interested in characterizing those relations by more than their lack of war. Perhaps by examining, for example, big-power relations between the Franco-Prussian War

[7]Evan Luard, *Peace and Opinion* (London: Oxford University Press, 1962), lists the 66 by category, pp. 35–37.

of 1870 and the outbreak of World War I in 1914, the peacemaking effort after World War I, the interwar years, particularly during the so-called Spirit of Locarno, and the years since World War II, we would be able to determine the reasons why war turns to peace, why peace persists over a period of time, and why war eventuates.

In our efforts to characterize peace we would probably look for what might be termed "tendency features" — that is, features that are frequent or are likely to characterize those periods in which there was no war among the countries being examined. We might well look to the national fabric (finding, perhaps, no national war footing but continuing armament) and to international intercourse (perhaps generally finding an increase in peaceful contacts and economic trade, the increased credicility of promises, and a decreased frequency of threats). This situation would especially interest us as we attempted to develop statements of the conditions in which war does not occur or in which peace continues to prevail.

When we study instances in which a spirit of cooperation predominates among states, we may find it useful to distinguish between cooperation among friends or allies on the one hand, and cooperation among enemies or adversaries on the other. This distinction seems promising because an alliance can be characterized by the cooperation of several parties against a third party whereas cooperation among adversaries is directed at a common problem rather than at another party. Presumably, the difference between friends and enemies here is a consequence of the amount and nature of interests shared, the amicability of their relations in general, and perhaps even the existence of an alliance that provides for continuing regularized cooperation.

Cooperation among Friends

Perhaps the most prominent instance of cooperation among nations is that usually designated "alliance," a term generally applied to an organization or a commitment of certain nations to take certain cooperative actions against another nation or nations under certain specified conditions. This definition distinguishes alliance from instances of cooperation among adversaries.

When we speak of alliances we have in mind such agreements as the North Atlantic Treaty, the Warsaw Treaty, and the

South East Asian Treaty. But there are, of course, other instances of cooperation among several nations directed basically at others but not so formalized. Perhaps the best example is the long-standing Anglo-American "special relationship" (as it is often called), which has been characterized by many and varied instances of cooperation through most of the twentieth century. Usage varies, but cooperation not formalized by a specific treaty is often referred to as an "alignment." Thus a developing nation that obtains most of its economic aid and political leadership or direction from a major power is said to be aligned with it rather than allied with it. Similarly, a nation that openly refuses to tie itself to one side or the other in the Cold War or in other regional confrontations is generally termed "unaligned" or "nonaligned."

To distinguish alliances from economic or other sorts of "nonsecurity" cooperation, as well as from collective security and nonalignment, we generally use the term to refer to a conditional commitment of a political or military sort exchanged by several nations and directed at some specified (although not necessarily named) nation. Such alliances generally establish organizations to oversee keeping of the commitment; they are usually formalized by a written agreement or treaty. It is with such alliances that we shall be concerned in Chapter 11.

Cooperation among allies will take many forms, among them promises of military assistance in the face of aggression (which may be the defining characteristic of this type of cooperation), military assistance, economic assistance, political consultation, and strategic and military cooperation.

Cooperation among Adversaries

Cooperation among adversaries, on the other hand, has as its objective limiting or eliminating the basic conflict between them or at least avoiding its manifestations in war and hostility. Thus the most likely instances of such cooperation will include the limitation of war, arms control and disarmament, international peace-keeping (for example, that undertaken by the United Nations in the Congo to try to keep the Cold War out of Africa), and joint nonsecurity activities (cultural exchange, economic trade, international organization participation, competition in the Olympic Games, and the like).

From this brief characterization and enumeration of possible instances of conflict and of two types of cooperation, we can see that no relations among any two nations are apt to be wholly cooperative or wholly conflictual. But by delving deeper into war, crisis, alliance, and other international political phenomena, we can become more familiar with their common and their distinguishing features. Having done this, we should be better able to categorize international political happenings and then to extend our analytical efforts to the stages in their life cycles. Focusing on the way a phenomenon develops over time, from its inception to its termination, should increase our knowledge of what particular stages to concentrate on and what possible determinants to look for as we attempt to explain why it occurs as it does. In so doing, we shall attempt to construct what can be termed a descriptive model of the phenomenon — a conceptual or analytical framework that portrays the stages over time and the various factors we believe might be determinant. For certain key stages, such as outbreak and termination, we shall probably wish to concentrate first on the decision process resulting in policy. For others, particularly the lengthy development of most negotiation and war, we shall seek to find more general patterns, such as conciliatoriness or intransigence in negotiation, or battlefield trends in war. In order to develop these models and employ them, we must first analyze the process and sources of national decision and the nature and patterns of multinational interaction. These will be the subjects of the next two chapters.

chapter 5

National Action
and Its Sources

The Sources
of Decisions
Once the United States had discovered missiles in Cuba, President John F. Kennedy had to decide what response the United States would make. There were several major alternatives. At one extreme the United States could simply accept the missiles and do nothing; at the other, it could invade Cuba, thereby bringing about at least a limited war in Cuba and perhaps a major intercontinental nuclear war with the Soviet Union. Among the intermediate responses, three were prominent. First, the United States could engage in what was popularly called "surgical removal" of the missile sites by precision bombing raids, thereby probably killing Russian construction workers and technicians and perhaps encouraging or forcing the Soviet Union to respond with a "surgical" or even a less precise attack on Americans either at home or abroad. Second, it could interrupt the flow of weapons and supplies from Russia to Cuba and attempt thereby to encourage the Soviets not only to cease building sites, but also to reverse their course and dismantle those already

constructed. Or, third, it could protest through appropriate diplomatic channels such as the United Nations, hoping that the Soviets would change their ways; and if not successful, could either accept the missiles or then attempt their removal using one of the previous strategies.

As policymakers debated among these alternatives that week in mid-October, each of these possibilities had its temporary advocates. But the alternatives soon came down to two choices: an air strike to destroy the bases, or a blockade to encourage reversal of Soviet actions. At first, opinion seemed to favor the air strike, but, as the week progressed, the decision finally reached was to blockade (or, in the legalistic phrasing of the proclamation, "quarantine") Cuba and threaten further action if the missiles and bombers were not removed immediately.

We can explain this decision in terms of the reasoning that went on among Kennedy and his advisers (and we shall when studying crises in Chap. 9) because we have a wide variety of accounts of that debate, by many participants in it. We can depict the process by which the final decision was reached as a rational one, although it would be less easy to say the same in the case of the Soviet Union. For one thing, we do not have extensive accounts by their participants from which to reconstruct the reasoning behind their decision. Indeed, particularly in view of the outcome — the Soviets, as a result of the U.S. blockade, were forced to withdraw the missiles — we would, if anything, be inclined to view their original decision as basically an irrational one. But such a conclusion conceals more than it reveals, and our first efforts at explaining the Soviet action (efforts we shall make in Chap. 9) will begin with the question, Why might the Soviets have decided rationally to plant missiles on the island of Cuba? Only if we cannot satisfactorily answer that question will we resort to "governmental irrationality" for an explanation.

The Assumption of Rationality

The reasons for assuming rationality are several. First, our efforts at constructing a generally applicable theory of international politics will be greatly enhanced, for it is much simpler to explain actions that are rational — especially because irrationality can take so many forms. For this reason alone, it would be sensible to employ the "rationality hypothesis" until we find it untenable in the face of our research. Further, our basic reasons for seeking a theory of international politics are to improve our understanding of the workings of international politics and to increase our ability to make policy recommendations. As a rule, rational behavior is more comprehensible than irrational behavior. Moreover, discussions of policy and recommendations about policy are generally based on the rationality postulate or assumption, for we are convincing only when our recommendations appear persuasive because they are based on rational argument.

We must of course remember that none of these arguments for making the rationality assumption is necessarily convincing, let alone accurate as a description of national behavior. But the assumption seems desirable at the outset, and it can always be revised should we find that evidence does not support it. In the meantime, by employing the rationality assumption, we can construct a model of rational policymaking that helps us to explain national decision-making behavior.

A Model of Policymaking

Our model of the policymaking process suggests that policymakers combine values or objectives from the political system with information obtained from their environment, and then calculate the best policy. When implemented, it becomes their state's action. This process is depicted schematically by stages in Figure 5–1. Because important actions are preceded by decision, all theories of international politics must in some way take note of this policymaking process. Some theories, however, avoid paying any significant attention to the process by making major assumptions about one or more of these stages. Because of their importance, we must look briefly at each stage.

Values and Objectives

The first stage of policymaking is that in which values are obtained through the particular state's political process. Actually, this is an assumption of our model. We can imagine a state where no such political process occurs, where political competition is nonexistent and rule is conducted by one unchallenged man. In such a state we would be interested not so much in its political system as the ideology, or the psychological nature of the

Figure 5-1.

MODEL OF A NATION'S POLICYMAKING PROCESS

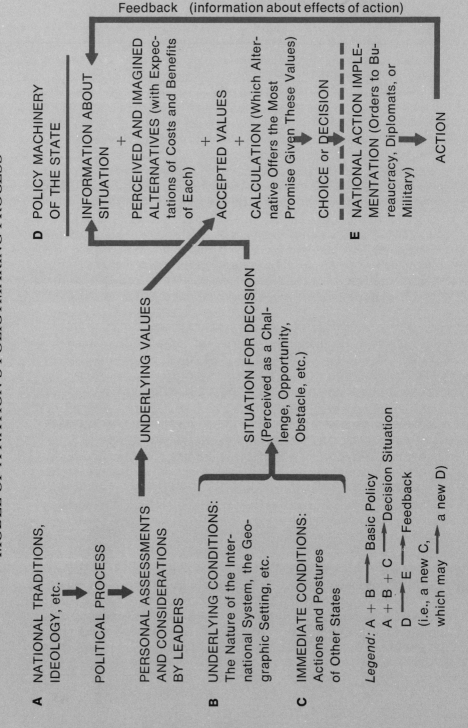

single ruler. We might well be interested in these factors even if there were political competition, for both aspects may be significant. The personal features of the leader or leaders (or perhaps more generally such features of their natures as whether they are generous or selfish) may be important in themselves if this elite is relatively free of pressure from others or of competition for office. Alternatively, the environment in which the system operates — everything from the populace of the state on through the international system in which the state acts — may also be significant. If we accept the arguments that public opinion or electoral sanction (the possibility of electoral defeat for the leaders) heavily influences policy, we shall obviously pay considerable attention to this level. On the other hand, if we accept the arguments of the systems theorists (which we shall examine more closely later) we shall pay particular attention to the systemic aspect of the decision environment — the nature of the international system in which the state acts — because we believe that it will determine the actions of the state.

Because our research to date is inconclusive, we do not yet know how much attention to give to each of these possible determinants of the values and objectives sought by the state generally or by a particular state. We would expect to learn much about this from studies of politics and policymaking in particular states — something undertaken comprehensively by students of comparative politics rather than by those concerned primarily with international politics. And until we have more such data and more such conclusions we must be tentative in assigning relative importance to these aspects. We may simply have to ask the state's policymakers what values they are pursuing (and perhaps where they got them) in order to arrive at some answer, for the only other way to find the values in particular cases is to deduce them from the state's actions — a dangerous and self-defeating activity.

There are some theorists who make significant assumptions about such values, and they merit attention. The first group includes those who believe that we can and do know what human nature is like (whether it is selfish or generous or some specific combination thereof). Some of them argue that international politics is as conflictual, even bloody, as it is because men are basically evil. On the other hand, those who hold the converse — that despite the constant bloodshed in human affairs, human nature is basically benign—must argue that something else is responsible for man's evil actions. They may, for example, maintain that the inevitability of political competition for office or influence, or the competitive nature of international politics without world government, is what makes good men act like savages.

Of the theories which argue that men are essentially brutish, perhaps the most prominent is the one developed by certain psychoanalysts who base their theories on the teachings of Freud, who wrote:

> men are not gentle, friendly creatures wishing for love, who simply defend themselves if they are attacked, but [in men] a powerful measure of desire for aggression has to be reckoned as part of their instinctual endowment. . . . Civilized society is perpetually menaced with disintegration through this primary hostility of men towards one another. Their interests in their common work would not hold them together; the passions of instinct are stronger than reasoned interests.[1]

This should not be taken to indicate that war is inevitable. Freud believed that the continuing progress of civilization, coupled with the increasingly dreadful form wars would take might well bring men to abolish war or at least at some point to cease fighting.[2]

Furthermore, it is clear that the institutional structure of society must be such as to allow politically effective implementation of the warlike attitudes of the populace if war is to take place because of men's nature. This is a very important point, for it indicates that psychoanalysis cannot itself offer a comprehensive theory of war—let alone of all international politics—because the politics of the society must also be important determinants of the resort to war in this theory.

Another major school offering theories about the nature of the political process to explain the occurrence of conflict in international politics (and, indirectly, of cooperation through alliances

[1] From *Civilization and Its Discontents*, reprinted in John Rickman, ed., *Civilization, War and Death: Selections from Five Works by Sigmund Freud* (London: Hogarth, 1953), pp. 50–51.
[2] See his interesting correspondence with Albert Einstein, "Why War?" in Rickman, *Civilization, War and Death*, pp. 82–97. For a comprehensive study of Freud's views, see Paul Roazen, *Freud: Political and Social Thought* (New York: Knopf, 1968), esp. chap. 4, "Politics: Social Controls."

and other such arrangements) is that of the "Realists." They postulate that any political unit (such as the state) will act in such a way as to "maximize" its power, which is defined in terms of the security of its territory. The prime exponent of "Realism" is Hans Morgenthau. Although his views have moderated somewhat over the years, he is still inclined to ascribe such territory-maintenance behavior to an inevitable drive for power, which is a product of man's basically evil or dominating nature.[3]

Whatever its basis or determinant, Realists tend to assume that the state will act in a certain militant and aggressive fashion — or, in our terms, will adopt certain values or objectives — just because it is a sovereign state in an anarchic world. This is not completely convincing because we see significant indications of cooperative behavior that are not always explainable simply as a selfish way to maximize national power. But even if we were impressed by some regularity in the adoption by states of such uncooperative objectives, we would probably find enough variation from the norm that would make us unwilling to make such a blanket assumption here and instead would seek evidence which would enable us to distinguish types of aggressive objectives.

Perceptions

But whatever the values or objectives we find nations adopting, whatever their sources or determinants, these values are but one component of policy. The decisionmakers must also gather information from their environment about the situations in which the actor or state finds itself and the various alternative actions open to it. We know from our study of international happenings that nations can often incorrectly perceive the environment — usually the interests and intentions, and sometimes the capabilities, of the potential adversary — as the Russians did in placing missiles in Cuba and as the Allies did in first believing

[3]See the various editions of his famous textbook, *Politics among Nations* (New York: Knopf, 1948, 1954, 1960, 1967) and also particularly his *Scientific Man vs. Power Politics* (Chicago: University of Chicago Press, 1946). Among the analysts of Morgenthau's work, who are legion, are Robert C. Good, "National Interest and Moral Theory," chap. 15 in Roger Hilsman and Robert C. Good, eds., *Foreign Policy in the Sixties* (Baltimore: Johns Hopkins Press, 1965) and Charles McClelland, *Theory and the International System* (New York: Macmillan, 1966), chap. 3. See also Alan James, "Power Politics," *Political Studies*, 12 (1964) 307–326.

that their airlift could not supply West Berlin through the winter during the Blockade. We also know that policy is originally made on the basis of whatever perceptions the nation or its policy-makers have, and that only after they attempt to act and are perhaps surprised by the consequences can they begin to sort out and assess these perceptions.

Because of the obvious importance of these perceptions and the obvious inaccuracy of so many of them, we are quite interested in learning why nations make such mistakes. Many explanations for this phenomenon have been proposed. Some argue that ideology distorts the perception and makes nations believe the success they desire to be actually possible or even likely. Others — particularly Marxists — have argued that perception is a function of one's class, which is an economic determinant. Still others have suggested more simply that some people are "naturally optimistic" or "naturally pessimistic" and that these inclinations strongly influence their image of the world by affecting their perception. Increasingly, "cognitive theorists," who study people's images of the world and the generation of those images, are developing theories that may help us to answer such questions.[4] And we may expect further contributions from the psychologists as their work progresses.

The Question of Rationality

Our third aspect of the policy process, that of actual calculation, may be more easily managed. Although we have very little notion of what factors determine values and perception, we do have some rather stringent notions of what is rational calculation, and hence we can assess rationality of calculation more easily. The term "rationality" has had many uses in the literature of psychology, politics, economics, and philosophy, but recently most scholars have come to agree upon a concept of rationality which views it as efficient means-end calculation. More explicitly, a person is said to act rationally when, fully conscious of the various ends he seeks and their relative importance to him, he as-

[4]For some of the interesting recent studies, see the essays in Part I of Herbert Kelman, ed., *International Behavior* (New York: Holt, Rinehart and Winston, 1965) and the special issue devoted to "Image and Reality in World Politics," *Journal of International Affairs*, 21 (1967) No. 1. See also Roger Fisher, ed., *International Conflict and Behavioral Science* (New York: Basic Books, 1964).

sesses the alternatives he believes open to him in terms of their expected costs and benefits (determined by the values he seeks) and selects that which maximizes total value or gains to him. Now, this statement of rational calculation is nothing more than a *definition*. It tells us nothing about the way people actually act; rather, it sets a *standard* in terms of which we can assess decisions. It was arrived at because we are convinced that people tend to want to be rational in this sense. Nobody likes to lose when he need not have if he had calculated better.[5]

No one will deny that in practice it is difficult to calculate rationally in this sense, for we generally have trouble deciding just how much of one objective we are willing to give up for a certain amount of another. Such knowledge is required by our definition which includes an awareness of our objectives and their relative worth. Further, as we know, we generally do not have perfect information about the situation and the available alternatives — partly because this presumes accurate prediction of a sort we cannot yet manage. But our requirement is only that, given our information, our choice be efficient if it is to be termed rational.

Now, no one will argue that in practice people always, or even usually, act rationally in this sense. Consequently, there have developed in recent years a number of theories which attempt to describe and account for the way in which people really act. Although many are well developed, these psychological theories of decision are still in the process of being tested, and so we do not yet have confirmed conclusions.[6]

But if we cannot always be certain about the values, information, and calculation that together produce a decision, we can be more certain of the decision produced because the decision becomes visible in commands, implementation, and action. The fact that it is much easier to observe and study action than its determinants has led some scholars — and many theorists of international

[5] See Carl J. Friedrich, ed., *Nomos VII: Rational Decision* (New York: Atherton, 1964), for various essays on and around this topic and citations of additional materials.

[6] See Ward Edwards, "The Theory of Decision Making," in *Psychological Bulletin*, 51 (1954) 380–417; Ward Edwards, "Behavioral Decision Theory," in *Annual Review of Psychology*, 12 (1961) 473–498; and Herbert Simon, "Theories of Decision Making in Economics and Behavioral Science," in *American Economic Review*, 49 (1959) 253–283. See also Ward Edwards and Amos Tversky, eds., *Decision-Making: Selected Readings* (Baltimore: Penguin, 1968).

politics – to attempt to ignore these sources of action and concentrate on international political interaction.

This may be the only possibility when we find that information on the actual decisionmaking process in the cases we are studying is not adequate, and hence we can only assume rationality, or, if we find that we do have adequate information, that the decision is irrational. Whatever the case, we shall be forced to settle for a "behavioral" focus, simply beginning with whatever behavior or action we find nations undertaking rather than with the reasoning behind it or the decision process from which it is the output. But in doing this, we shall probably never be fully convinced by our conclusions or confident that we really do understand why nations act as they do. For this reason, it is desirable to attempt to consider the possible causes of national action even if we must make certain simplifying assumptions about informed rational conduct. If we find that these assumptions prove inadequate, we can then either skip the decision stage and concentrate on interaction, or we can attempt to rework those assumptions. This is, in fact, what we generally do even when we are not carefully rigorous in our attempts to explain international politics.

Thus, when we ask why a man or a state took a given action, we are often satisfied by the answer that it was a sensible or rational act under the circumstances. This answer is generally substantiated by elaboration of the believed interests or objectives of the actor and of the expected costs and benefits of the various acts that might have been taken in view of the actor's capabilities.

Sometimes the act taken appears irrational, until we find that the actor had faulty information or had miscalculated with accurate information. Or we may conclude that something other than calculation on merits seems to have determined the action. Thus, for example, the decision may have been rational but may not have been carried out accurately or rationally; or by making what are referred to as "side payments" such as bribes, economic interests may have lobbied to achieve a decision in their interest but not in the interest of the state; or by bargaining or blackmail political interests may have lobbied to achieve a decision in their interest.

Such instances of decisions being affected by interest groups can be viewed as cases when other considerations seem to enter the decision beyond the act and its consequences for the organization that takes it. Thus a president might in foreign affairs act in a way that helps his chances for reelection rather than in a way that accords with the national interest. Of course, he might argue that his reelection would be beneficial to the country in the long run, and although this would appear to be a far-fetched argument, it could be correct.

Sometimes, however, rather than finding an explanation of action in terms of rational decisions, we encounter events that cannot be easily and satisfactorily reduced to decisions. For example, although the outbreak of war can generally be treated as a collection of decisions, the outcome of the war cannot easily be. The parties in a war, for example, might decide to continue or end the war, but their decisions will probably be the product of the developing interplay among the parties, (the reciprocal destruction or infliction of pain, for instance). Here we would probably not be satisfied (if someone answered our question as to why the war came out as it did) with the response that the parties to the war decided to end it then and there.

Thus, rather than merely presuming rational decision as an explanation of international political occurrences, we may ask a series of further questions: Why was this act rational? What conditions made this the rational choice? Why did the man or the state act rationally (in this means-ends efficiency sense) rather than otherwise? Did the adversary lack information or make an error in calculation? Were there external factors or interests influencing the decision? Any of these questions may arise when we look at action in terms of decisions about policy.

Levels of Description

The differences that are inherent in looking at international politics in terms of interaction rather than in terms of national actions are part of the more general fact that, depending on the point of view and interest of the persons doing the describing, there are various ways to describe the same political event. Thus, to take a homely example, a headache will be described as a painful feeling by the person who has it, as a state of physical tension by an examining doctor, as a manifestation of anxiety by a psychiatrist, and as a symptom to be removed by a purveyor of aspirin. The same event or occurrence or condition at the same point in time may receive multiple descriptions, none of which is necessarily incorrect and each of which is a consequence of the point of view and interest of the one making it.

In a somewhat similar way, an occurrence in international politics can be described differently by various analysts. A student may view a war as an intriguing subject for study, whereas a national official views it as a challenge to his country, and a representative of the United Nations views it as an affliction of the international order, and these differences are understandable. Further, one event at a given time or over a given period of time can be described at different levels by the same scholar.

Thus we might describe the Cuban missile crisis as a collection of decisions by the leaders primarily of the United States and the Soviet Union. The Soviet leaders decided to place missiles in Cuba; then the leaders of the United States decided to continue to keep an eye on Cuba and discovered the Soviet preparations. The American leaders then decided to attempt to get the missiles removed by ordering American forces to blockade the island and by insisting on the removal of all traces of them. The Soviet leaders then decided to remove them on condition that the American leaders promised not to invade Cuba, and thus a settlement was reached by the two sets of leaders. This is a description of decision making by leadership in two countries.

We could also describe the crisis as the consequence, not of decisions by leaders, but rather of the actions of nations. The Soviet Union put missiles in Cuba, the United States discovered them and blockaded the island, and the Soviet Union removed them when agreement was reached that the United States would not invade Cuba. This skeletal description does not mention anything about decisions on either side—just actions. We could be more specific and describe the actions of individual leaders and diplomats as they carried out plans and conferred on a settlement, discussing not the actions of a nation so much as the actions of individuals within a nation or within both nations. Or, if we were describing war, we might describe it as a collection of decisions by leaders on one side or both, as the actions of armed forces or even of soldiers themselves (which is the way newspapers generally describe wars), or as the actions of a nation (which is the way foreign policy analysts generally describe it), or as the actions of several nations (which is the usual international political analysis of war).

All these ways are incomplete as well as misleading. Thus, for example, the description of leaders' decisions does not tell us, except perhaps by implication, if and how they were carried out, while the analysis of the actions of armed forces does not tell us what decisions were being implemented by the actions. The approach based on the actions of several nations is perhaps even more misleading for several reasons. First, in most instances, it is not the whole of a nation that acts but rather parts of the nation; indeed sometimes there is significant dissent and even noncooperation within the nation. Further, the actions of the nation are not always controlled — that is, what happens may not be the "conscious" action of the nation at all, but rather the insubordinate action of several members of the populace (as in the escapades in the movie *Dr. Strangelove*). Moreover, in a crucial sense, nations themselves do not act; only people act. It is important to remember this, because people, even acting for nations, are subject to considerable influence by various factors and can easily make mistakes. We must also consider the possible impact of the group within which decisions may be made. Social psychologists find that people may become bolder and more daring in groups than when acting alone, and this possibility too should be kept in mind in accounting for decisions.

These suggestions may seem to suggest simply that we must be careful not to exclude certain important factors when we attempt to describe an event or a type of happening. But there are more important considerations. To use our analogy again, just as the doctor is interested in the headache as a physical condition with mental effects and the druggist interested in it as a removable symptom, so at times we will be interested in describing international political happenings as collections or staged progressions of decisions, and other times as collected actions.

There are various reasons for this. First, for some kinds of analysis we must have certain kinds of data. To analyze decision-making that leads to war, we must have data on decisions that have been made, while to analyze which side wins a battle we must have data on the actions of each side regardless of the decisions that preceded them. Furthermore, consistency of description will be important when we attempt comparative analysis of different instances of the same phenomenon. Typically, historians and journalists and even students of foreign policy and international politics will tend to wander from one type of data to another (and then from one type of causal argument to another) without always recognizing that they are indeed on different levels and hence that they cannot really be compared. Therefore they do not always contribute satisfactorily to our increased understanding of the phenomenon under examination.

In describing the Cuban missile crisis, many Americans used to say that "Khrushchev put missiles in Cuba" and "the United States made him take them out." Now it is obvious that it was not Khrushchev himself who put them there, but perhaps he did decide they should be put there. On the other hand, some students of Soviet politics have argued that internal domestic conditions — political infighting—resulted in the placement of missiles, and hence that Khrushchev not only did not do it, but was not even the one who determined that it should be done. Now, until we have studied the case, we cannot decide whether or not the responsibility was Khrushchev's; but if we describe the happening as his doing, we are less apt to realize that it is possible that someone else forced him to make that decision.

This problem of level is particularly important when we attempt to assign casuality to some factor. Just as Soviet foreign policy in the 1950s and early 1960s was often ascribed to Khrushchev, French policy was often ascribed to de Gaulle; British policy at that time was rarely attributed to Lord Home, the British Prime Minister. Later it became popular to ascribe Russian policy to internal political considerations but to continue to ascribe French policy primarily to de Gaulle rather than to internal French politics. All these causal ascriptions may prove correct, but we would only be safe in reaching that conclusion if we have undertaken careful study—not because we have found it easier to describe the events in these varying terms. If we do find them to be the case, however, we shall be interested in knowing why one person can be so influential in a nation's foreign policy at one time and not at another, and why the leader will matter in one country and not in another.

These are but a few of the multitude of questions that will concern us as we attempt to discover why international politics happens as it does. It is clear that in order to be able to study this subject accurately we must be able to gather all the relevant data (something that may be precluded by careless or presumptuous description of the sort we have been examining) *and* to organize that data effectively.

Individual, Group, Set of Groups

To help us in this, we shall find it useful to distinguish among various possible *levels*, or *units*, of description to describe various happenings.[7] Basically, the three types of units are the *individual*, the *group*, and the *set* or *collection of groups*. In terms of foreign policy and international politics, these will usually take the form of the leader, the state, and the society of states, often referred to as the international system. In reality, of course, the levels will not be that clear-cut. Among the individuals, for instance, will not only be leaders but also influential citizens of various countries and "international" citizens such as the Pope or the Secretary-General of the United Nations. Similarly, we may describe an event or a situation in terms of nations, but we may also wish to descend into sublevels of the nation, for example, the government, the political system as a whole, the economic system, interest groups, or the military. And finally, when we are at the international level we may wish to speak of regional or other subinternational groups—alliances, such as NATO, economic blocs, such as the Common Market, international organizations, such as the United Nations, and so on—that do not include all nations.

Some events will be more easily and more usefully described at some levels, and others at other levels. Most international events, particularly wars and diplomatic activities, can be described at the leader level. But such happenings as trade and the Olympic Games (which may at times concern us because of their political effects), while they can sometimes be described in terms of individuals, cannot satisfactorily be described in terms of the decisions and actions of leaders. We can obviously describe wars in terms of leaders, nations, or such subgroups as the military forces. But it is less easy to describe wars in terms of the competing economic systems—even though it is quite possible that economic factors will have a major effect on the outcome of war.

---

[7]Although students of international politics have far from exhausted this problem, useful work includes Kenneth N. Waltz's pioneering study, *Man, the State, and War* (New York: Columbia University Press, 1959); David Singer's article, "The Level-of-Analysis Problem in International Relations," in *World Politics*, 14 (1961) 77–92; and James Rosenau's article, "Pre-theories and Theories of Foreign Policy," pp. 27–92 in R. Barry Farrell, ed., *Approaches to Comparative and International Politics* (Evanston, Ill.: Northwestern University Press, 1966).

The major levels of description that are likely to concern us are listed in Figure 5–2.

We could go on dividing the three major units into subunits, but we must now consider the various levels that may be important in determining what happens in international politics. Our concern thus far has been mostly with what we call "levels of description"—levels at which we can describe and analyze any particular happening or type of happening. But description is merely a prerequisite for understanding. We shall also be concerned with what might be called *levels of determination* or *levels of explanation*—levels that may prove to be the determinants of the way things happen, or that we may use to explain why they happen.

Levels of Determination

As mentioned, we may wish to describe a crisis or a war in terms of the decisions of the leaders of the participant nations, in order to ask then, why did they make these decisions and take these actions? There are many possibilities. Perhaps it was certain alarming information they were given that led them to decide as they did. Or perhaps it was the result of an unconscious drive for power stemming from an abnormal parent-child relationship (as a Freudian psycholanalyst might argue).

Some people maintain that the subconscious is the major determinant of a man's attitudes and actions, while others reject it, citing many other possible determinants. Some would argue the *role* a man plays determines his behavior more than anything else. For example, in the 1964 American presidential election, many believed that Lyndon Johnson and Barry Goldwater would follow radically different foreign policies (to say nothing of domestic policies), while others argued that although Goldwater sounded more militant in his campaign speeches, he would find, once he were elected, that the President could not act so impetuously or so freely because the *office* of the Presidency (the role) would severely limit and even determine his actions. Interestingly enough, as it turned out, many of those who feared Goldwater's election because of his militant stand on Vietnam were markedly surprised to find that Johnson's foreign policy increasingly resembled Goldwater's. It is not immediately clear why this proved to be the case, but the fact that it occurred might suggest that

Figure 5-2.

MAJOR LEVELS OF DESCRIPTION
(And hence, possible levels of determination)

THE INDIVIDUAL

(Generally a Decisionmaker
within a State)
  —Subconscious Mind
  —Conscious Mind
    (esp. the decision process)

THE GROUP

(Generally a State)
  —The Governmental System
  —The Political System
    (i.e., governmental system + interest groups
    and politically active populace—esp. voters)
  —The Interest Groups (military, business,
    industry, trade and professional associations,
    unions, etc.)
  —The Economic System

THE SET OF GROUPS

(Generally a Group of States)
  —An Alliance
  —An International Organization
  —The International System
    (plus its subsystems, such as the
    "superpowers" or the uncommitted nations)

perhaps elements other than the idiosyncrasies of the leader determine a nation's foreign policy.

Beyond a leader's role there are the governmental system and the political system—both possible determinants of political behavior. At these levels, some have argued that democracies tend to be peaceloving whereas dictatorships tend to be warlike. Others have suggested that it is the economic system that determines foreign policy—capitalist states act one way and socialist or communist states another.

At the international system level, some have argued that certain kinds of international systems produce certain kinds of international relations, but that other kinds produce others. Thus some have said that a tight bipolar system in which nations are clustered around two separate poles (as was true after World War II when the United States and the Soviet Union formed the poles), will result in greater world stability because there is little that is "up for grabs", and, since each leader can control its weaker allies, there is little to dispute. Others have said that a more flexible or loose multipolar system, in which more nations form poles, will result in greater overall stability because there is more possibility for realignment to keep a balance between the strongest nation and the others and to allow others to be neutral if they desire so long as they are not threatened. We shall return to such questions in coming chapters.

Thus there are multitudes of possible determinants that can be analyzed and organized in any way we wish. One such way, which we shall employ, is in terms of these three general units: the individual, the group, and the set of groups. But this is only a first step toward the kind of analysis we wish to do. For although we have now discovered a number of possible "levels of determination," we have not yet begun to decide which levels do in fact determine happenings. That is, do the subconscious minds of leaders, or political systems, or economic systems, or international systems, or some other factors actually determine the way things happen? And even when we are able to determine the key level, we must then examine what *part* of the level is the key. For example, if the subconscious is crucial, is it due to the relations with one's parents or with one's lovers? If the political system matters, is it the governmental structure or the degree of awareness of the population? If the economic system, is it the relations and means of production or the international quest for markets? And then we must attempt to discover *how* each part matters — what particular condition in that part makes what particular thing happen internationally under given conditions.

At the moment, these challenges seem overwhelming. But once we develop a better understanding of various methods and types of explanation, and of causal analysis, the problems will seem more manageable, and we can then make progress in actually determining why international politics happens as it does. For the moment our concern is to remember that we may describe these happenings at various levels of analysis and that we will soon wish to examine each happening in terms of various possible levels of determination. If we can keep our data organized and selected in terms of these important categories, we should be much better able to confront the real problems of causal explanation.

chapter 6

Interaction
and Its Outcomes

The Nature of Interaction Various factors may account for the discrepancy we sometimes find between a nation's foreign policy and its desires. For one thing, the nation's perceptions of world conditions may be inaccurate. For another, its calculations about which possible policy would maximize attainment of its objectives may be faulty. Alternately, as we have noted, there may be problems in the implementation of the policy: the diplomats and soldiers may not act according to orders, or communications channels may break down preventing orders from going through. All these problems can be considered accidents which might have been prevented with greater effort or care.

There is, however, another fundamental obstacle not nearly as easy to correct or allow for. Even if all three policymaking stages — perception, calculation, and implementation — are perfect, it is quite possible that the countries with which a nation is interacting will not behave as expected, or, to phrase it technically, that the outcomes of interaction may not be as anticipated. If the problem is not in perception, calculation, or implementation, it must be in mistaken beliefs about the way the world works — erroneous or incomplete notions about what makes nations act as they do. This problem can be termed, in our language, that of a faulty or inadequate theory of international politics. For it is a nation's theory of international politics — tacit or implicit as it may be — that tells it what to expect as consequences of the various actions it considers undertaking.

A nation implements its foreign policy by taking action outside its borders (action of which we shall examine in detail shortly). As this external national action is perceived and reacted to, interaction occurs. Generally, we expect that reaction to be action also, but it can, of course, be inaction, as occurs when a nation threatened by another refuses to acknowledge the threat in an effort to deprive it of its force. The process is illustrated schematically in Figure 6–1.

Cooperation and Conflict as Interaction   The reaction of one nation to another's action may produce an instance of cooperation, or it may result in conflict. Instances of conflict are the most obvious in international politics: war, crisis, debate at the United Nations. As instances of cooperation we might think of peace, alliance, and international arms control agreements. The term "cooperation" here means "acting or working together for a common purpose," and the term "conflict" means "a sharp disagreement or collision in interests, ideas, and perhaps actions."

But these distinctions are overdrawn, for most international political occurrences are not instances of pure conflict or pure cooperation but, rather, contain elements of both. Cooperation may occur in cases where parties discover and act from common or coinciding interests. Conflict may occur over ends or over means. It is quite possible to imagine parties sharing the same objective but differing over the best way to attain it. Thus neither the United States nor the Soviet Union desires a major nuclear war, for obviously both would suffer massive damage from one, but if we can believe the statements of the respective leaders, there are substantial differences over the best way to prevent such a war. The many proposals offered the parties include disarming, strengthening the United Nations, ending colonialism around the world, making West Berlin a neutralized city, opposing aggression

Figure 6-1.

NATIONAL INTERACTION PROCESS

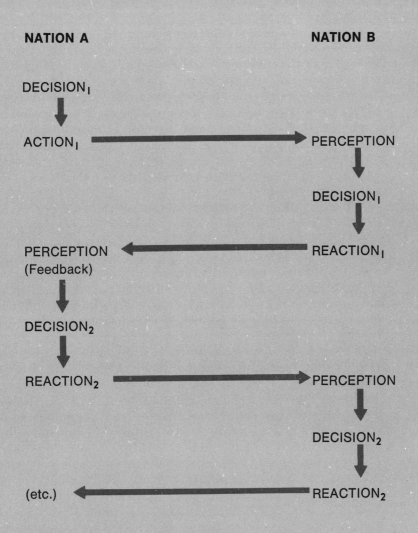

NATION A

DECISION$_1$

ACTION$_1$ ⟶ PERCEPTION

DECISION$_1$

PERCEPTION (Feedback) ⟵ REACTION$_1$

DECISION$_2$

REACTION$_2$ ⟶ PERCEPTION

DECISION$_2$

(etc.) ⟵ REACTION$_2$

NATION B

Note: Interaction may consist of anything from diplomatic communication to bombing. These actions constitute wars, crises, etc., each of which will have a specific pattern composed of some particular version of this interaction.

in small countries like South Vietnam, and threatening devastation of the other's country if it should execute or perhaps merely plan an attack on the one.

These differences arise partly from differing information about the state of conditions in the world (such as the strength of each side's military establishment, the basis of the unrest in the underdeveloped third of the world, and the intentions of each side toward the other). They are also the result of divergent beliefs about the dynamics of world politics (such as what effects a stronger United Nations could have on the superpower confrontation, whether or not an end to colonialism would pacify the underdeveloped world, and what kind of action and statements by one power will satisfactorily deter the other from taking actions unacceptable to the one).

It is important to distinguish these two sources of difference, for they correspond to the two major stages of our effort to understand international politics. Differences in information about the conditions in the world are basically problems of description of a sort that could be eliminated if only each side could improve its study of conditions at the time. Difference in beliefs about the way the world works (or, in social scientific terms, different theories of international politics) cannot be so easily resolved, for they are not static but dynamic problems. Even a comprehensive and accurate picture of the world and its politics today would not of itself resolve these differences, for it would not enable the party to determine what it is that makes the world change over time. Only careful analysis of cause and effect in international politics offers any promise of resolving these types of differences — differences that presently exist not only among nations but among scholars.

Differences in information, or differences in theory or understanding, may help to account for variations in means even when nations share a common objective. But another factor is probably even more important in determining such conflict over means. Nations (and other actors) live in a world of scarcity, in a world where their desires cannot all be satisfied. Most nations will understandably seek to retain what they possess in territory and natural resources, but few nations seem to be fully satisfied with what they have; most are interested in obtaining more.

Sometimes a nation can achieve this through more efficient or extensive exploitation of the resources within its borders. The industrial revolution that all advanced states underwent is a manifestation of this kind of internal activity. An increase in the production of military weapons and in manpower training is military instance of action intended primarily to maintain and increase the nation's possessions or capabilities within its own borders, without relying heavily upon external assistance or plunder. Of course, no nation, even when it is primarily developing itself internally, can wholly divorce itself from reliance on others, whether for raw materials or machine tools in industrialization, or for armaments or political support in militarization. Nevertheless, it is generally possible to develop internally in many ways without major dependence upon other nations.

But when such internal development is not promising, a nation will be tempted to resort to external assistance (aid) or to mutually beneficial exchange (trade) where these are attainable, or perhaps, if it is less costly than the former, exploitation and conquest.

This, at least, is the type of behavior we would expect from nations which behaved like rational people living in a world characterized by limited resources and relatively unlimited wants. But this is too simple a characterization of the sources and manifestations of national conduct in world politics, and most of our additional study will be an effort to improve on this characterization.

This condition of scarcity, where few have everything they wish, underlies the conflict in international politics. When resources are scarce, each party not only desires them but also comes to desire that the other not obtain them because they are scarce. The competition that ensues, in which two parties seek the same scarce objective, becomes transmuted into conflict as the two parties shift their effort from obtaining the objective to preventing the other from capturing it. The situation is similar to a footrace where the contest is considered competition as long as both runners are simply trying to reach the finish first and win the race. But if one runner should at some point attempt to trip the other in order to make him unable to reach the finish first, competition has turned to conflict. In some sports such conflict is allowed within limits. Thus, while runners may not trip each other, football players may block each other. But in all such contests there are rules that limit the extent to which conflict may be added to competition—and the existence of such rules is indeed what makes these events *games* rather than anarchic conflict.

In international politics there is no universally accepted rule maker and no referee, so that it is very hard to get nations to create — let alone observe — rules to govern their international conduct. But although difficult to achieve, it does at times occur. Certain types of cooperation exist among nations at peace who may trade, align, and otherwise help each other; and other types exist even among nations in conflict, who may observe international law, accept limitations on wars they are involved in, and even make and observe international agreements.

If this is a world of limited resources — which should be broadly defined to include not simply material goods but also such nonmaterial goods as prestige and power — and less limited desires, it is hardly surprising that there should be much competition among nations. And if this is a world of few international rules to govern national conduct, with no all-powerful referee and enforcement agency to see that what rules do exist are not violated, it is hardly surprising that there exists so much conflict. Indeed, virtually every international occurrence will have conflictual aspects — if not in its very nature, then in the reason for its occurrence. Thus war will be conflictual in its very nature, whereas foreign aid will be conflictual in only its motivation (which is generally, at least in part, the struggle for allegiance or at least self-sufficient neutrality of the weaker states).

But we must not ignore the extensive and vital role cooperation plays in international politics. Most — indeed probably all — nations share desires for world survival, reciprocated national restraint in situations where mutual destruction threatens, mutual assistance, and mutually profitable exchange or international trade. Such agreement or concord tends to lead to cooperation where both parties are aware that they share desires and where existing conflict, institutions, or norms do not inhibit cooperation. Cooperation with a nation considered in many ways an adversary can be curtailed by conflicts such as war or by institutions such as laws forbidding trading or fraternizing with the enemy. And such inhibitions are strengthened by the tendency, shared by major participants in the great wars of this century, to conceive of war as total.[1]

---

[1] See Robert Osgood, *Limited War* (Chicago: University of Chicago Press, 1957), pp. 28–45; Robert W. Tucker, *The Just War* (Baltimore: Johns Hopkins Press, 1960), esp. pp. 11–93; and Paul Kecskemeti, *Strategic Surrender* (Stanford, Calif.: Stanford University Press, 1958), for treatments of this tendency and its consequences.

The basis of cooperative action is concord, or coincidence of desires. But how is such agreement discovered? It may be realized by both or all parties independently. Or it may be realized by one party and communicated to the other by word or by deed, such as the restraint in the mid-1960's on the development of civil defense measures and the long-lasting mutual restraint in deploying anti-ballistic missile capabilities. When such self-restraint is recognized and emulated by the other side, concord has been discovered and expressed, and cooperation has been achieved through reciprocated action.

The Forms of Interaction

The external action of a nation may be in the form of a pronouncement, or it may be in the form of an allocation or commitment of material resources such as men or goods. We can best understand the different types of action possible by inquiring into the various objectives or directions of such actions.

Much, if not most, of what a nation does can be viewed as an effort to maintain or increase its own capabilities or assets with possible future international encounters in mind. When those encounters take place, they will be either bargaining encounters (in which goods or deeds or pledges are traded) or efforts to destroy the bargaining assets or capabilities of another. Among instances of bargaining are treaty-making, foreign aid, foreign trade, and diplomatic conversation. Instances of the destructive type of activity include war, subversion, and propaganda.

But what are the instruments a nation may employ toward obtaining these objectives, thereby getting what it wants in international politics? The fundamental elements are words, goods, deeds, and weapons. For the purposes of our study, it is useful to distinguish three processes of interaction: discussion, exchange, and coercion.

Discussion involves the employment of words as information or arguments conveyed to affect opinions and beliefs. Exchange involves the trading of some combination of goods or deeds, or both, in ways that each party finds beneficial. And coercion involves the use of goods and force (often in the form of the use of weaponry) to affect behavior more directly. These distinctions are not perfect, and it will not always be clear just where a given interaction sequence fits. But the distinctions do enable us to examine more closely the natures of these various types of interaction in an effort to increase our understanding of the patterns of international politics and the elements of national action that constitute them.

Discussion

When nations are still in the talking stage of a given interaction sequence, they may use argument—the presentation of new evidence or considerations by one nation to another with the intention of altering ideas, images, opinions, or intentions. Nations, like all other speaking parties, use argument almost every time they converse. But such argumentation takes varied forms, depending on whether it merely conveys information about the environment in which they both operate—and hence over which neither has direct control—or whether it conveys information about one nation's intentions that are conditional on the reaction of the other. The latter type are termed threats and promises.

Threat

The term "threat" is often used loosely, as in "threatening to resist attack," where the threatened action is clearly in the interest of the threatener should the undesired action be undertaken by the one threatened; we would call such a "threat" an "argument," because it is intended to bring relevant and credible information about one's own incentives to the attention of another.[2] Thomas Schelling, perhaps the leading analyst of threat in bargaining and strategy, offers a strict definition: "The distinctive character of a threat is that one asserts that he will do, in a contingency, what he would manifestly prefer not to do if the contingency occurred, the contingency being governed by the second party's behavior."[3] This emphasizes the importance of the credibility of the commitment to carry out the threat should the prescribed conditions for doing so develop.

Of the three basic types of threat the most common is the *deterrent* threat—so characteristic of military strategy—which

[2]See Thomas C. Schelling, *Strategy of Conflict* (Cambridge, Mass.: Harvard University Press, 1960), p. 123.
[3]Schelling, *Strategy of Conflict*, p. 123.

takes the form; "Do not do something undesired to me or I will do something undesired to you." A second type of threat, which might be termed the *desistent* threat, takes this form: "Stop doing something undesired to me or I will do something undesired to you." The desistent threat tends to be less credible than the deterrent threat because the undesired action has been carried on with impunity thus far, and, should the command to desist go unheeded, it is more difficult to imagine the threatener taking action (which he would prefer not to) that heretofor he has refrained from doing, and indeed, has repaired from even threatening. The third type, the *compellent* threat, is likely to be even more difficult to enact. It takes the form: "Do something desired to me or I will do something undesired to you." It shares the credibility problems of the desistent threat in that the one threatened has previously refrained without punishment from doing the good desired by the threatener. But its difficulty is compounded because often the only way to become credibly committed to an action is to initiate it, so the threatener often has to administer the punishment *until* the other acts, rather than *if* he acts.[4] And such action is obviously likely to be disquieting to and provocative of the one threatened.

Responses to Threats

Of course, the *making* of a threat does not in itself constitute interaction. There must first be a response, of which there are four possible types: *submission, defiance, counterthreat, and integration.*[5] Submission produces agreement — on the terms of the threatener. Surrender and appeasement, including unilateral gestures of pacification, are instances of this response. Defiance produces disagreement, which then may lead to conflict should the threatener carry out his threat. Counterthreat ("If you do something bad to me, I'll do something bad to you.") creates a situation of deterrence if it succeeds. Counterthreat may then itself elicit any of these four responses to threat, or it may elicit a response which seeks to vitiate the counterthreat and thereby revitalize

[4]Schelling, *Strategy of Conflict*, p. 196.

[5]This analysis has been much influenced by the already cited works of Thomas Schelling and Kenneth Boulding. Here the debt is to Boulding's "Towards a Pure Theory of Threat Systems," *American Economic Review Papers and Proceedings*, 53 (1963) 424–434.

the original threat. Thus if one nation threatens the other with attack by nuclear missiles in order to deter it and the other then makes the same threat as a counter, the first threatener may undertake civil defense or anti-missile defense as a counterdeterrent measure to vitiate the counterthreat. The fourth possible response to a threat, the integrative response, will become clearer when we consider the integration interaction below. It transcends the level of the immediate conflict, moving to a level of commonality. A primary characteristic of the threat-response interaction, whether the threat elicits submission, defiance, or counterthreat, is that the nation threatening considers itself better off after making the threat, and better off if the other side submits, but probably worse off after defiance or counterthreat.

Promise

The other fundamental instrument employed in discussion is the *promise*. The unconditional promise ("I *will* do something to or for you at a future time.") would be classed as altruism, encouragement, or reinforcement if it were beneficial (which it need not be). It is the *conditional* promise that interests us here.[6] But there is an important difference. It is true that, just as a threat can be deterrent, desistent, or compellent, so a promise can be conditional on another's refraining from action, ceasing action, or undertaking action. But, whereas a threatener gets what he wants or *else* he gives, a promiser gives *only if* he gets. It is true that the threat contains an implicit promise, but that promise is an implicit promise that "if you do not do something undesired, I will not do something undesired"; otherwise the conditional nature of the threat would have no effective power, for the one threatened could anticipate the threatener's doing something undesired even if he himself refrained from doing something undesired.

There is a further difference between threat and promise, especially in international politics. Credibility is a problem for both, and so the capacity to commit oneself irrevocably to respond as threatened or promised will encourage compliance. But if such irrevocable commitment is impossible, as it usually is in international politics and most other human endeavors, the threatener

[6]Kenneth Boulding, *Conflict and Defense* (New York: Harper & Row, 1962), p. 253.

can be helped by an adversary's perception of divergent national interests and presumption of some malevolent interest and intent in an adversary, whereas the promiser must somehow create or encourage trust in himself on the part of the adversary.

We might be inclined to believe that "trust" is something given only by naïve, credulous, and altruistic individuals. But on closer examination, trust seems to be a product of the inevitable interdependence of men's investment of themselves in other men and in collectivities that exist within a given system. Such interdependence based on investment in the system is the permissive condition of effective actions like promise and even threat, and so is at the very base of military deterrence as well as other international political activity. We shall soon return to interdependence.

Responses to Promises

The interactive response to the promise is conversely comparable to the threat-response type. It too employs goods, but it does not employ force as a promised gift. The responses a conditional promise may elicit include acceptance, rejection, acceptance coupled with a threat for noncompliance, and perhaps an integrative response. If one party accepts the promise (and acts in accordance with its terms), the party that made it must then either carry it out or break it (and then face whatever consequences might result). Rejection of a promise implies inaction by both parties — and here the difference between threat and promise is manifest, for rejection or defiance of a threat entails implementing the threat or lessening the credibility of future threats (and perhaps promises as well). Acceptance coupled with a threat for noncompliance indicates that the promiser will succeed in eliciting the desired behavior but will be encouraged then to keep his promise by the other party's threat. The integrative response, once again, raises interaction to a level of greater commonality.

Exchange

Exchange as a form of interaction consists in the granting or withholding of trade, whether of material or of behavior. Such exchange is mutually beneficial — that is, after exchange each party considers itself better off than before, although perhaps to different degrees. Such trade is clearly a basic part of international relations, for it has always been fundamental to human society. It can serve as an instrument of national policy through national decisions to permit or prohibit or regulate trade of materials by its citizens or institutions, or decisions to engage in or abstain from exchange of behavior (where one nation does something desired by another in exchange for the other's doing something the one desires). If such exchange is perceived to be in the interest of each participant we would expect that it would be undertaken as a desirable national policy rather than as an effecting action, but the nation might determine that controlling such "natural flow of commerce" could effect greater national good because it would provide another possible instrument of effective action. Although most such interaction involves the trade of material goods, it may involve the exchange of goods for deeds.

Such transfer action may be either *ex ante* (in which case the goods are transferred before the desired action) or *ex post* (taking place after it). *Ex ante* transfers are undertaken in order to bring about desired action, and may take the form of either assistance or resistance. If assistance takes such forms as grants of access or sanctuary, it can be viewed as permission designed to increase the capacity or choice of the nation being assisted, and may well be temporary. And if it takes such forms as grants-in-aid or bribes, it may be encouragement in the form of *ex ante* rewards, the continuance of which is dependent upon benefit to the nation making the transfer. Resistance or opposition, which may take the form of denial (of access, sanctuary, assistance, or other desirables) or of discouragement (by taxation, penalty, or other such *ex ante* punishments), is intended to prevent undesired action.

Ex post transfers take the forms of reward and punishment. Although rewards and punishments may follow compliance or noncompliance with threats and promises, they are distinctively transfers when they are undertaken without threat and promise and when they serve to reinforce desired behavior and discourage the undesired in repeatable situations in a continuing relationship. Thus transfer may be used to assist or impede before the act, and to reward or punish after the act, in each case in an effort to affect the future behavior of another.

Coercion

The third basic form of interaction, coercion, may involve either deployment of forces (a form of nonlethal conflict) or employment of forces in order to destroy or at least demonstrate the capacity to destroy. Not all such coercive action involves direct interaction. We have seen that nations sometimes prepare for future interaction by acting unilaterally to muster resources for eventual employment. Another very important action of nations, however, is what may be termed "fate-control" or "fate-manipulation" in which a nation will act independently of its adversary to deploy forces elsewhere or to obtain commitments from other states that will serve to foreclose possible alternatives for the adversary in the future. Alliances can be viewed in these terms as efforts by some states to control the possible behavior of an adversary without directly interacting with it; the preventive deployment of military forces as well as programs of foreign assistance may well fall in the same category. The important point here is that we cannot ignore foreign national actions just because they do not result immediately in direct interaction with adversary states. These actions may be setting the stage—or, perhaps more appropriately, setting the boundaries—for future interaction, and particularly for future attempts at coercion.

It should be clear that although exchange interactions are primarily cooperative (but contain large elements of competition that set the terms of trade), coercion interactions are fundamentally conflictual, containing elements of cooperation that set limits to the scope of the conflict and the extent of the harm done. The discussion interaction clearly contains even larger elements of such cooperative limitation, for it is confined to words rather than to deeds and force. Depending on the predominance of threats or promises, it may be largely cooperative or conflictual.

But the relative degrees of conflict and cooperation in all such interaction will depend very heavily on the response to the instigation. If that response is at the same level as the instigation, the degree is thereby set. But it is possible for the respondent to any action to attempt to alter the level by converting the interaction into an integrative or a disintegrative one.

An integrative response to a threat "establishes community between the threatener and the threatened and produces common values and a common interest."[7] Thus the integrative relationship involves a convergence in the images and utility functions or desires of the parties involved toward each other. Its obvious tool is persuasion, but it may also employ the gift of goods (as usual,

---

[7]Boulding, "Towards a Pure Theory of Threat Systems," p. 430.

including behavior) and the positive disuse of power (as in acts of mercy). In an integrative relationship, both parties, discovering commonality and undertaking social construction, believe themselves to be better off and more similar than before their interaction.

Perhaps the best examples of the functioning of the integrative system are to be found in social cooperation among people of different races, creeds, or national origins. Examples are less easily found and less unadulteratedly integrative in international relations, perhaps because of the relative weakness of the societal elements of international society. Nonetheless, there are certainly integrative aspects to many alliances and alignments — particularly, for example, the World War II alliance between the United States and the Soviet Union against Nazi Germany. And it is argued by some theorists that international organizations like the United Nations and the International Labor Organization (to take two different types) encourage the gradual development of integrative responses by nations. Indeed, some believe that even economic integration will prove to be a prelude to and even a source of pressure toward broader political development of societal integrative relationships.

But integration has its opposite: disintegration. And it would be highly unrealistic and politically dangerous not to recognize and appreciate its role in societies at any level. Encouraged in part by argument and denial of goods, it is still fundamentally dependent on the use of force, which tends to overcome commonality and emphasize differences among parties and so tends to result in social destruction and the conclusion, generally too late, that each party is worse off than it was before undertaking disintegrative initiatives or responses.

In order to understand the nature of interaction, we must also ask what the basis of interaction is — that is, what are the fundamental conditions beyond conflicting interests that make it possible for actors to make threats and promises which tend to keep the system from disintegrating and perhaps even tending to encourage integration.

A principal difference between a society grounded in developed legal codes and institutions and an underdeveloped society like the international "order" is the incentive for a member to remain in the developed society, and the difficulty of getting out, regardless of the punishment applied for wrongdoing. The very possibility of usefully employing punishment and reward depends on the continuing desire or necessity on the part of the constituents to remain within the community.

As a basis for punishment, interdependence keeps the punished party tied to the system provided he is reinstated after punishment. As a basis for reward, interdependence makes it possible for one party to help another, simply because they operate as constituents of a system in which the actions of each will affect the others. Thus, the nature of this interdependence is a reliance on one another.

There has been a considerable development of communication and transport in the twentieth century, affecting military affairs, international trade, international finance, personal relations, and even global values,[8] which might suggest that interdependence has increased in this century. But there has been a concomitant emphasis in recent years upon autarky (or self-sufficiency) militarily where possible, and economically (emphasizing development and diversity). This, coupled with the consequences of multipolarity politically and financially (for example, the multiplication of monetary standards: gold, sterling, and the dollar), may have decreased this fundamental interdependence, at least for the major powers.[9]

The basis of interdependence would seem to be the making, whether necessary or voluntary, of an investment in or commitment to the system. In this sense, interdependence is like trust and hence results in the creation of opportunities for influence. Such influence is manifest in the reward and punishment delivered by the system or its constituent parts to individual members.

The autarkic tendencies displayed by large powers would seem to undermine the interdependence as well as the possibilities for reward and punishment by the international system. But this contention probably tends to overemphasize the dependence in interdependence. For although the large powers are able to get along alone in most respects and at least for a time, they

---

[8]See Ernst Haas and Allen Whiting, *Dynamics of International Relations* (New York: McGraw-Hill, 1956), chap. 1, for a discussion of "the fact of interdependence and its denial."

[9]See the argument by Kenneth N. Waltz in his review article, "Contention and Management in International Relations," *World Politics*, 17 (1965) 720–744, for a brief but suggestive partial documentation of the case against increasing economic interdependence, on pp. 735–737.

may also have or adopt interests extending beyond their borders. The United States, for instance, encounters other nations resisting Communist inroads abroad; these nations become dependent on American assistance in resisting; and because the United States needs them for their resistance, they come to be able to exercise considerable effect on the United States — within limits. In this way large powers become dependent on small states while small states continue to be dependent on them. Further, the important factor is not interdependence, but patterns of interaction, or, more specifically, of transaction, which bring about "interadvantage." That is, the attainment of goods (in all senses), even if they are luxuries, depends on relations with other members of the system. The point is that international intercourse is advantageous; hence reward will be appreciated and punishment will hurt if they affect the nature of that intercourse. Continued international intercourse will be desirable, heightened intercourse (reward) will be appreciated, and exclusion from the society will be dis-favored. It is these considerations that form the basis for effective interaction among members of the international system.

These, then, are the constituents and bases of interaction among states. The interaction process will have continual out-puts — the results of the threats, promises, trades, arguments, destructive actions, and other types of interaction — that will result in continuation of the interaction or in its termination and the consequent "isolation" of the parties previously involved. *Some* of these outcomes will terminate engagements, such as crises or wars or negotiations, but most will simply be stages in the development of those engagements, and these outcomes will be perceived by the actors involved and presumably will affect their subsequent behavior, serving as what we now often call "feedback" — or information about the operation of the system that is fed back into the system to make adjustment possible.

The Uses
of Interaction
Analysis

Multinational interaction will be an ongoing or continuous series of stages composed of the types of interaction we have analyzed briefly here. We en-gage in this sort of analysis in order to break down phenomena into smaller parts so that we can understand the mechanisms of international effect. Such decomposition also gives us units out of which we may build notions of patterns in the practice of international politics. These patterns may be fundamental processes such as integration-disintegration, or they may be more specific, such as escalation-deescalation, initiating-responsive, commitment-independence patterns. If we can detect these patterns of interaction in crises, wars, alliances, and other international political happenings, we may be able, with this shorthand, to describe the development of such phenomena when we attempt to account for their outcomes. In other words, we may be able to find linkages between certain outcomes and the patterns of interaction leading up to them. Thus perhaps crises tend to terminate in war if the interaction within a crisis is escalative, or perhaps the nation that takes and keeps the initiative in a war will tend to prevail in it, or perhaps an alliance to which nations actively commit their forces will be more likely to last than one among nations insisting on continued independence of their military forces. These propositions are at this stage nothing more than crude hypotheses, but they are hypotheses that we can develop only if we are able to detect patterns in the interaction of states in international relations. Hence, such analysis of interaction may play an important part in advancing our ability to study and learn about international politics.

PART III
EXPLANATION

chapter 7

From Analysis
to Explanation

The Nature When someone says something which
of Explanation we do not understand, we often ask
him to explain it, meaning that we
would like a paraphrase. When he says something we understand but find too sketchy or elliptical, we often ask him to explain
it, meaning that we would like him to elaborate. Encountering
a poem that includes a symbol, we may ask for an explanation
of that symbol, meaning that we want to know what the symbol
stands for. And when someone does something that surprises us,
we often ask him to explain his action, meaning that we wish
him to state his aim in doing what he did. We use the word "explain" in all these senses. Although diverse, they share one feature: in each case we are in some way puzzled by the instance or
evidence we have received, and so wish to know more in order
to remove the puzzlement.

When we as scholars use the term "explanation" we, too,
are concerned with eliminating puzzlement, but our meaning
and our objective are more precise. Historians not only recon-

struct or describe an event, but often attempt to explain it as well. When they do so, they are endeavoring to tell what caused it. Social scientists generally deal not with individual events but rather with classes of events. The historian will attempt to explain World War I by telling what caused it, whereas the international political scientist will attempt to explain war by telling what causes war as a phenomenon manifest in such instances as World Wars I and II and the Korean conflict.

When we attempt to explain such a phenomenon we generally move backward in time to the conditions that preceded it. This is only to say that we do not engage in explanation by saying that what happens today is caused by what will happen tomorrow. Sometimes there is confusion about this point. Some people understandably wish to argue, for example, that a war is caused by the fact that someone or other *expects to win it* — something that can happen only after the war has occurred. War may indeed be caused by such expectations, but the important thing to remember is that although today's war is won tomorrow, the expectations of victory that brought about today's war arose yesterday. Thus we say that events are caused by previous conditions or happenings, and so when we attempt to explain why something happens we look backward in time.

We may also range from one level of determination to another in our effort to discover what has caused an event or a class of events. Thus we generally describe war on the nation-state level of analysis: the parties to a war are generally states and they interact as states, attempting to change each other's behavior or government. We may be able to find the causes of war at this same level — perhaps, for example, in the conflict of objectives between nations. But many theorists have argued (as we shall see in more detail later) that wars are really caused not by characteristics of nations as nations, but rather by the objectives of their leaders as individuals (who may be power-mad or crusading) or by the nature of their economic systems (which may be capitalist and need to conquer sources of raw materials or markets for their finished products; or which may be communist and desire to create one international socialist economy). Such explanations of the phenomenon of war do not stay on the nation-state level, but rather move to the individual or the economic-system level (among many other possible levels). Thus we may find ourselves explaining happenings on one level in terms of conditions or happenings on other levels.

But how far backward in time must we go, and on what levels will we settle? What, in other words, constitutes an acceptable explanation? This will depend on several things—the degree of our puzzlement, the extent of our knowledge, and the eventual objective we have in seeking such explanation.

The Acceptability of an Explanation If we are deeply puzzled, we may have to go far indeed. Thus, if we notice how peaceable a student is, how docile a baby can be, how oblivious to international politics two lovers are, or how friendly participants in the Olympic Games are, and then remember how prevalent war is and wish to find out why, we may require comprehensive explanations across time (even to the Garden of Eden) and across levels to the very nature of man to satisfy ourselves. If, on the other hand, we notice the ferocity of partisans at an athletic contest, bitter quarrels among brothers and sisters, virulent denunciations of some nations by others, and the armed readiness of almost all nations, we will be much less surprised by the prevalence of wars and may require only some indication of the kind of incident that can trigger such resentment and bring about employment of war machines.

Similarly, if our question is the most general one of why war occurs at all, our explanation will have to be much more fundamental than if our question is the more limited one of why war occurs at one particular time rather than at another. (Of course, the actual explanation of why war occurs at a particular time may turn out to be more comprehensive than that of why war occurs at all, as we shall see later.)

What sort of explanation we find acceptable will depend, too, on the degree of our knowledge. The more we know about why things in our world happen as they do, the more easily we are likely to be satisfied. This will be so because explanation is in a sense a process of subsuming the particular event or class of events under a more general type. Thus if we are satisfied that we understand why conflict becomes violent under certain conditions, explanation of war requires only that we discover that conflict exists or arises among nations and that those conditions conducive to the transition to violence come to exist. If, on the other hand, we are continually baffled by the fact that conflict exists at all or that conflict sometimes becomes manifest in violence, explaining war will probably require that we also explain the sources of conflict in general and the causes of the transition to violence. In a sense, explanation consists in showing that something unknown or not understood is actually an instance of something known or understood, so the more relevant things we know or understand, the easier or less comprehensive explanation will be.

Finally, our eventual objective—the reason for seeking such explanation—may also determine what sort of explanation is acceptable. If our only objective is to understand why things happen as they do, we may be satisfied with a limited explanation in terms of the antecedent and causal conditions. But if we wish to develop an ability to *control* happenings, we must discover those antecedent conditions that might be subject to our control. Thus if we know of ways to reduce tension among nations (such as through increased Olympic competition and cultural exchange), we shall require an explanation of the occurrence of war that goes far enough backward from the conditions in which the first shots or missiles are fired to a time when such preventive measures might actually have time and opportunity to operate in reducing tensions.

It is also likely (though not always necessary) that if our objective is not simply understanding but prediction, we shall need different and probably more comprehensive explanations. As some scholars have pointed out, for example, evolutionary theory gives us a good understanding of the development of species, but it has not enabled us to predict what new species will arise.[1] We shall be examining this question and the problem of prediction in some detail in Chapter 14.

Types
of Explanation

Typically, in the past, the major, if implicit, objective of scholars was the removal of their own particular puzzlement about why things happened. This may have been so largely because scholars neither were very good at prediction nor were

[1] See on this point Michael Scriven, "Explanation and Prediction in Evolutionary Theory," in *Science*, 130 (1959) 477–482; but see also Carl Hempel, "Aspects of Scientific Explanation," *passim*, pp. 331–496 in Carl Hempel, *Aspects of Scientific Explanation and Other Essays in the Philosophy of Science* (New York: Free Press, 1965).

able to recommend impressive strategies for the control of future happenings, rather than because scholars were not interested in prediction and control.

Whatever the reason, the emphasis on removing individual puzzlement tended to a highly personalized criterion of satisfaction which, of course, was not always shared by other scholars. If the questions asked were different according to each mind, the solutions were even more so. The knowledge, or contention, thus developed was not easily transferrable to others, for it is rare that any two people's perplexities are identical. Furthermore, this psychological criterion for explanation offered little possibility that scholars could agree on any common explanation of a general phenomenon or even of a given instance of that phenomenon. This approach offered no general *criterion* by which scholars could agree that any one explanation was better than another. Each individual would have his own solution — the one that best satisfied his own curiosity. There could be no disagreement that a given explanation did or did not satisfy a given scholar or reader so long as the solution satisfied his own particular criterion.

This concentration on the idiosyncracies of individual explanations is somewhat overdrawn, but the portrayed weakness of that approach is not; without criteria for choosing among competing explanations as contributions to the advancement of knowledge, a discipline cannot progress. The problem is made the more obvious, if no less tractable, by the clear contrast with what explanation involves in the physical sciences. There, an event or a class of events is considered explained if it can be subsumed as a case under a general principle or law — in other words, if it can be classified as a specific instance or class of instances in a more general category. We discussed this approach in our examination of the nature of scientific theory in Chapter 3. It provides accepted criteria for deciding whether a purported explanation qualifies as an acceptable explanation, and for selecting among alternative explanations in terms of their consistency with broader scientific laws.

Unfortunately, as we are well aware, the social sciences have not yet been able to approach such consistency and rigor in explanation. Those who claim that we will never be able to, because of the nature of the problems dealt with, will continue to use the idiosyncratic approach of concentrating simply on attempting to remove puzzlement. Others, more optimistic about the prospects for cumulative social science, have been contending that the traditional approach must be abandoned completely in favor of the "scientistic" approach that employs the same criteria used by the physical scientists. But while it would be disastrous for the progress of social science were we to stick entirely with the traditional approach, adoption of the approach of the physical sciences *in toto* has not proved useful.

We should recognize the limitations as well as the contributions of the traditional approach. Were the criticisms of the traditionalists by the social scientists wholly accurate, we would not now be able to claim to know anything interesting or important about international politics or any of the other social sciences. But this is clearly not the case. The problem is not so much that we have no knowledge as it is that we cannot be *confident* of that knowledge because it has been derived or developed in this traditional way. In other words, there is no way to test or confirm the claims of the traditionalist, and so what we have is largely suspicion rather than knowledge. But even in the physical sciences, confidence in knowledge is actually a matter of degree, for the scientists continue to make progress that makes previous beliefs no longer so impressive and acceptable. So it should come to be in the social sciences. But for this to happen we must attempt to move beyond the traditional approach toward science.

What such progress will require is the acceptance of criteria for assessing competing explanations — or, in the words now popular among students of science — acceptance of a *paradigm for explanation*. That paradigm need not be the rigid requirements of deductively organized general laws under which particular instances can be subsumed. This is clearly asking too much, at least at this stage. What is required at this point is clear and open recognition of the role that theory must play in explanation and extensive efforts to make explanation and the theories upon which it is based as explicit as possible so that by being tested against other cases of similar phenomena it can be assessed. Let us examine this further.

In Chapter 5 it was suggested that we will tend to shift our focus from reasons to causes. Even if we do so, we are still engaging in the traditional forms of social explanation, rather than in the forms that might be drawn from explanation in the physical sciences. Simple notions of explanation, when they range beyond reasons, are generally put in terms of the discovery of cause and effect. What we wish to discover, it is said, is the cause of a given happening, or the effect of a given happening. This language seems to suggest some necessary connection between cause and effect. The eighteenth-century Scottish philosopher David Hume, in his *Enquiry Concerning Human Understanding*, attempted to disabuse men of the notion that there was something intrinsic that connected cause and effect. He described an instance in which one billiard ball hits another and then that other ball moves. Most of us would easily say that the first ball caused the second to move. But Hume argued that all we could legitimately say was that there was a conjunction in time between the collision of the two balls and the movement of the second ball. If we have observed the same phenomenon over a number of cases, we may conclude that there is a connection between the collision and the movement. But that connection exists only in our minds; or at least we cannot satisfactorily say that there is a connection between the two outside our minds. This argument has led many to say that causes are connected with effects not because the world is held together by some sort of "cosmic glue" but because our *theories* connect cause and effect.[2]

Whatever our views about this rather abstruse but interesting philosophical debate about the nature of causality we would like a great deductive theoretical system in which strict laws of regularity enable us to explain both classes of political events and individual events in terms of laws that follow from the general principles of international politics. But if we are not likely to have such a general theory of international politics in the near future (and indeed may never have such a general theory), what might we have in its place?

Although nothing will adequately replace such a general theory, any progress we can make toward such a general theory, or toward partial or subtheories of classes of events, say, crises or wars, will be an improvement on our present state of extensive ignorance and even more extensive casual intuitionistic analysis. We must be careful that we do not claim to be or act as if we were more rigorous than we are. But we wish to make sure that

[2]For the literature and debate on this question, see Daniel Lerner, ed., *Cause and Effect* (New York: Free Press, 1965).

we are as explicitly rigorous as we can be, so that our understanding of international politics can progress more rapidly toward well-developed and extensive explanatory theory.

From Explanation to Theory

Our great problem in the study of international politics today is that we do not have satisfactory general theory. If we did, we could apply it to explain any and every event, as well as to predict and perhaps even control those events. We share all the perplexity of men of the past and we have even more ambitious objectives of explanation and control in a world of increasing complexity and accelerating change. However, to attain any of these objectives, even the limited objective of replacing our puzzlement with understanding, we must find a way to develop the required general theory of international politics. In attempting to develop that general theory, we shall examine the nature of explanation. In one sense, we shall be attempting to develop general theory by explaining things, yet all the while explaining events by applying general theory. Impossible as that formulation sounds, it is not really, for in practice, explanation and theory-building are inextricably linked: each complements the other, and the two advance together as each contributes to the improvement of the other. How, then, does this cross-fertilization occur?

We cannot generally know what goes on in the minds of decisionmakers, and hence what the reasons for their actions are. And even if we could, we would find that such knowledge would not necessarily satisfy our need for increased ability to predict and control as well as to understand. Thus we must shift our focus from the decisions to the circumstances or conditions in which decisions are made, and even more generally to the patterns of national interaction that combine to make up international politics. When we study the various phenomena such as war and crisis in this way, we may well be able to reach conclusions about just what causes them to occur as and when they do. But even so, we must be tentative in our contentions, for we cannot always be confident of their accuracy, nor can those to whom we relay them. Rather than begin by seeking cause and effect as such, we may be inclined to shift the emphasis of our study toward the conditions under which events occur. If we do so, we shall attempt to find correlations between the presence of specified conditions and the occurrence of specified events.

Explanation by Correlation

If we described comprehensively the conditions that were present before the occurrence of one event (for example, the conditions preceding the outbreak of World War I), we would not have grounds for claiming to understand why the event occurred unless we had general principles to tell us that, under conditions like these, this phenomenon always, or at least usually, occurs. Our basic effort is to develop general principles about regularities or correlations like this. Thus we must examine other specific instances of the same general phenomenon and see whether the same conditions occurred before each of them. (For example, we might study the conditions preceding the outbreak of World War II, the Korean conflict, and the Vietnam situation as well as World War I.) We would expect to find that some of the conditions would be similar and others would be different. What would we do then? We know that the result of these conditions was generally the same in each instance — the same general phenomenon (war) occurred after each of these collections of conditions. Thus if we found some conditions present in each instance we would begin to suspect that they were causally related to the phenomenon. Those conditions that varied from instance to instance would seem to be *either irrelevant* to the happening *or alternative* possible causes.

For example, if we studied many outbreaks of wars we might find that economic unrest always preceded its eruption, and also that either political unrest or political unanimity existed in the states as well. It would then appear that economic unrest was causally important and *either* that political factors did not matter and could vary independently of any effect on the outbreak of war, *or* that either political unrest (which perhaps led the leadership to seek diversions abroad) or political unanimity (which perhaps enabled a leader to venture forth acquisitively) can be causally important. We would then examine more cases in an effort to see which one of these possibilities or hypotheses was accurate.

When we attempt to discover what similar conditions precede different instances of the same phenomenon we are attempting to discover the *correlation of factors and outcomes* that will offer us some *order* in the world, or at least some order in our way of looking at it. This sort of study will require two things: comprehensive listings of the conditions or factors, and "translations" into common terms of the conditions that *appear* to be different. Thus, for example, there are various kinds of tension in international relations, and it may be important, although difficult, to recognize the different versions as different instances of the same thing—just as we have seen that wars may vary considerably in appearance while sharing those features we consider essential to war.

Eventually, of course, we hope to discover correlations between factors and outcomes—that is, we seek regular co-occurrence over various instances of particular types of factors. This regularity or correlation should enable us to produce statements of the form

> x (an international political happening) will occur
> after or when a, b, c (conditions or factors) occur.

We may actually be reduced to qualification of the "will" into a probability or tendency statement of the forms

> x will occur in a (specified) percentage of cases . . .

or

> x will tend to occur . . .

Only time and our continuing efforts will tell us what the limits of this correlation analysis will prove to be.

It should be clear, however, that this type of analysis is but the first step toward an understanding of why things happen as they do. Our statements of regularity will lack the causal linkage generally supplied by additional phrases beginning "because . . ." All we shall have discovered will be that a given phenomenon will occur under certain conditions. These conditions may be such that our general knowledge or our other theories about the way the world works make them appear sensible. Thus, we tend to expect trouble when there is economic or political unrest, and so perhaps we would not be mystified should we find a high *correlation* between war and these conditions.

On the other hand, we might, to take an extreme case, discover that war would correlate highly with the presence in positions of power of men with a certain hair color. The chances are that this would not be comprehensible, or at least would not lead us to cease our research satisfied that we understood why war occurred. It might be that war correlated highly with the presence of gray-haired leaders, and we might conclude that this was because gray-haired men, being old, have little but fleeting glory and excitement to live for and therefore are more venturesome and hence more apt to launch wars. But even if this correlation were discovered to be true (and its truth is not obvious), we would probably not be satisfied that our quest was over.

It seems most likely that, when we have undertaken our correlational analysis, we shall wish to continue our efforts to establish linkages between conditions and the happenings they result in through some sort of causal analysis. Such analysis is both quite complex and often still of questionable validity; hence we shall have to pay careful attention to its logical problems as well as to the research problems it raises. But if we stop with correlation and neglect causal analysis, the only linkage between condition and happening, the only answer to the additional question of why the happening follows the conditions, is that it always has happened this way. This is a reason for belief, not for the happening.

The Uses of Correlation

This is not to minimize such achievements. For although causal explanation is not strictly possible with only correlation analysis, prediction may well be possible. When we predict we generally begin with a statement of present conditions and then in some way move forward into the future. If we have for our use a number of propositions telling us that under certain conditions a certain international political happening will occur or will tend to occur, and we find in describing present conditions that one or more of our principles begins with these conditions, it is not difficult to predict that the specified phenomenon will occur. (Of course, whether or not such a phenomenon does actually occur will depend on our accuracy in perceiving present conditions and on the validity of our correlation propositions.) Thus prediction may prove quite possible even without causal explanation or understanding. However, we shall probably be more confident as well as more understanding of our predictions if we can base them on causal explanation rather than on simply correlational principles. And there are reasons for believing that prediction will be easier if we can employ theories rather than just correlation principles. Nonetheless, it is encouraging that even such limited progress as correlation analysis may permit some significant activity such as prediction.

It is, as we have said, explanation that gives us the intellectual basis or the knowledge to enable us to understand why things happen as they do and to understand why predictions that we might make on the basis of correlation analysis prove accurate. Such explanation is based on discovery of the necessary and sufficient conditions for each event and then for each class of similar events. But even before we have attempted such explanation openly, we shall be presaging it in our correlation analysis.

The Practice of Correlation Analysis

The decision as to which conditions to concentrate on in describing the conditions that precede a given phenomenon must be based to some extent on our previous suspicions about what factors are likely to prove causally relevant. If we did not select (either from experience or intuition or common sense) certain factors or features on which to concentrate, we would have to describe everything about the world at the stage preceding the happening in which we are interested.

If we were trying to describe the conditions preceding the occurrence of the Cuban missile crisis, no one would even consider including such conditions as the colors of the ties the participants were wearing, the standings in the National Football League at the time, the rate of incidence of malaria around the world, and the existing regulations on marijuana. These conditions are considered "clearly irrelevant" precisely because, as educated persons, we already believe we have a fairly good notion of what generally is significant and what is insignificant in accounting for world events. There are also, however, many factors that we might be inclined to dismiss but perhaps should not—such as the weather (which in the Cuban missile affair delayed American detection of Soviet emplacements in Cuba by preventing photo-reconnaissance missions for some days). This should serve as a caution against our getting too exclusive too early in our quest for relevant conditions in our descriptions of happenings.

But what criteria do we, or should we, adopt in selecting what to include in our descriptions? Clearly we will rely in large part on our previous suspicions about causation. This is both necessary and perhaps proper if we remember that we are doing it and we allow for it (at least in retrospect) in our work. This reliance may be more misleading in the description of any given incident than in the collective description of many instances of the same general phenomenon. For we may well expect that in describing the conditions contributing to crisis, for example, the weather in some instances will prove important, and in others the personal friendships of national leaders.

But these "idiosyncratic" features will probably drop out of our "equations" about crisis, not because they are unimportant in individual cases, but rather because other features seem to be generally more important at this stage in our inquiry — perhaps the personalities of the leaders, the state of technology, the types of governments involved, the nature of diplomatic communications at the time, the configuration of alliances, and the degree of international tension and so on. Our analysis may not always be able to account for all the peculiarities in the event, but if it can cope in each instance with such general features as these, it may be able to take account indirectly of idiosyncratic features that become manifest in the actions of leaders, the capabilities of states, and the interactions of politics.

Typologies

For our study of the conditions of various happenings, we must have in mind what are often called *typologies* or *conceptual schemes* with which to seek and organize data. It is here that the levels of analysis or description we considered in Chapter 5 may prove useful as guides to possible data and categories in which to place such data when we encounter them. Thus, for an international political happening we will probably seek to examine such levels as the subconscious and conscious minds of the leaders, the requirements of actors' roles, the governmental, economic, and political systems of the states involved, the material factors (possessions, capabilities, features of the states), the regional transnational organizations existing, and the nature of the operating international system.

But we shall also have certain unique interests as products of the nature of the phenomenon being investigated. For crisis we shall be particularly interested in the diplomatic channels available, for wars we shall be interested in the strategies adopted, and for alliances, commitments stipulated in legal documents. Thus in a sense, as we attempt our analysis by conditions, we must develop our own particular typologies of possibly relevant data. Then, if we do so and are successful in gathering data about existing conditions, we may begin the further task of establishing through causal explanation the linkages between these conditions and the events.

The Linkage between Correlation and Causation

After careful study of the conditions under which an international political event (or a type of event) occurs, we may well be able to expect or anticipate its occurrence when we encounter those conditions. But we may nonetheless remain puzzled about *why* it occurs under those conditions. If we find that crises arise or tend to arise when one nation challenges the basic interests of another in a way that requires rapid response, we already have the beginnings of an understandable explanation of why a crisis occurs. But if we find that crises occur the day after every fifteenth full moon over Washington, we would continue to be puzzled as to why crises occur—indeed, our original perplexity would be in a sense compounded by our new problem about what full moons might have to do with crises. In any case, we shall wish to move beyond knowledge or belief about the conditions under which a given international political phenomenon occurs toward an explanation of *why* it occurs under those conditions and perhaps as well to knowledge of why those conditions themselves occurred or existed. How, then, might we do this?

When we encounter an event that interests us—say the Cuban missile crisis or the Korean conflict—we begin by describing it in some detail. This would enable us to place it in some *class* of events, such as the class of crises or of wars. If we know enough about that class of events (or, in our terminology, that phenomenon) to satisfy our curiosity, we may stop there. Thus if we had wondered why the Cuban missile affair occurred and, upon discovering that it was an instance of crisis, we were able to apply a theory of crisis that told us enough about the reasons for its occurrence, we would stop with the classification.

But at our present state of knowledge, in which we do not yet have adequate theories of crises, wars, alliances, and other international political phenomena, we would probably seek to go further, studying the conditions that preceded the event. Obtaining these developmental data about the phenomenon, we can then engage in comparative study. If we compare statements of the conditions preceding various instances of the class of events (the Berlin Blockade, the Berlin Wall, the Suez crisis, and the Cuban missile crisis, for example), looking for regularity or recurrence of conditions, we may be able to develop a statement of the conditions of this class of events. This statement will enable us to describe the development of the type of event (a crisis or a war) and may well enable us to predict its happening where we find these conditions.

We may have general principles of international politics, widely accepted by scholars in the field, which tell us that what we consider crises are simply one manifestation of international political interaction which can be understood in terms of certain causal principles about the behavior of men, of groups, or of groups of groups. Thus if we have an experimentally verified principle stating that any nation (or perhaps any nation's leadership), when challenged by an action threatening its very security, will respond in an aggressive fashion, and we can see that our crises fall into the category of international political happenings, we may be satisfied by this subsumption of our collection of cases under this general law of international politics.

However, we may not yet be satisfied. We may wish to know something more about the response of the original threatener, for this may be what differentiates a crisis from a war in our study. Then if we should find a principle that says that the response of the threatener is such as to perpetuate the tension without escalating it in such a way as to require surrender or war, we may be satisfied.

But again we may ask the additional question about its development as tension-ridden interaction in which the ordinary time frame or perspective of international political interaction is shrunken or telescoped. And if we can be satisfied about that, we may then ask about the eventual resolution of the crisis — or its eventual escalation into war.

In each of these questions or inquiries we may be satisfied by the presentation of an established general principle that subsumes our particular class of events, or we may further ask why that general principle is true. We have been satisfied that it applies, but we have not been satisfied about the reasons for its holding true in general. In other words, we wish in some sense to discover the causes of the cause of our particular happening or stage in our phenomenon. And if we make such demands we are simply engaging in further causal explanation of general principles.

It is also possible — indeed, likely, given the present state of our knowledge and strong beliefs about international politics — that we shall not have such accepted general principles about international politics. What may we do then? We still wish to know why crises occur and develop and terminate as they do, but we cannot subsume them as a class of events under general principles of international politics.

We may then in a sense escalate our own study, engaging in comparative study of various other international political phenomena, such as wars and alliances, looking eventually for statements of the conditions of the class of phenomena (crises, wars, alliances, and so on), rather than simply for statements of the conditions of the class of events that constitute one phenomenon, such as crisis. We might then discover that the same conditions, or at least the same types of conditions, or perhaps the same types of determinants (such as the economic, the geographical, or the psychological) hold across these various types of international political happening.

The Limitations of Correlation Analysis

What we have been doing, when we undertake this sort of study of a class of events or of a class of phenomena, is inductive study in an effort to establish regularities in conditions so that we can make lawlike statements of this form: "Under conditions a, b, and c, x will result." If we are able to establish such general statements or laws, we can then explain a particular instance (that is, a case in which an x resulted) if we find conditions a, b, and c—for our law tells us that this result x is to be expected under these conditions. This is the type of explanation often called deductive-nomological,[3] which is generally argued to be the ideal type of explanation in the natural sciences and which many have hoped could be attained in the social sciences as well.

Because we still have a very long way to go toward satisfactory general theory, we shall find that the theoretical propositions we have or obtain or develop are likely to be qualified or hedged in various ways. We shall probably find, as this book has been arguing implicitly, that the most profitable way to proceed is to develop statements of the conditions precedent to various types of happenings—conditions which appear to be determinants of those happenings. These statements must be of some generality, for generality is a basic trait of any proposition that seeks to link together features or conditions of events that are in themselves all distinguishable from one another. Thus if we are developing statements of the determinants of the outbreak of a crisis, we clearly must omit specific features of the crises we are examining, such as the names of the nations involved and the times at which the crises take place, for the very nature of generalizations is to find what is common to distinguishable happenings.

It is also likely that these statements will contain alternative conditions. Thus they may state that a crisis will occur when either of two sets of conditions exists. These two sets may eventually prove to be collapsible into one more general set of conditions, but because at the time we do not know the determinant that underlies them both, we may have to settle temporarily for such duality.

Furthermore, our statements are very likely to be not strict laws but, rather, probability or tendency statements. A probability statement is one which states that in a specified percentage of cases, certain conditions will have a specified outcome. A tendency statement is less specific, stating that if certain conditions are present there is an unspecified tendency for a certain outcome to result. Most of our generalizations will be of this form. This

---

[3]We have already considered deduction, the logical process by which a conclusion is derived from certain premises. The term "nomological" is used by philosophers of science to refer to general laws. Thus a deductive-nomological explanation subsumes the particular instance under a general law. For further discussion, see any of the works on the philosophy of science cited above, or see Richard Rudner, *The Philosophy of Social Science* (Englewood Cliffs, N.J.: Prentice-Hall, 1966).

might be the case because there is some underlying randomness in the universe that makes it impossible to predict accurately. But few really believe this. Rather, we suspect that we are limited to such probability statements because we have not yet fully discovered all determinants of the happening, or because we have not yet fully understood the relations among these determinants that bring about the conclusion or happening. Thus we expect that, as our knowledge increases, our uncertainty (and hence our reliance upon probability and tendency) will decrease.

Reliance on such tendency statements is one of the major compromises we must make in our efforts to move from a traditional approach in which most analysis lacks general statements and in which most general statements available are much too general to be true or useful in rigorous explanation. It would be splendid if we could shift from such analysis directly to rigorous scientific analysis in which we would simply apply comprehensive deductively organized general theory to particular instances in order to explain their occurrence. Unfortunately, we have no such theory, and we must now attempt to develop and construct it. We could not begin such a task if we did not have firmly in mind the requirements for explanation of international politics, for that is the first task of theory and also the best way to begin trying to construct such theory from a study of some of what actually happens in international politics.

chapter 8
From Explanation
to Theory

The Need for Theory   If we had a comprehensive general theory of international politics, it would be relatively easy to explain why wars occur or why the Cuban missile crisis developed as it did. As we have said, we seek such theory because we believe it can make major contributions not only to our understanding of past events, but also to our ability to predict and ultimately influence or control what happens in the relations among states. But such theory cannot be simply found, it must be carefully developed or constructed. Our concern in this chapter, as we approach our detailed study of crisis, war, alliance, and cooperative control, is how to create such theory—how to employ our social scientific tools of reason and analytical concepts in turning the data of historical and contemporary study into international political theory. We shall approach this task by attempting to explain various happenings. But in order to do that effectively, we must first consider the strategy and tactics of theory-building.

There are two fundamental stages to any rigorous, scientific

123

inquiry: discovery and validation (or confirmation). We must first find the knowledge or contention we desire, and then attempt to see whether or not it is correct.

The Nature of Discovery

We do not yet know enough about human thought processes to be able to speak definitively about the ways the mind arrives at principles or propositions about happenings. We do know that at the outset there is some sort of curiosity or interest — arising presumably out of perceptions like observation, reading, or discussion — which leads us to formulate a very tentative hypothesis. This hypothesis may in fact vary from a substantive nature — "wars are caused by economic disorder" — to a procedural nature — "the way to learn about the causes of war is to study certain aspects of history, such as economic conditions." But in any event, it arises from our innate desire to convert ignorance into suspicion, which in turn initiates the process of discovery.

Hypothesis

Hypotheses are tentative propositions, usually expressed in the traditional "if . . . then . . . " form — "if there is economic disorder, then there will be war," or "if war is to occur, it will be preceded by economic disorder" — designed to be tested against the observable facts. There are various ways of testing a given proposition. In many instances, we can simply examine various cases (other than those that might have stimulated our original formulation of it) and see if it adequately describes the consequences in those cases where the conditions exist. (For example, do we find that all historical instances of economic disorder result in war?) Another sometimes useful approach is to make predictions on the basis of the hypothesis and then see whether they prove to be correct. (Thus we might look around the world for instances of economic disorder and see whether they eventuate in war; or in the more limited formulation of the hypothesis we might look at the conditions that preceded any war that has broken out to see if they included economic disorder.) In a sense, any of these activities is a prediction. Where we examine other cases from the past, we have predicted that we would find certain things to be true when we studied their history. Where the instance is past, we sometimes refer to our activity as "postdiction" or "retrodiction."

These research activities are actually deductive in the sense we have spoken of previously. That is, the proposition implies certain things, and we first make that deduction and then compare it with reality. Thus, if our hypothesis is that "economic disorder results in war," this implies that where we find economic disorder we will also find war. After deducing this from our general proposition, we test this deduction against our data, and discover whether or not it is accurate. If we should find that it does not hold up—if we find an instance where there is economic disorder and war does not follow—then we conclude that the hypothesis is not correct, and we attempt to discover why by considering other possibilities, such as the possibility that other conditions may prevent war if they coexist with economic disorder, or the more basic revision that there is something even more fundamental which causes war. This process of revising our hypothesis in the face of contradictory evidence is inescapable in rigorous study of complex phenomena.

But one way or another we eventually develop a proposition that does seem to correspond to the evidence. The questions then are, When do we stop testing it, and What criteria of satisfaction do we apply? There are no single answers to these questions. Some have suggested that a certain number of instances in which the hypothesis does apply should satisfy us that it always does. But we can see that just because all previous instances have worked does not necessarily mean that all future ones will. As the philosophers of science are fond of pointing out, the fact that all crows we have seen thus far have been black does not tell us that the next one we see will be black. This is an instance of what is generally referred to as "the problem of induction," and it is important to recognize that it is a real problem for research and theory-building of the sort we seek to do. We must remember that certainty will not be absolutely justified, no matter how many tests we run or how many corroborating instances we find. On the other hand, we should also realize that the more tests we run, and particularly the more varied the tests, the more confident we can be about our proposition.

This testing could go on forever, but what usually happens is that the law of diminishing returns sets in—eventually, the increased confidence that results from the most recent test seems to be less valuable to us than the benefits of some other activity. If we are attempting to develop a theory of international politics, we may, for example, stop testing our proposition(s) about the causes of war in order to move on to our propositions about the causes of crisis or of alliance.

Eventually, by repeating such activities for the various aspects of the subject being studied, we arrive at a set of propositions that seem to us rather well tested. If they appear almost wholly certain, and if we wish to sound like physical scientists, we may then refer to them as "laws" — laws of international politics rather than laws of nature. But in any event, we have a collection of propositions and we seek to develop a theory out of them.

A theory is, in the language of science, a collection of propositions systematically organized. Usually in the physical sciences such organization is deductive: the propositions are arranged so that certain specified assumptions imply the propositions, or so that the specific propositions can be deduced from more general assumptions.

Actually, rather few general theories in the physical sciences are deductively organized and highly developed, and there are far fewer in the social sciences. Indeed, only economics, with its classical and neoclassical theories of economic man and his activities, can claim to have a developed deductive theory.

The other social sciences, including international politics, have what might more accurately be viewed as nondeductive theories. These have sometimes been referred to as "concatenated theories"[1] or "factor theories,"[2] and they are distinctive because they are not logically constructed in such a way that one can deduce each proposition or law from underlying assumptions. Rather, they take the form of tendency statements — "war will tend to occur when there is economic disorder" or "alliance will tend to occur when there is military weakness." Such statements are not easily combined into a theory, let alone organized deductively. But they do tell us what factors to look for in trying to explain or predict certain happenings. And they may eventually be developed into absolute statements rather than tendency

[1]See Abraham Kaplan, *The Conduct of Inquiry* (San Francisco: Chandler, 1964), pp. 298–299.
[2]See Quentin Gibson, *The Logic of Social Inquiry* (London: Routledge, 1960), pp. 144–154.

statements, and into deductively unified rather than concatenated statements.[3]

As we have said before, we might attempt to develop a deductive theory by making certain basic assumptions, such as "all nations seek to maintain their territorial integrity at any cost" and "nations will seek to expand their territorial boundaries when they believe they can succeed in doing so." From such crude general assumptions we might deduce propositions about the conditions under which wars, alliances, and crises might arise. If we were systematic and if we added definitions and other assumptions to our basic formulation we could develop a crude theory of international politics. Indeed, some of the so-called realists of the early postwar years attempted such a feat. The problems with these kinds of theory arise in their application, for they are too simple to fit reality satisfactorily (as we can see when we examine the "realist" theory), and so we must keep adding more salvaging and clarifying assumptions until the deductive beauty of the theory has all but disappeared.

The alternative to such deductive activity is the inductive collection of various propositions through efforts to unify them into a theory that, even if it is largely probabilistic (composed of probability statements) or very uncertain (composed of tendency statements), does suggest what seem to be the key factors contributing to international political happenings.

We have been speaking thus far as if these two approaches are mutually exclusive. But it does not take much thought to see that the deductive approach is dependent for its start on some study of the world to be explained, and such an examination will be inductive. Nor is it hard to see that the principle on which we attempt to organize our factor or tendency propositions is our desire to develop a theory that is deductive in shape—that is, in which the propositions are logically related to each other and to basic assumptions from which they follow. No intellectual endeavor can long exclude either of these two fundamental approaches to the discovery of theory. Individuals may have preferences and may excel at one rather than the other, but our social scientific study requires a continuing, if perhaps alternating, interplay between a combination of the two if it is to succeed.

---

[3]For a useful statement of the problems involved, see Eugene Meehan, *The Theory and Method of Political Analysis* (Homewood, Ill.: Dorsey, 1965), chap. 5.

Confirmation   But how, then, are we to recognize such success? Success in theory-building is to be realized or discovered through confirmation or verification of the theories we develop. But how are we to know when our theory is confirmed? We have already recognized that, because of the problem of induction, we can never be absolutely certain that our theory, even though it has explained and predicted everything thus far, will continue to explain and predict everything in the future. In other words, even if our theory does all we wish of it now, we cannot assume that it will continue to do so. How then might we say it had been confirmed or validated?

One answer sometimes given is that theory is never confirmed, it is only disconfirmed.[4] If instances are found in which our theory's propositions or the deductions from them do not correspond to reality, then our theory (or at least some part of it) has been disconfirmed. If we examine the history of science, we find that it has been largely the history of disconfirmation of prevalent theories and their replacement by other theories which have in their turn been disconfirmed and replaced. Each replacement has been superior to the previous one, and presumably each has more closely approached truth or reality.

If the study of international politics, or of politics in general, could reach the stage where it proffered and disconfirmed theories in this manner, we could indeed celebrate progress in our field. In the meantime, we must address ourselves to the matter of degree of confirmation. Each further testing of a proposition inspires further confidence in it, and that testing which is significantly different from previous testings, whether in extent or in type of case or in some other dimension, reassures us all the more. This attitude seems quite justified — particularly to one who employs such theory (whether in his governing or in his writing) — because we must have some sort of theory, we must select among competing theories, and in those circumstances we prefer the theory with the better record of doing what we wish it to do.

In a sense, then, confirmation is a matter of an individual's being satisfied, and that satisfaction clearly depends on the individual's objectives. We have said that among our objectives are likely to be an understanding of why the world works as it does,

---

[4]For the classic statement of this argument, see the works of Karl Popper, esp. *The Logic of Scientific Discovery* (New York: Basic Books, 1959).

contributions to further research, prediction of future happenings, and perhaps contribution to the controllability of the world. It is a rare theory in any field that contributes equally to the achievement of all these objectives (except for those theories that contribute nothing equally to all of them). There are many instances of theories that explain well but do not enable prediction (evolutionary theory is a prime example), and there are others that do not explain well but do enable at least some useful prediction (classical economic theory is sometimes argued to be an example)[5]. In international politics, none of our theories is well enough developed and tested to be subjected to such demands, but some are rapidly making progress and we can expect these demands to be applied increasingly to our theories. When we attempt to discover how well they meet them, we are evaluating our theories, and that evaluation will play an ever more important role in our deliberations. This growing evaluation will be one sign that our discipline is progressing.

Our Approach All students of international politics confront the same world and can share the same data, and all have the same fundamental objective of understanding that world, even though some do not go beyond this objective to attempt to develop theory and to predict the future. All of us must develop concepts that help us to manage the data. Some students will concentrate upon the policymaking within participant states, whereas others will emphasize the interaction among states. But all will tend to find it convenient, if not essential, to talk in terms of certain basic phenomena that recur in one form or another throughout history. We have chosen to single out crisis, war, alliance, and cooperative control for special attention, among many other such phenomena, including negotiations, trade, arms races, foreign aid, and even the Olympic Games. Our criteria for this selection have been two: the importance of the phenomena in international politics, and the extent to which they reveal fundamental aspects of the conflict and cooperation that underlie all of international politics. We might have chosen other phenomena for concentration, as various schol-

[5]See Milton Friedman, *Essays in Positive Economics* (Chicago: University of Chicago Press, 1953), chap. 1.

ars do, but there can be no dispute that these four are crucial components of international politics which no serious student of the subject could long neglect.

If the topics we shall study in detail are rather ordinary, the approach we shall use is not. Most books on international politics are basically designed to convey information about the subject matter, or, more specifically to present what the author believes to be the truth about that subject. But in this book, since it is methodologically oriented, we do not seek to convey specific information as such. We are attempting to develop certain ways of thinking about international political events so that we can improve the prospects for development of international political theory. If we had a comprehensive general theory of international politics, it would be the subject of the next four chapters: each chapter would present the elements of that theory relevant to the understanding of the phenomenon under consideration. Indeed, if only we had a theory of crisis, or a theory of war, or one of alliance or of cooperative control—a theory that was general and widely accepted as highly accurate—each chapter could be devoted to presenting the relevant theory. But the work of scholars is still so fragmentary and tentative that we do not yet have any theory about these four key phenomena. What we have, rather, is relevant work, useful approaches, competing hypotheses, and speculations. The important thing is that there is a variety of useful material in these approaches and hypotheses and speculations, and that the discipline now shows signs of progressing in the direction of theory. Greater unity of purpose and approach is required as well as more imagination and rigor in study. These are demands that even the beginner can meet if he has assistance. The next four chapters are designed to offer various aspects of the assistance required, each tailored to the demands of the particular phenomenon under consideration, but all coupled to encourage development of the broad range of skills that should permit us to undertake and pursue our own study of these phenomena. From there, we can also pursue our own study of phenomena not considered in this book.

Thus we begin with the study of crisis. Crisis has recently become the subject of interesting and useful study by scholars. But at this point we have nothing resembling a theory of crisis. What we do have is considerable information about a number of crises and the first tentative hypotheses about the conditions under which crises arise and terminate. Consequently our effort in this chapter will be to begin from scratch in attempting to develop the desired propositions about outbreak and termination. We shall go through the process of examining one event – the Cuban missile crisis – in order to develop tentative hypotheses and then improve and extend these hypotheses by studying another crisis – the Berlin Blockade. We shall then examine the state of our tentative knowledge and consider what extension of our study and what testing of our results seem desirable. This will leave considerable opportunity for scholars and students to advance our understanding of crisis, and it will also indicate, step by step, how we can go about studying a phenomenon on which little theoretical work has been done.

We shall then turn to a long-standing favorite phenomenon of students of international politics – war. Here our problem as social scientists is just the opposite, since there exist multitudes of theories, most of which are underdeveloped and apparently conflicting. Here our effort will be to determine how to go about examining and comparing competing theories while learning from them about the great variety of factors that determine what occurs in international politics.

Following these two examinations of interaction that is basically conflictual, we shall turn to interaction that is primarily cooperative. Our first subject here will be alliance. There are many studies of particular alliances, each of which purports to explain why the alliance under examination was born and why it developed as it did, but few of which are related to each other in the theoretical contentions that underlie them. Thus our approach to alliance will be to take an explanation of the establishment of one alliance – the Warsaw Pact, for instance – and derive from it a general theoretical explanation that we can then test against a number of other postwar alliances in order to see whether it appears to be a satisfactory general theory of alliance creation and, if not, what changes appear merited by the evidence.

We will then examine an instance of cooperation, not among friends but among adversaries. Such cooperative control is ever more desirable in an age of complex and interrelated antagonisms and shared interests in survival. There are not many instances of major programs of cooperative control, however, so we shall take one such type, arms control, and attempt a rather speculative study directed toward conclusions about the conditions under which we might expect it to be achieved by the major powers in the future. This should be a useful study because it will require us to apply what we have learned about international politics in general and, in other cases, to a type of phenomenon that has existed thus far only in occasional minor instances but which may well become of major significance in international politics in the coming decade. Such a study should prove useful because it is the kind in which our ultimate interest in prediction and control of future developments in international politics may be developed and exercised.

Our focus upon crisis, war, alliance, and cooperative control, and our varying approaches to each, should enable us to understand better the major ways scholars confront their data in attempting to develop and improve their explanations and their theories. In the course of our study, we should acquire much useful information about international politics as well as the requisite skills for engaging in useful study ourselves. If we expect to learn the conclusive truth about the causes of each of these phenomena, though, we shall be somewhat disappointed. No one, not even scholars who have spent their lives at such study, can yet lay claim to such definitive knowledge. On the other hand, if we are attentive to these studies we shall probably find the subject so interesting, and the analytical skills easily enough acquired that we can then carry these and other related studies further toward such conclusions.

PART IV

THEORY-BUILDING

chapter 9
Studying Crisis

The Outbreak of the Missile Crisis Why did the Soviets decide to put missiles and short-range bombers in Cuba in the summer of 1962? That question still intrigues students of international politics, just as it must have puzzled and troubled American policymakers who had to decide how their country should respond when the missiles were discovered in mid-October. A crisis begins with a sudden alteration of the status quo — or at least with the discovery of such an innovation. We expect a crisis-initiating decision to be a product of the existing situation coupled with some new considerations or capabilities. Consequently, we shall look first at the objectives and expectations of the party that attempts to alter the status quo, seeking an explanation in terms of reasons that would answer the question, Why did the nation initiate the crisis?

In the case of the Cuban missile crisis, one way to attempt an answer to that question is to determine the nature of these weapons systems in order to find out how they might change the

crisis

decision

military situation. One of the weapons to be introduced into Cuba was the medium-range ballistic missile (MRBM), which had a range of about 1000 miles and could be moved from one site to another and made operational in about six days. By October 14th, when these missile sites were discovered, several missiles may have been operational; by October 28, when the Soviets agreed to withdraw them, perhaps twelve to eighteen could have been fired. The second system was the intermediate-range ballistic missile (IRBM), with a range of about 2000 miles, but requiring permanent installation. None of these sites would have been ready to fire before mid-November. The third part of the Soviet arsenal in Cuba was the IL-28 bomber, operational immediately. The accompanying map illustrates the position of Cuba and the superpowers.

When the reconnaissance flight of the U-2 uncovered the development of missile bases and the presence of bombers in Cuba on October 14, American policymakers had to determine how serious a threat they were. The answer might contribute to an explanation of why the Soviets decided to attempt to install the weapons. There was at first considerable difference among analysts about their significance. Some believed that the proximity of the missiles made little difference to the United States because of its overwhelming nuclear and missile superiority at that time, but others pointed out that much of the American manned-bomber force of the Strategic Air Command was based in the southern United States, where it would have a warning of only several minutes if missiles were launched from Cuba. It was also argued that, apart from the immediate military significance of the placement of the missiles, the political impact of such a sudden shift in the strategic balance might be considerable, giving the Soviets political opportunities in other parts of the world — particularly among the underdeveloped nations. Thus the Soviets might have hoped for both political and military gains.

But why might they be so desirous of such gains as to risk a direct nuclear confrontation with the United States? The answer to this question may lie in international political developments in the year and a half since Kennedy had taken office. Khrushchev's latest efforts to compel the West to abandon Berlin began with his pronouncement that West Berlin must be made a free city and followed with his construction of the Berlin Wall in July of 1961. Since that failed, the Ulbricht regime in East Germany

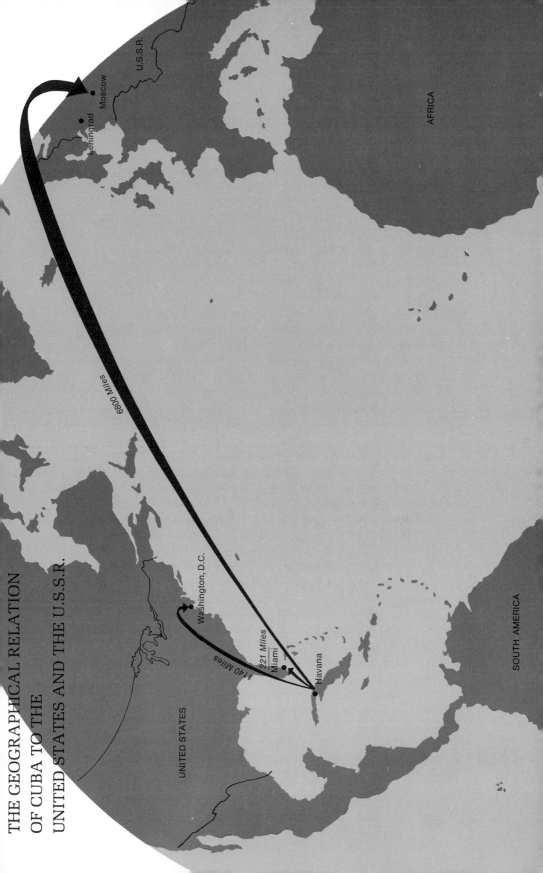

THE GEOGRAPHICAL RELATION
OF CUBA TO THE
UNITED STATES AND THE U.S.S.R.

faced an internal crisis that threatened its survival. The Sino-Soviet dispute had worsened and former Soviet ally Albania was siding with China. Meanwhile, the Soviet Union had not made up for this obvious failure with significant gains in allegiance among the underdeveloped states. Further, Soviet resources were under domestic pressures because the expenses of the space race and defense left little for expanded consumer production and agricultural development following several poor harvests.

On the other hand, successful emplacement of the missiles and bombers in Cuba would significantly increase the size of the military threat that the Soviet Union could pose to the United States, would undoubtedly increase Soviet leverage over Berlin and shake NATO, and would also encourage further subversion in Latin America. Moreover, such Soviet success would meet the Chinese argument that the Soviets were weak and lacked effective leadership in dealing with the West.

These are all possible—and rather obvious—reasons for a Soviet effort to put missiles in Cuba. But there were also important possible costs. If the missiles were discovered in time, the United States might attempt to compel their removal before they were operational; in any event the United States might force a showdown after discovering them even if they were already operational. The Soviets obviously decided to run these risks. In view of the outcome, we are particularly puzzled as to why.

The most likely possibility seems to be that they poorly predicted the American ability to discover the missiles and perhaps also the country's reaction should the United States discover them. The Russians, too, may not have appreciated the historic importance of the Western Hemisphere to the United States, Soviet ideology possibly preventing the Russian diplomats from understanding the American commitment to preventing or eliminating such a major foreign intrusion into the hemisphere. Such considerations move beyond reasons to conditions that might help us explain why rational Soviet calculation might have produced such a mistaken assessment.

We might go farther in seeking conditions that contributed to the information and calculation that seem to have been the basis of the Soviet action. Some have suggested that the explanation lies in miscalculation not by Khrushchev but by a militant faction in the Soviet government (presumably the military or a militaristic clique), coupled with a temporary political weakness of Khrushchev which enabled this faction to prevail at the time and insert its miscalculation into the policy machine. It has also been suggested that irrationality by Khrushchev was the explanation—an explanation sometimes inferred from Khrushchev's raucous behavior at diplomatic cocktail parties and at conferences, including the shoe-banging episode at the United Nations.

It is not our purpose at the moment to settle on one or some combination of these possible reasons and conditions as the actual explanation of the Soviet move into Cuba. Rather, we consider these various possibilities to bring to mind the variety of possible determinants and the likelihood that we shall want to examine not only reasons but also more fundamental conditions in our effort to understand the outbreak of a crisis.

The second obviously significant component of a crisis that we seek to anticipate and explain is the response of the nation that is challenged. In most cases a nation will have a variety of possible responses, and we expect its selection among them to be affected by such considerations as its view of the nature and extent of the challenge, its own interests, its capabilities, and the results it expects from the various alternatives. One feature that tends to characterize crisis is a narrowing of the alternatives of response so that a nation is forced either to accept the changed status quo or to escalate the confrontation so that the risk of violence increases significantly. Thus some of the alternative responses that usually exist might not be present in a time of crisis.

As we have seen, once missiles were discovered in Cuba, the United States had several major alternatives. At one extreme it could simply accept them and do nothing. At the other, it could invade Cuba, thereby bringing about at least a limited war in Cuba and perhaps a major intercontinental nuclear war with the Soviet Union. Between these extremes there were three possibilities. It could engage in what was popularly called "surgical removal" of the missile sites by precision bombing raids, thereby probably killing Russian construction workers and technicians and perhaps encouraging or forcing the Soviet Union to respond with a "similar" attack on Americans in the United States or elsewhere. It could interrupt the flow of weapons and supplies from Russia to Cuba and thus encourage the Soviets not only to cease building the sites, but also to reverse their course and dismantle those already constructed. Finally, it could protest through appropriate channels, such as the United Nations, hoping that the Soviets would change their plan. If unsuccessful here the United States could then either accept the missiles or adopt one of the strategies designed to encourage their removal.

As policymakers debated among these alternatives that week in October, each of the options had its advocates. But the basic choice soon came down to the air strike to destroy the bases or a blockade to encourage reversal of Soviet actions. At first, opinion seemed to favor the air strike, but, as the week progressed, the decision was to blockade (or, in the legalistic phrasing of the proclamation, "quarantine") Cuba and threaten further action if the missiles and bombers were not quickly removed.

Again, we are interested in the reasons behind the selection of one alternative rather than another. There were really two decisions, the first being whether to do anything at all and the second being what to do. The decision to attempt to get the missiles withdrawn was reached, according to our accounts of the debates, on the same grounds that presumably encouraged the Russians to attempt the installation—the military and political implications of a sudden change in the strategic balance of power. It does not surprise us that the United States decided to resist emplacement. Only if we believe that any such resistance would make a major war highly probable might we be surprised by such a decision. And although there were those at the time—inside and outside the government—who did indeed suspect such a danger, the general contention seems to have been that American military superiority in the area, coupled with intercontinental missile superiority, would give the Soviets pause if they were inclined to react violently to American resistance.

The decision against an air strike seems to have been heavily influenced by two factors: the danger that killing Soviet citizens would force the Soviets to react violently, and the belief that a surprise attack would be similar to that suffered by the United States at Pearl Harbor in 1941, and thus would be morally unacceptable and politically damaging to American relations around the world. It was recognized that blockade, coupled with the conditional threat of further action, although possibly less was more attractive since it greatly decreased the risk of immediate general war.

In this case we find that the American calculations – or what we have been told of them[1] (which is more than we can determine about the calculations which underly the Soviet decision) – are understandable, and perhaps even predictable. Thus we are less inclined to look for instances of misinformation and miscalculation in the American case than we are in studying and attempting to explain the Soviet decision. Nonetheless, we may still be interested in the underlying conditions that made this particular American decision seem rational and sensible. Some of these conditions were reflected in the reasons offered above: the presence of Soviet troops and technicians in Cuba who would be targets of any strike; the American local naval superiority in the Caribbean and the American global ICBM superiority; and the presence in office of individuals particularly sensitive to the undesirability of an American surprise attack.

Other factors may lie deeper. We are told that domestic political considerations were never raised in the decisionmaking.[2] Yet we know that Cuba was a politically sensitive issue in American politics: in their election TV debates Kennedy had chided Nixon for letting Castro establish himself and turn Communist; and in turn Kennedy had been in office during the abortive Bay of Pigs invasion, which was embarrassing both because it was a failure and because that failure was in part attributed to the Kennedy's refusal to have the United States participate actively in the invasion even though it encouraged its launching. Further, various Republican senators had been warning off and on that Castro was establishing or allowing Soviet bases in Cuba – even missile bases – while the administration denied this. Thus the decisionmakers may have been motivated in part by political considerations which would have made taking no action less likely even if military and international political considerations had not suggested so strongly that resistance be offered.

Again, deciding just which factors actually determined the American decision to quarantine would require a major historical

[1]The most helpful account is that of Elie Abel, *The Missile Crisis* (Philadelphia: Lippincott, 1966). Useful information is also to be found in the memoirs of three of Kennedy's assistants: Roger Hilsman, *To Move a Nation* (Garden City: Doubleday, 1967); Theodore Sorensen, *Kennedy* (New York: Harper & Row, 1965); and Arthur Schlesinger. *A Thousand Days* (Boston: Houghton Mifflin, 1965).
[2]See Hilsman, *To Move a Nation*, pp. 196–198.

study. Our concern is not so much with a comprehensive, accurate explanation of this decision as it is with discovering the various factors involved, and then seeing if they are also present in other crises so that we will know what we must ultimately take into account in developing a theory of crisis.

The Outcome

Besides its outbreak, the other major aspect or stage of a crisis that will interest us is its outcome. Crises may end in various ways. The missile crisis ended in a negotiated resolution, the Berlin Wall crisis ended by subsiding without negotiation, while the Suez crisis of 1956 and the Middle East crisis of 1967 ended in war. Whatever the outcome, we can view it as a product of decisions on both sides or by all participating parties to bring about or accept such a termination. Thus again we can ask what reasons led each party to settle as it did.

Such questions are not easily answered. As was noted before, we expect the outbreak of a crisis to be a product of the given situation plus some new desires, expectations, or other considerations (and perhaps some new capability) on the part of the initiating party. Somewhat similarly, we expect the outcome of a crisis to be a product of the way in which the crisis has developed.

Thus in the missile crisis the Soviets were informed that the United States had uncovered the missile sites and was blockading Cuba and threatened worse actions if the Soviets did not withdraw the offensive missiles. In other words, part of the Soviet plan of secretly introducing the missiles had already failed; the other part — the expectation that the United States would accept the missiles or at the most protest their presence — had been proved mistaken. Further, the development of the crisis indicated that the United States could effectively blockade Cuba so that the remaining missiles and supplies could not be brought in. The Soviets were caught in the middle of an action whose success depended on its completion. On the face of it, therefore, one might expect them just to pack up their missiles and go home. But, as we well know, no state finds retreat easy. Indeed, after the Soviets failed, the Communist Chinese accused them of both "adventurism" (overly risky gambling) and "capitulationism" (giving in or folding when in a hole). Thus the Soviets faced competing considerations: the failure of most of their efforts plus the desire not to be humiliated. It is when a nation is in such a dilemma that negotiated settlement is a particularly attractive prospect.

The United States found itself in a somewhat similar situation. It had succeeded in breaking the back of the Soviet military venture. But the Soviets did already have the light bombers and a number of MRBMs (increasing numbers of which were operational every day) in Cuba, and there was no peaceful way in which the United States could itself remove those. Thus Soviet cooperation was highly necessary to avoid war with the Soviet Union.

There were long days during the crisis, as the various accounts portray, when neither side could tell what the other would do. While each stood ready to intensify its efforts while at the same time looking for signs of weakness or else willingness to compromise in the other side, the crisis led gradually to a negotiated settlement in which the weapons were removed and the United States agreed not to invade Cuba.

Thus an immediate answer to why the Soviets agreed to remove the missiles might be because they failed to introduce their entire intended arsenal and the United States threatened to destroy those parts of it already there—something the Soviets did not look forward to. And the answer to why the United States agreed to allow the Soviets to remove the missiles gradually might be that it would achieve the fundamental American objective of getting the weapons out—and avoid open conflict. However, the United States would be unhappy with a pledge not to invade Cuba, since it had encouraged and abetted that the year before. Indeed, the Soviets eventually claimed that they had been victorious in the confrontation because they had succeeded in what they claimed they had set out to do: protect Cuba from invasion by the United States. American analysts do not believe this was the basic Soviet objective, although it is not hard to understand why the Soviets would seek to make the claim afterward to avoid admitting they had been defeated by American resistance. In any event, whatever the truth may be, we are able to construct reasonable propositions to account for the actions of each party in deciding to settle on this particular outcome.

Other underlying conditions were probably important also. The relative military strengths of the two nations in the Caribbean, which is off American shores and many thousands of miles from Soviet shores, significantly favored the American stance. But the internal strength of Castro's regime and the presence of Soviet troops combined to make the prospect of an American invasion or even merely an air strike less attractive than it would otherwise be. The support the American allies and even many of the nonaligned nations gave to the American position both strengthened the United States and made it less likely that the Soviets could gain political capital in other countries by their venture. These and other conditions also seem likely to have contributed to making the outcome a negotiated settlement rather than a surrender, or a standoff, or a war.

We are at this point beginning again to consider not simply reasons in the minds of policymakers but also conditions in the world that may have entered whatever calculations policymakers undertook. There are other conditions that probably did not enter such calculations but almost certainly affected the outcome, such as the nature and availability of communications channels through which a settlement could be negotiated. The first American statement to the Soviet Union was presented by the Secretary of State to the Russian Ambassador just before Kennedy addressed the nation to reveal the American discoveries. Subsequently, the United Nations Security Council met at the request of both parties. In the next few days, Russians in Washington and Moscow spoke to other diplomats and to American citizens indicating they would run the blockade. Meanwhile, U Thant, the Secretary-General of the United Nations, exchanged letters with both parties. Then, significantly, a staff member of the Soviet embassy in Washington spoke to an American radio-television correspondent, whom he happened to know, and first suggested terms similar to the eventual settlement. Shortly thereafter in rapid succession two letters from Khrushchev arrived at the White House, the first conciliatory and the second bellicose. The American decision to answer the first letter by "accepting" terms like those mentioned by the Soviet diplomat and to ignore the second letter resulted in a letter from Kennedy to Khrushchev stating such an offer and shortly thereafter a response agreeing to such terms. It is quite clear that the outcome was influenced—particularly in its timing, but also apparently in its nature—by the happenstance existence of such varied channels of communications between the superpowers— channels that have since been further developed by the establishment of a direct telegraphic link between Moscow and Washington known as the "hotline." Thus in considering why the outcome took the form it did and occurred when it did, conditions such as communication channels probably merit consideration along with the conditions that influence the substantive considerations of each party.

Thus far we have generally been examining reasons rather than conditions. It is usually not difficult to translate reasons into immediate conditions. For instance, if the Soviets introduced missiles into Cuba for the purpose of increasing their nuclear capability against the United States without having to build more long-range intercontinental ballistic missiles, the condition of their introduction was a desire on the part of the Soviets to increase their capabilities without building more missiles. But there can be problems with such conversion or "translation." It is, as we have already seen, often very difficult to figure out just what the reason was, let alone what the condition incorporating the reason was. In the case of the American response to the Soviet missiles, we have several detailed accounts of the deliberations and hence we can simply report such reasons. But in the Soviet case, no one has written about their deliberations in implanting the missiles and in removing them. Consequently we are left to infer their reasons based on the actions the Soviet Union took.

Because of this problem, we are more inclined to move a step farther back and look for the conditions which preceded the action—conditions we can describe relatively easily—and assume that those underlying conditions influenced Soviet decisionmaking and that we can therefore ignore or skip the reasoning and move directly from the conditions to the actions.

Thus we point out that the Soviet Union, as stated, had suffered various foreign policy reversals in the preceding months (over Berlin and Communist China, particularly), and that Soviet resources were hard pressed by the demands of the space race and defense as well as by domestic manufacturing and agricultural needs. We also look to the Soviet role in the world, as a revolutionary or revisionist power seeking to displace Western influence in the developing nations. All these factors (and perhaps others) seem to us potentially relevant to—or, more accurately, likely contributory causes of—the Soviet decision to put missiles in Cuba.

We may also wish to go farther, considering the character of the Soviet leader—often thought to have been impetuous—

and of the Soviet government—one that can conduct its foreign policy in secret but that tends toward considerable bureaucratic infighting over policy questions and personal power. We could go on, but such is not our purpose.

Developing Propositions about Crises

Our actual objective, although closely related to an explanation of the Russian and American actions, is somewhat different. Eventually, we hope to develop a theory of crisis, a collection of propositions about the actions of states that bring about and resolve crises. These propositions should enable us to predict, or at least to tend to expect crises to develop and be resolved in various ways. And if they are satisfactory, the propositions should also enable us to understand why and when crises develop and terminate. This is of course a gigantic order, and we would be fooling ourselves if we expected this study, or any study, to produce such a satisfactory theory of crisis, let alone satisfactory theories of war, alliance, and cooperative control. Although it will take considerably more systematic study by scholars of international politics to develop satisfactory theories, we can make some progress toward that objective here.

The first step is to formulate our descriptions of events systematically. We would like to have propositions with a form something like this:

Crisis will occur when conditions *a, b, c*, . . . exist.

Actually, however, we must reduce our objectives somewhat for now since our list may not be complete. Thus we may decide to turn our proposition around to read:

When a crisis occurs, we shall find conditions *a, b, c*, ...

This allows us to add more conditions as we become convinced they are relevant, and does not encourage us to hope to predict the occurrence of crisis before our proposition is satisfactorily comprehensive and accurate.

Another modification we may wish to make is to change our verb form from "will" to "tends to." This also protects us from having too strong expectations early in our study, before our collections of conditions are sufficiently complete and accurate. While admitting that we are not yet certain, we are claiming that we have considerable evidence that these various conditions matter.

But how do these propositions arise in the first place? How do we first get these suspicions, how do we collect evidence, how do we determine what conditions matter? Ordinarily, when seeking propositions about the occurrence of something as frequent as crisis, we read the scholarly literature in the field and see what factors are believed to matter in producing it. But unfortunately scholars have been preoccupied with other happenings—particularly war—and have not studied crisis systematically. We have many studies of particular crises,[3] but we do not have much comparative study of crisis in which efforts are made to generalize about the causes of its outbreak and termination. Thus we must attempt our own systematic study, so that we cannot expect great accuracy from our first conclusions. But we can develop an idea of how to go about such comparative study, plus the ability to develop propositions that will be worthy of further test in our own additional work. In a sense, our primary question is how to undertake the study of history, or of historical writing, in the service of theory-building.

In this chapter we have been familiarizing ourselves with the broad outline of events in the Cuban missile crisis both to obtain a better idea of the nature of a crisis and to have some raw material with which to develop propositions about conditions

[3]See, for example, on the Cuban missile crisis, Abel, *The Missile Crisis;* Hilsman, *To Move a Nation;* Henry Pachter, *Collision Course* (New York: Praeger, 1963); on the Berlin Blockade, W. Phillips Davison, *The Berlin Blockade* (Princeton, N.J.: Princeton University Press, 1958); Lucius Clay, *Decision in Germany* (New York: Doubleday, 1950); Jean Edward Smith, *The Defense of Berlin* (Baltimore: Johns Hopkins Press, 1963)—which includes a comprehensive bibliography; on the Suez crisis of 1956, Hugh Thomas, *Suez* (New York: Harper & Row, 1967); Terence Robertson, *Crisis* (New York: Atheneum, 1965); Anthony Eden, *Full Circle* (Boston: Houghton Mifflin, 1960); G. Wint and P. Calvocoressi, *Middle East Crisis* (London: Penguin, 1959), among many others; on the Middle East crisis of 1967, Robert Donovan, ed., *Israel's Fight for Survival* (New York: Signet, 1967); William Stevenson, *Strike Zion* (New York: Bantam, 1967); Peter Young, *The Israeli Campaign 1967* (London: Kimber, 1967); David Kimche and Dan Bawly, *The Sandstorm* (London: Secker & Warburg, 1968); Walter Laqueur, *The Road to War 1967* (London: Weidenfeld and Nicolson, 1968); and others forthcoming.

resulting in the outbreak and resolution of crisis. Now we must begin to put these data to use. To know just which data to concentrate on, we must have what is referred to as a *descriptive model* of crisis—a representation of the stages of its development and the particular aspects to which attention should probably be given to explain that development. Then we must "fill in the blanks" of that model for the Cuban missile crisis, and from those data we shall attempt to fashion hypotheses about conditions or factors which may be important determinants of its eruption, development, and outcome. As we progress, we shall find it essential to make distinctions not only among stages of crisis and among determinants of crisis, but also among types of crisis. Eventually we hope to acquire a collection of propositions about the conditions of crisis in order to assess their apparent accuracy and the degree to which they seem to explain the development of crisis. Because this is a large task we cannot expect to complete it comprehensively here.

A Descriptive   Figure 9-1 presents the major stages of
Model of Crisis   crisis and the major possible determi-
                    nants of each stage. As we have seen,
when a nation's policymakers make a policy decision they will examine the situation as they perceive it, assess their nation's capabilities, consider their believed interests and objectives, and then make that decision among available alternatives after calculating their likely costs and benefits. Once decision has been made they must attempt to get it carried out through formal channels. If it is a foreign policy decision, implementation will almost certainly involve the diplomats and perhaps the army.

The first decision of interest concerning crisis is the decision to initiate one. In order not to omit any major determinants of that decision, we should investigate at least these conditions:

1. The nation's beliefs about or images of its adversaries' interests or objectives and capabilities

2. The international configuration (the status quo) that constitutes the external environment in which the decision is made—and particularly any recent changes in it

3. Internal conditions such as idiosyncrasies of the leadership, the nature of the political system, political conditions, and

Figure 9-1.

DESCRIPTIVE MODEL FOR THE STUDY OF CRISIS
(And the matters of concern for analysis)

INITIATION
—Permissive Conditions (See Fig. 5-1)
—Possible Determinants (See Fig. 5-1)
—Substance of Decision
—Way in which decision implemented
—Action by which decision expressed
1. threat
2. movement

RESPONSE
(Same as for Initiation, but special attention
to the nature of the response)
1. Is response low-level (increasing tension,
pressure, discomfort, etc.)?
2. Is response high-level (forcing to war or
ceding victory)?

INTERACTION PROCESS IN DEVELOPMENT
—What patterns can be found?
1. Is initiative maintained by one party?
2. Are the flows of information between the
parties explicit or tacit?
3. What uses are made of threats, promises,
commitments, etc.?
—Key choices of escalation or de-escalation
(perhaps analyzed as initiation/response
were, above)

TERMINATION
(Same as for initiation but analyzed for both parties)
—Nature and Consequences
1. war
2. return to *status quo ante*
3. surrender or acceptance of new *status quo*
4. abatement without settlement

economic conditions—all of which should contribute to determination of the nation's objectives and its believed capabilities

Regarding the decision and the action itself, we shall want to
know not only these possible determinants, but also the substance
of the decision and the way in which it was implemented.

The external action that follows the decision will in turn
become the major new input into the decision process of the
other party. Concerning the decision to resist that instigation we
shall want information about the same possible determinants and
knowledge of the decision itself, its implementation, and the
action in which it is expressed.

At this point in interaction, a crisis clearly exists. We could
pursue our study of it by continuing to examine each determinant for each decision by each party, but for economy we shall
avoid such detailed study and concentrate instead on the pattern
of interaction between the two as the crisis develops. In studying
the pattern we shall look for repeated instances of one party having the initiative, for flows of information from one party to the
other through explicit and tacit communication, for uses of threats,
promises, commitments, and other instruments of effect, and for
key turning points in which one party or the other chooses to
escalate or deescalate the crisis.

Finally, as the crisis terminates, and because termination
is itself a major turning point, we shall be concerned again with
the determinants of the decisions to bring it about. And of course,
we shall be interested in the nature of that termination, particularly in relation to the original situation or status quo ante.

We can be somewhat more explicit in categorizing possible
actions and interactions in the development or life cycle of the
crisis. First, a crisis may be initiated either by action or by a threat.
The missile crisis was initiated by action, as were the Berlin Blockade crisis and the Berlin Wall crisis. But the first Berlin crisis of
1961 was initiated when Khrushchev threatened to sign a separate peace treaty with East Germany, a treaty that would include
turning control over access to West Berlin to the East Germans
and hence, the West believed, endangering it. "Action crises"
and "declaratory crises" may differ greatly.

Further distinctions may be made among possible instigations of action crises. One promising set was developed by Allen

N. Ferguson,[4] who viewed the crucial question to be whether or not the action of a party tended to force the other party to choose between going to war and ceding the victory (surrendering). An action of this sort can be termed a high-level action, intended to terminate the crisis in war or cession. A low-level action simply increases tension, pressure, or other uncomfortable qualities but allows the adversary to respond similarly with a low-level, or nonforcing, action. A crisis of this sort can go on indefinitely un-less very gradual escalation eventually reaches the high-level point.

Thus in the Berlin Blockade, which we shall examine in more detail shortly, the Soviets clearly thought that their action of interrupting ground traffic to Berlin would prove to be a forc-ing initiation, for they did not believe that the airlift commenced by the allies could long supply the city. However, the Allies proved the Soviets wrong, and the continuation of the blockade, coupled with the continuation of the airlift, created a pattern of inter-action that was low level and could have continued indefinitely. Similarly, Khrushchev's threats about expelling the West from Berlin in 1961 did not force cession or war, and hence constituted low-level initiation. The Allied response of refusal to be pushed from Berlin qualified similarly. In the missile crisis, the Russians apparently thought that the introduction of missiles would be viewed as a *fait accompli* that would have to be accepted unless the United States were willing to attack Cuba. However, they proved to be wrong in this belief. Kennedy's response of a quar-antine was basically a forcing response, allowing the Soviets to turn their ships around or to run the blockade, which would presumably initiate war. The Kennedy response did indeed bring about a negotiated settlement very quickly once the Soviets con-cluded that the United States was not bluffing and would indeed go to war if forced to.

Crises, we have observed, may end in war, as did those in the Middle East of 1956 and 1967. Or they may end in a return to the status quo ante, as the Berlin Blockade crisis and (over-all) the missile crisis did. Or they may result in surrender or accept-ance of the instigator's change in the status quo, as the Berlin Wall

[4]Allen N. Ferguson "Tactics in a Local Crisis," in *Journal of Conflict Resolution*, 7 (1963) 130–140.

crisis did. Or they may end in an abatement without any sort of settlement, as Khrushchev's various threats to expel the Allies from West Berlin did. We are particularly interested in discovering to what extent termination depends on the pattern of interaction, as well as on the more obvious factor, the strength of the two sides. Put in policy terms, are there ways of seizing the initiative or structuring the interaction so as to prevail in a crisis even though one party is not stronger than the other? Study of the conditions of crisis termination may help to answer this sort of question.

The Outbreak of Crisis

The first and most obvious answer to the question, When will a nation initiate a crisis? is: When it decides to do so. This is not a helpful answer, for we will then wish to know what considerations will lead it to such a decision. The most immediate answer to this second question is: When it believes that this action will benefit it. While this answer may appear somewhat more interesting than the first, it is no more helpful. For by assuming that a nation will act so as to benefit itself (or, as analysts often put it: to maximize utility), this answer simply forces us to go another step backward and ask either what considerations will lead a nation to value one course (in this case, instigating a crisis) over others, or (if we wish to emphasize conditions rather than reasons) what conditions will lead a nation to act to maximize utility.

This is a problem that pervades the analysis and explanation of international politics, as it does that of other activities. If we simply *assume* that people act rationally, or selfishly, or irrationally, or altruistically, or whatever, we cannot then use this contention to explain why they do what they do because it is an assumption. Only if we find some way of testing and confirming our assumption may we then employ it this way. And finding ways to confirm such assumptions, as we have seen in previous chapters, is extremely difficult if not impossible.

Thus we may have to conclude that it is better to bypass the decision phase as such in our analysis. This leaves us two types of alternatives. One is to say that the study of factors determining or influencing national decisions about foreign policy and action is best left to students of foreign policy rather than to students of international politics. Some argue that international politics starts with interaction, and therefore we should simply take whatever inputs into international politics we get from nations as givens, and explain the development and outcome of interaction. But if we do this, we shall probably remain puzzled as to why nations do what they do externally. The other possible approach is to attempt to develop propositions about the conditions likely to exist in the world, or the nation, or perhaps the leadership of the nation at times when that nation takes a given action internationally. Progress in this approach to the study of international politics will often be limited by our lack of satisfactory studies of the determinants of foreign policy in specific countries and of the determinants of foreign policy in general, but we may be more satisfied than we would be if we looked only at multinational interaction. Thus it seems desirable to proceed as far as possible in developing propositions about the determinants of such foreign policy decisions as that to initiate a crisis and that to respond to such instigation.

The Outbreak of the Missile Crisis: The Soviet Instigation

At this stage, we have one crisis with which to begin our efforts — the Cuban missile crisis. What reasons and influences led the Soviet Union to decide to place missiles there? We have already speculated about this on the basis of what evidence we have, coupled with our general suspicions about what motivates nations. We found that the international political position of the Soviet Union had been weakened by its failure to succeed in forcing the Allies out of West Berlin and by increasing dissension from its foremost ally, Communist China, as well as by its continuing inability to obtain increased allegiance or support from the underdeveloped states. At the same time, the Soviets' chief adversary, the United States, after the disaster of the Bay of Pigs, had "stood firm" in Berlin, had increased its military superiority over the Soviet Union through mobilization of some reserve military units and through increased production of ICBMs, and was apparently making headway in its relations with the underdeveloped states through foreign aid and such innovations as the Peace Corps. We might summarize the international political situation and relations between the United States and the Soviet Union this way: The United States had recaptured the initiative among the neutral nations and was increasing its military superiority while the Soviets found their military position weakening and their influence over their allies and the neutrals declining; furthermore, the West had forced the Soviet Union to back down from its aggressive threat in Berlin.

It may be that such international political conditions will prove to be adequate in explaining the outbreak of crisis. But many argue, as we have seen, that internal political conditions must also be considered. We know how dependent the American administration is on domestic support; we also believe that the Soviet regime depends, albeit not as much, on popular support (in the absence of which it might face revolution, because elections do not offer the populace an opportunity to change regimes as they do in the United States). Further, we know that there are periodic power struggles within the Soviet hierarchy, and that such struggles are usually fought out over policy issues.

note

At the time of the missile crisis, the Soviets had faced serious agricultural problems and a continuing demand for more consumer goods. These factors plus those of the expensive space and arms races produced considerable pressure on scarce Soviet resources. Putting missiles in Cuba seems to have promised increased military capability without a major expenditure (the Soviets already had the missiles, probably aimed at Europe), and also held out gains in prestige and influence in the third world without further costly expenditures for foreign aid and subversion.

leader

Moreover, if Khrushchev was under pressure from more militant members of his hierarchy—as any leader in any country is almost always likely to be—this bold initiative would be likely to placate them or at least weaken their criticisms if it succeeded.

The other major factor sometimes believed important is the idiosyncrasies of the leadership—in this case, Khrushchev himself. He had the reputation of being a tempestuous and impetuous man—derived largely from his behavior in personal encounters. This may have played a role in the development of the missile crisis once it had begun, as we shall see, but it seems unlikely to have influenced the instigation, which had to be planned and engineered for three or four months and was hence unlikely to be determined by a leader's impetuous behavior.

We could go into considerably greater detail about each of these categories of possible cause as well as add other elements, such as the role of the military, the impact of geography and technology, and the role (or lack of it) of the United Nations and other nonnational bodies and individuals. But our effort is to develop general propositions rather than elaborate explanations of the sort the historian constructs. If we have left out any major factors we may hope that our comparative study of other crises will point them up so that we may attempt to add them then.

Developing a Proposition about the Soviet Instigation

At this point, we must take our specific information and convert it into a general proposition about the conditions under which a crisis will or may break out. The first requirements of such a general proposition, obviously, are that it not be highly bound by names and time. We could truthfully say that a crisis breaks out in October 1962, or that a crisis breaks out when the Soviet Union puts missiles in Cuba, or various other quite specific propositions. But if we did, our proposition would not be applicable to other crises at other times involving other states. This does not mean that our proposition must apply to the years before Christ, or to a crisis between countries like San Marino and Andorra (if one can be imagined). We expect the vast changes in international relations and in the nature of states in the past two thousand years—or even in the past one hundred years—to limit the applicability of our propositions, just as we expect the vast differences in capability and world role between the Soviet Union and Andorra to limit that applicability. But once we have developed a proposition, we will want to attempt to test it against other crises of the postwar years, such as the Berlin Blockade, the Berlin Wall, Suez, and the *Pueblo* affair. Thus we must avoid specificity that would make that impossible.

We might generalize the Soviet decision this way: "A nation will initiate a crisis when it seeks to improve its military position relative to its adversary, to reverse a previous loss of political initiative, and to increase its influence among uncommitted states." Or we could convert this into a statement of conditions: "A crisis will occur when one nation takes action that seems likely to improve its military position relative to its adversary, to reverse a previous political setback, and to increase its influence among the uncommitted." Or, somewhat more generally, we could say: "A nation will take action which instigates a crisis when its military position relative to its adversary is weakening but may be strengthened by new deployment, when it has recently failed to achieve a political victory in a confrontation with that adversary, and when its influence with the uncommitted has suffered from initiatives by its adversary."

Which of these formulations we adopt at this time is not in itself significant. Our selection should depend on the usefulness of each in providing a statement that can be tested against other cases and that enables us better to understand and perhaps anticipate the outbreak of a crisis.

But we have not finished formulating our proposition, for we have yet to include internal political considerations. The chief domestic factor we found was great pressure on resources, coupled perhaps with pressures from political rivals. Thus we might hypothesize that "a nation will instigate an international crisis when it faces great problems of resource scarcity and an alternative political ruler or faction threatens the leadership." Or we might say that "an international crisis will occur when a nation's resources are strained and its leadership is threatened, if there arises an opportunity for it to attempt a change in the status quo that, if successful, may lessen each of these dangers."

Now we must attempt to combine our international and our domestic conditions. We might then arrive at a formulation such as this: "A nation will take action which will instigate a crisis when that action promises to lessen the strain on resources and the threat to the leadership domestically, while improving its military position, countering a recent international setback, and increasing its influence among the uncommitted."

Stated in terms of a possible solution to all the major problems facing a regime, it is hard to imagine why any nation does not instigate a crisis whenever it can—until we remember that a distinctive feature of a crisis is its high risk, not only of failure to achieve such objectives, but also of a positive setback in achieving others. At present we are simply trying to describe the conditions in which a nation takes action that instigates a crisis. We presume that a nation will undertake such action only if it believes that the likely benefits will outweigh the likely costs or, more accurately, that the probability that the action will be successful, coupled with the benefits expected from success, is high enough to make the risk of failure and its costs worth taking.

This statement quite clearly applies to the Cuban missile crisis, which is hardly surprising since we have developed it specifically out of our explanation of that crisis. We have already seen that other formulations of it—and indeed quite different formulations—might also apply to the missile crisis. Selection among such alternatives depends on their usefulness in portraying the conditions we find preceding other crises.

The American Response

But a crisis does not exist until another party has in some way recognized and responded to the instigator. If the United States had failed to uncover the presence of missiles in Cuba, or had decided to let the missiles remain, the status quo would have been changed, but there would have been no crisis at least then. Thus we must now resume our consideration of the outbreak of crises by describing the conditions under which the United States chose to resist the Soviet initiative.

We concluded above that the United States viewed the emplacement of missiles as a direct threat to its national security, and also that it was concerned about the political impact of a Soviet success in Cuba on the security of Berlin and on the attitudes of the uncommitted nations of the world. We could then state, as our generalized principle derived from the American response in this crisis, that "a nation will respond to an action that instigates a sudden change in the status quo if it views it as a threat to its military security at home and its political position among its allies and the uncommitted." But, as we have said before, absolute certainty about how a nation views or will view a given happening is most difficult, and we wish therefore eventually to develop propositions that will depend on statements of conditions rather than on portrayals of a nation's attitudes.

Thus we might reformulate this proposition to state that "a nation will respond to a change by another nation in the status quo if that change alters the military balance between the two nations unfavorably and shifts the initiative in the contest for influence in the world to the instigator."

We have not yet, however, considered the nature of the response we should expect. This cannot be done satisfactorily until we have examined a variety of crises in which these responses varied. If the nation should respond to such an initiative by launching a war, there would have been either no crisis or perhaps a very brief crisis while the nation was deciding to launch a war. Since our concept of crisis involves actions short of war by either side, we shall hope eventually to be able to generalize about the conditions in which we might expect various possible types of crises, such as those involving military deployments (missiles in Cuba) and those involving only diplomatic threats (orders to leave Berlin or be forced out).

In developing comprehensive propositions we must test one crisis against another to see whether the propositions are accurate and promising. There are multitudes of crises available for comparison, and we must first decide which sorts of crises to employ as our first test. The Cuban missile crisis was basically a confrontation between the Soviet Union and the United States. We would expect that a proposition developed from such a crisis would apply to a similar crisis such as the Berlin Blockade, so we could sensibly begin our test by applying our propositions to that crisis. To do so we must first examine what actually happened in Berlin.

The Berlin Blockade

In a series of agreements among the "Big Three" of World War II, the United States, the Soviet Union, and Great Britain mapped out their plans for the postwar state of Nazi Germany. The conferences — Yalta, Teheran, and others — planned the eventual denazification, demilitarization, and democratization of the nation. Zones of occupation for all of Germany had been created, and the city of Berlin was divided into four wedge-shaped sectors, each of which was to be garrisoned by one of the occupying powers. Supreme authority in Germany was to be exercised by an Allied Control Council sitting in Berlin and operating on the unanimity voting principle.

Cooperation, however, did not continue once the common enemy was defeated. Various unilateral Soviet measures on reparations policy and territorial settlement had upset the Allies, but none so much as Soviet refusal to agree to the currency reform that would curb runaway inflation. It seems likely that Stalin believed that the best solution to the German problem would be to destroy Germany as a great power once and for all. But when the Allies seemed interested in incorporating West Germany's military and economic strength into their total potential, Stalin became increasingly concerned and modified his unilateral exploitation of East Germany. Instead he began to strengthen the economic and political structure of East Germany and demanded

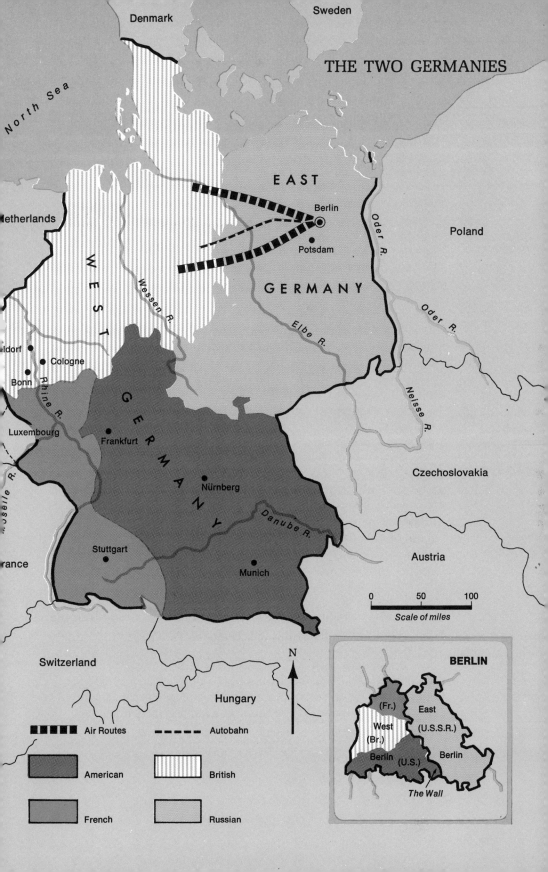

THE TWO GERMANIES

Denmark

Sweden

North Sea

Netherlands

EAST

Berlin

Poland

Potsdam

Oder R.

GERMANY

W E S T

Wessen R.

Elbe R.

Oder R.

ldorf

Cologne

Neisse R.

Bonn

G E R M A N Y

Rhine R.

Luxembourg

Frankfurt

Czechoslovakia

oselle R.

Nürnberg

Danube R.

rance

Stuttgart

Austria

Munich

0   50   100
Scale of miles

Switzerland

N

BERLIN

Hungary

(Fr.)

East

West
(Br.)

(U.S.S.R.)

Air Routes   Autobahn

Berlin

Berlin

(U.S.)

American   British

The Wall

French   Russian

that the two parts of Germany be reunited on Soviet terms, which would grant the Russians greater gains than Western nations would obtain from the controlled reunification.

Soviet intransigence in the Control Council and the Council of Foreign Ministers, coupled with Communist policies in East Germany, convinced the Allies that the Soviets had no intention of coming to an acceptable agreement on the administration of Germany. American, British, and French representatives, convening in London in February 1948, arrived at the London Agreements, which they announced on June 7th. These recommendations called for coordination of the economic policies in the three Western zones, German participation in the European Recovery Program (the Marshall Plan), and the German drafting of a constitution for a German Federal Republic.

The first communiqué was issued from London on March 8, and the Soviets walked out of the Allied Control Council in Berlin on March 20. With the Control Council dead, the Western authorities lost no time in taking advantage of this opportunity to institute currency reform in the Western zones. The first such law was announced on June 18, 1948; others followed in rapid succession, producing the remarkable economic recovery of not only West Germany, but Western Europe as well.

The Soviets were thus faced with two possible policy alternatives: they could continue with the bolshevization of East Germany and eliminate the Western enclave in Berlin, or they could try to force the Allies to accept a four-power agreement on Soviet terms. Either policy could at the outset be pursued by blockading West Berlin. And the selection among these long-range policies could rest largely on Western reaction to a blockade, for a successful blockade would force the Allies to decide whether to stay in Berlin and accept the Soviet program or withdraw from Berlin and complete the division of Germany.

In 1947 the Soviets began to prepare the way for a possible blockade by repeatedly predicting in the Soviet-controlled press the Western withdrawal from Berlin. In addition, they claimed that Berlin was part of the Soviet zone, attempted to discredit the democratic *Magistrat* ruling Berlin, took measures to consolidate Soviet control over the eastern sector of Berlin, and finally instituted controls that gradually strangled the movement of people and goods between Berlin and West Germany.

After walking out of the Allied Control Council, the Soviets,

on April 1st, imposed rail and road restrictions on Allied traffic
from the Western zones to Berlin because of "technical difficulties." The Allies countered with a "little airlift" to supply occupation forces in Berlin. Then, following announcement of the
London Recommendations, the Soviets halted rail traffic between
Berlin and West Germany for two days on June 11. The next day
the highway bridge on the road to Berlin was closed for "repairs"
and on June 16 the Soviets walked out of the Allied Kommanda-
tura. On June 18 the Allies announced currency reform for West
Germany but not for Berlin; and then on June 23 the Soviets or-
dered currency reform for East Germany and for all of Berlin.
The Western powers responded the same day by ordering currency reform in West Berlin. And on June 24 the Soviets imposed
a full blockade on Berlin. The next day the Allies decided to
begin supplying Berliners, as well as the occupation military
forces, and on June 26 the great Berlin Airlift began. The Soviet
Union and the three Western Allies (the United States, Britain,
and France) were locked in a major crisis.

Explaining the Outbreak of the Crisis

What, then, are the conditions that preceded the Berlin
Blockade? Will our generalization derived from the Cuban missile crisis hold up when tested against this instance? Among the
international conditions we found present in the Cuban case
were opportunities for the instigating nation to improve its military positions, a chance to counter a recent international setback,
and the means to increase its influence among the uncommitted
nations.

There can be little doubt that driving the Western nations
from Berlin would remove a thorn deep in the Soviets' Eastern
European side. It would not have resulted in a more favorable
posture against the West, for Communist boundaries with the
West would have remained the same, and there would have been
no better military deployment for the Soviets. What would have
happened, however, would have been a weakening of the credibility of the commitment of the United States to the defense of
Europe, and of the three Allies to the defense of West Germany.
In this sense, then, the position of the Soviets would have been
militarily improved.

Furthermore, this might have had the effect of impressing

on the uncommitted nations the dynamism of the international communist movement. At this time there were few uncommitted nations and most of those that subsequently joined this "third world" were then colonies of the major Western powers and were still in the process of seeking independence. The Soviet Union, however, had recently increased its control over the nations of Eastern Europe. The last vestiges of democratic politics disappeared in Poland and Hungary in 1947, and Czechoslovakian democracy was overthrown by Czech Communists in a movement that began on February 25, 1948.

But if the Soviets had been gaining influence and control in Eastern Europe, they had been losing it farther south. In May 1947 the United States Congress, under the "Truman Doctrine," appropriated $400,000,000 for economic and military aid to the pro-Western governments of Greece and Turkey for what was to prove a successful repulsion of Communist insurgents. And the next month the United States announced the Marshall Plan, by which it would provide $15 *billion* in aid to European states for postwar reconstruction. Furthermore, the Soviets had been contending with the refusal of Yugoslavia's Premier Tito to toe its line. Thus the Russians faced a situation in which they were losing influence on the fringes of their bloc while at the same time consolidating power within it. In these circumstances, expelling the West from Berlin and thereby unifying East Germany in the Soviet bloc might be a particularly attractive way of overcoming the recent setbacks farther to the south.

An additional consideration which appears to have been important was the Soviet army strength in Central Europe, which far exceeded that of Western forces. The military indefensibility of West Berlin itself, coupled with this Soviet superiority on the ground in Germany and the believed weakness of Western air transport, served as general conditions that could encourage such a venture.

What, then, of domestic conditions within the Soviet Union? The proposition we derived from the missile crisis suggests that we should find internally a strain on resources and some threat to the country's leadership. That there was a strain on resources so soon after the termination of the Second World War was both true and expected, although it is not obvious that the Berlin Blockade would have contributed significantly to lessening that strain. (Indeed, the counterblockade the Allies then imposed, as we shall see shortly, simply added to it.) We have, however, no evidence that Stalin was subject to particular domestic political pressure at the time of the blockade. Indeed, what pressure may have arisen subsequently seems to have been a result of the failure of the militant Soviet policy to produce anything but remobilization in the West.

Applying Our Proposition to the Outbreak

How, then, does our proposition about the conditions preceding crisis fare in its test against the Berlin Blockade? We have not found that the action taken to instigate the blockade promised to lessen the strain on resources and the threat to the leadership. Thus these "domestic" factors do not seem generalizable. And there are not obvious substitutes either. The major "domestic" factor that may have been important was ideological hostility, which can be expressed in terms of the international conditions we have considered. It is possible that there were domestic considerations of which we continue to be ignorant; hence we would not wish to be too conclusive in rejecting the inclusion of such conditions. But because we have not found them clearly present in this instance, it seems sensible to view them as possible contributory factors rather than as essential factors preceding crisis — at least until we have more conclusive evidence of their importance.

There is, moreover, another possible way to reconcile the apparent difference in domestic conditions. As we know, in the case of the Berlin Blockade, the Soviet action in substance was designed to force the West to leave Berlin, whereas their action in Cuba was designed to place themselves in a militarily advantageous position relative to the United States. Perhaps if we study other crises we shall find confirmed a proposition that links the nature of domestic conditions with the type of action pursued by the instigator. For example, we might eventually settle on a proposition like this: "A nation will undertake to change the status quo in a way that advances its offensive military capability when it faces a strain on its resources and a threat to its leadership. A nation will undertake to change the status quo in a way that serves to decrease the adversary's favorable position when international considerations prevail over domestic conditions."

Of course, we cannot be confident of this distinction without testing it against a variety of crisis instigations, both of the apparently offensive kind (Cuba) and of the apparently defensive kind (Berlin). But such linkage of preceding conditions with the type of instigation is one way of coping with apparent divergences in conditions and at the same time attempting to make our propositions more revealing.

There is significantly greater similarity in the international conditions preceding the two crises. Although the instigating action did not promise great improvement of the Soviet military position, it could have been advantageous. Indeed, it was partly the strength of the existing Soviet posture that enabled the Soviet Union to be confident of success. It is quite clear that the Russians had suffered significant setbacks in their efforts to increase their political and military position in areas contiguous to those they controlled; it is also clear that they might have expected a victory in Berlin to have significant benefits in terms of decreased Western prestige and increased Soviet influence among other areas in which the West was involved.

Thus the international aspects of our general proposition seem to survive this first test, and we may be somewhat more confident of our statement that "a nation will take action that changes the status quo in a way that instigates a crisis when its military position relative to its adversary is weakening but may be improved by new deployment, when it has recently failed to achieve political victory in confrontations with the adversary, and when its influence with nations outside its sphere of influence has suffered from initiatives by its adversary."

At this point, we return to the question of the conditions that precede a challenged nation's decision to resist, and thereby bring about a crisis. We have concluded from the Cuban case that "a nation will respond to a change in the status quo by another nation if that change alters the military balance between the two nations and shifts the initiative in the contest for influence in the world to the instigator." In the Berlin situation we are dealing not with one nation but with three—but three whose policies did not diverge significantly. The change in the military balance, we have concluded, would not have been of great significance in itself, for Berlin was not a useful outpost militarily (although it was of significance to intelligence-gathering). But the impact of withdrawal from Berlin on the confidence of Europe, and hence on its solidarity in the face of the Soviet Union, would probably have had much the same effect. Furthermore, the initiative the West—particularly the United States—had seized through the Truman Doctrine, the Marshall Plan, and the principles underlying these new approaches to problems of political and military security was certainly threatened by the prospect of defeat in Berlin. Thus the conditions that make the American response in Cuba understandable can also be found in the Berlin situation fourteen years earlier, and so our proposition seems applicable.

Some Tentative Conclusions

What, then, have we learned? We have developed several propositions about the outbreak of crisis that seem to fit the two crises we have examined and help us to understand why they arose. Because the cases are so similar—in each the Soviet Union attempted a major change in the status quo and the United States resisted—we are very much interested in additional testing of the propositions.

One obvious variation that would be interesting would be cases in which the United States attempted such a change and the Soviets resisted. Unfortunately for our analysis, we have no such clear cases. There are numerous instances in which the United States sought to alter the status quo, but each time it was against a weak nation that was at most a client state or supporter of the Soviet Union. Examples of this type include the American cooperation in the overthrow of a communist president in Guatemala in 1954, the American sponsorship of the Bay of Pigs invasion of Cuba by anti-Castro exiles in early 1961, the American invasion of Santo Domingo in the face of rebellion against a military regime favored by the United States in April 1965, and the American decisions to fight actively in South Vietnam and to bomb North Vietnam. The periods preceding the American decisions in each of these cases constituted crises of sorts, and the periods immediately following American intervention can be viewed as potential crises while the Soviet Union decided whether or not to intervene. But in none of these cases did matters develop so that the superpowers directly confronted each other, or even made major threats to each other. Consequently, we would expect conditions to vary somewhat, and these conditions would be worthy of study.

Also important would be cases of the opposite type, in which the Soviet Union attempted to change the status quo and the United States decided not to resist. These cases include the Soviet ① activities in undermining democratic regimes in Eastern Europe in 1947 and 1948, ② the Soviet suppression of the Hungarian revolt in 1956, and the ③ increasing Soviet involvement in Cuba prior to the Bay of Pigs invasion.

Before we could be highly confident of the accuracy and broad applicability of our propositions about the conditions under which crisis confrontations arise, we would wish to examine all these instances in which crises did not arise. For clearly we would hope that our propositions would be accurate enough that when the conditions they contain exist, crisis occurs. But until scholars undertake much more extensive systematic study of crisis, we are left able to state only the conditions that are to be found when crises occur — not necessarily the conditions that always lead to crisis. In other words, our propositions may help us to understand the outbreak of a given crisis, but they will not necessarily enable us to predict it. Nonetheless, increased understanding of the outbreak of crisis is progress, and if we attempt the same sort of study of cases in which crises might have occurred but did not occur we should be able to improve the predictive value of our work. We shall return to this problem again in our coming chapter on prediction.

If we were concentrating extensively on the study of crisis, we would examine, not only superpower confrontations and superpower nonconfrontations, but also crises involving primarily the middle-range powers, such as the Suez crisis of 1956, and also the more frequent crises involving smaller and often uncommitted nations, about which we rarely hear. But our major focus in this introductory study must be on the interaction of states and the effects that interaction has on the outcomes of crises, wars, alliances, and cooperative control. In an effort to see whether we can generate and test propositions about the outcome of crisis, we must turn now to an examination of our several crises as they developed.

The Development of Crisis

Our attention thus far has been focused on the foreign policy decisions and actions of parties to a developing crisis. We could analyze the whole of the crisis in this way, asking at each point, Why did each nation take the action it did? But as we have already seen, it is often difficult to reach definite conclusions to such questions. We usually find ourselves noting the action taken and then asking what might lead a rational person or a rational state to do such a thing. This is unsatisfactory both because it involves a high quantity of speculation and because it does not allow for irrational decision or for poor implementation of rational decision.

All that we are quite sure about is what action was indeed taken. We strongly suspect that each action taken in turn affects the action taken by the adversary—if only for the very sensible reason that nations do not generally seem to act randomly or purposelessly. Thus we expect the development of a crisis to be heavily dependent on the moves made that instigated it.

The Missile Crisis

In the missile crisis, once the United States discovered and revealed the presence of missile sites in Cuba and announced her intention to obtain their removal, both sides acted in ways designed to enhance their positions. The United States established the naval blockade of Cuba and moved strike forces to the Caribbean area to prepare for possible air attack or invasion. And the Soviets sent submarines to accompany their ships across the Atlantic and pressed on quickly with efforts to make their missiles in Cuba operational. Furthermore, both parties alerted other elements of their armed forces and each side readied its diplomatic forces. The United States immediately approached her allies to brief them and gain their support. The Soviets began communicating their firm resolve to available Americans and to America's allies. And both sides began a continuing confrontation at the United Nations.

Such activities generally involve both deployment of military forces and diplomatic communications. The Berlin Blockade extended over a year, and the pattern of interaction coupling deployment and diplomacy can be seen quite clearly in this extensive interaction.

The Berlin Blockade

The Soviets responded to the Allied Airlift in late June by first exerting pressure on elected all-Berlin German authorities.

If they yielded, the West would be gravely weakened, for it would no longer have even a formal vestige of control in Berlin. But almost to a man these officials remained firm. The Soviets then issued the first of a series of invitations to negotiations on the German problem as a whole, cut off the East Berlin supply of electricity for West Berlin, and increased the effectiveness of the transportation interference. Allied councils were divided on the best and, indeed, on the possible response. Knowing that Berlin was militarily indefensible, they regarded the airlift as only a device to gain time for diplomatic negotiations. After a week it began to appear that the airlift might be able to provide the city until winter: 450 flights by 150 planes were transporting over a thousand tons of food and supplies each day. Nonetheless, it was clear to the Allies that negotiations must be immediately undertaken. On July 3 Western representatives visited the Russian commander, Marshal Sokolovsky, who seemed to suggest that the terms for ending the blockade were not an end to currency reform but rather an end to Western efforts to establish a separate West German government. On July 7 the airlifting of coal began — a gift of western German states. But the pinch was already being felt as restrictions were imposed in preparation for the coming winter. General Lucius Clay, the American commander in Berlin, told Washington that in his opinion the Soviets did not want war and therefore the West could afford to take the necessary risks of sending an armored column down the autobahn to force its way through the blockade. But Washington decided instead to appeal to the United Nations, still emphasizing its legal rights of access to the city.

In these early days the Allies were fundamentally split. The French favored withdrawal from Berlin if a suitable formula could be worked out, whereas the Americans contended that Allied rights of occupation were not negotiable. The British took a middle view. Consequently, reconciliation of the Allied differences took time, and the Allies could not act rapidly. Nonetheless, they did impose a rather feeble counterblockade to prevent rail traffic between the Soviet zone and non-German countries through West Germany, but the major decision about the military response to the blockade was long in the making. American policy had to take into consideration two important military factors: America's monopoly on the atom bomb and her desperate weakness in conventional forces. These factors determined that any military action resting on ground efforts would be obviously bluff; hence realistic efforts would have to be backed by the bomb – the credibility of which was somewhat unclear. The immediate step taken by America was the dispatch of sixty B-29s to Britain July 17 and another thirty or so in August. These planes were popularly known as "atomic bombers," and although they were unlikely to be used immediately, they at least reversed the policy of withdrawing American forces from Europe and increased the immediate striking power of the West. They might therefore set some limit to Soviet extensions of her actions against the Western position in Berlin.

Meanwhile, however, the Allies were very much interested in negotiation. Meetings in Moscow began August 2 and resulted in the Moscow Agreement of August 30, which provided for the introduction of Soviet-sponsored currency under four-power control in all Berlin. The communiqué contained a directive to the military governors in Berlin, calling upon them to arrange the agreed currency reform and the removal of traffic restrictions. All the while the Soviets had been intensifying their efforts to demoralize the West Berliners and to subvert the democratic governmental bodies of the city. When the military governors met in Moscow on September 1 to 7 it became quite clear that the Soviets had no intention of honoring either the spirit or the letter of the Moscow Agreement. But Allied opinion that the airlift might be able to supply Berlin through the winter was spreading and the morale of the West Berliners seemed relatively immune to Soviet threats and promises. It became clear that the Soviets were in no hurry to lift the blockade. And when it became equally clear that the Western powers would not alter their policies in West Germany itself, the Soviets concentrated on their second objective: control of all Berlin.

When the negotiations proved unsatisfactory to both sides, each resorted to the same course it had pursued before. In October the Allies formed the Combined Airlift Task Force to synchronize American and British airlifting in order to increase the flow of goods to West Berlin. This bred increased optimism about the future even though winter was coming on. On October 20 the West German Parliamentary Council began to meet in Bonn to draft a constitution for West Germany. As the Allied powers drafted an occupation statute to define their role in a new West German state the Communists intensified their efforts to cement their control over the eastern sector. On November 30 a "rump Assembly" met there and split the city government by establishing a new *Magistrat* that appointed Fritz Ebert mayor. The Soviets recognized the legality of the new regime two days later, after the real *Magistrat* officials had been barred from their East Berlin building by police. The legal city government was thus forced to abandon its authority in the eastern sector and the split was formal. Nonetheless, the scheduled elections for a new *Magistrat* were held in West Berlin December 5 and resulted in an overwhelming, 80 percent support of the three democratic parties despite Communist efforts.

Diplomatic negotiations proceeded through the fall. On September 29 the Western powers submitted the Berlin dispute to the United Nations, and on October 4 the Security Council began consideration at a Paris meeting. On October 25, after prolonged efforts by disinterested Council members, a "neutralist" draft resolution calling for settlement on the terms of the Moscow Agreement was vetoed by the Soviet Union. A month later the Council established a Technical Committee to study the Berlin currency problem. The fast pace of diplomatic efforts elsewhere during the autumn continued unabated. *Aides-mémoire* were exchanged in Moscow and notes were circulated among the four governments involved. But no progress was made, and it seemed that the Soviets were engaging in these various diplomatic maneuvers to keep the Western powers at the conference table until the blockade forced them to make appreciable concessions.

Slowly, however, the Western stand became firmer. The two chief antiblockade measures — the airlift and the counterblockade — were strengthened. Even more important, Western nations continued to pursue three extremely significant programs in Europe that, although not specifically directed against the blockade, probably played a greater role in the long run in bringing it to an end than did the counterblockade. The Marshall Plan, coupled with the Western currency reform and German industrial vigor, gave birth to the "economic miracle" of West Germany. Plans for the West German State were completed by the spring of 1949 and the formation of defensive alliances progressed with remarkable speed. Talks that led to the formation of NATO on April 4 were begun in the latter half of 1948, and talks that resulted in the defense agreements among Britain, France, Belgium, the Netherlands, and Luxembourg signed April 7 made considerable headway. All these developments came to a head in the autumn of 1948. As the airlift produced greater confidence for the Allies and greater defiance from the Berliners, the West refused to yield in the Berlin conference of military governors. The Soviets failed to depose the legally elected *Magistrat,* and the Western Allies made considerable progress in coordinating their own defensive efforts. Consequently the Soviets seem to have decided to concentrate on consolidating their position in East Berlin, although they undoubtedly still hoped to obtain West Berlin by a tightened blockade.

As the new year opened it began to look as if the Western resistance had succeeded and the Soviets would have to seek a convenient opportunity to remove traffic restrictions without demanding appreciable concessions from the West. But they seemed to be in no hurry to end the blockade. On January 31 Stalin answered a question put to him in writing by J. Kingsbury Smith, European manager of the International News Service, by saying that there would be no obstacles to lifting the blockade if the West postponed the establishment of a West German State pending a meeting of the Council of Foreign Ministers to consider the German question as a whole. The ommission of any mention of the currency problem led Ambassador Philip Jessup to inquire on February 15 of the Soviet representative to the Security Council, Jacob Malik, whether this omission was accidental. A month later Malik informed Jessup that it was "not accidental" and Soviet-American negotiations progressed rapidly. Nonetheless, Soviet and East German political behavior remained outwardly unchanged. The West, however, began to take the offensive. As the airlift succeeded in supplying Berlin through the winter the Allies tightened their counterblockade, extending it on February 4 to all truck traffic between the Western zones and the Soviet zone. Moscow began to speak of the importance of reopening German trade and of again seeking German unification or at least the withdrawal of foreign troops. In the third week of March the Jessup-Malik negotiations produced a tentative agreement to lift the blockade and the counterblockade. On March 21 Malik reported that if a date were set for the meeting of the Council of Foreign Ministers, the restrictions could be lifted in advance. After details were discussed jointly with Britain and France, an official statement was released in the four capitals on May 5 announcing that the blockade and the counter blockade would end on May 12 and that the council meeting would take place in Paris May 23.

The Termination of Crisis

We have now examined the development of two different crises. Just as we expect some new condition or consideration to provoke a crisis, so we expect the outcome of a crisis to be heavily dependent on what happens during it — that is, on its development. It is difficult to organize or schematize the developments in a crisis even though it is relatively easy to observe and study them — easier, at least, than studying the decisionmaking within the countries involved — because they are constituted by a series (or two series) of actions.

One scholar has suggested that careful attention to the patterns of interaction in a crisis is likely to pay dividends in better understanding of its outcome and, indeed, of the nature of crisis itself. As he has written:

> Prominent international crises are complexes of events which can be dissected, up to a point, to yield numerous sequences of related acts. A crisis temporarily narrows the focus of international politics and accelerates events in the public view so that there is very little difficulty in tracing sequences of action in which Event A calls forth Event B which calls forth Event C, etc., until the track is finally lost. After a number of such sequences have been traced and studied, similarities or identities of form in some of them may appear.[5]

Unfortunately, scholars have not yet attempted such study comprehensively and comparatively, although the raw materials for it are at hand in studies of individual crises.[6] We are thus forced to attempt again our crude development of propositions about the conditions preceding termination of crisis. We are concerned not only with the fact that the crisis terminates, but also with the way it terminates — in war, in negotiated settlement, in deterioration, or in capitulation. And we shall hope that our efforts will at least bring us close to propositions linking certain

---

[5]Charles A. McClelland, "The Acute International Crisis" in World Politics, 14 (1961) 182–204, at 191.
[6]But see, for an early preliminary effort, Charles A. McClelland, "Action Structures and Communication in Two International Crises: Quemoy and Berlin" in Background, 7 (1964) 201–215. And see McClelland's further effort, "Access to Berlin: The Quantity and Variety of Events, 1948–1963," pp. 159–186 in J. David Singer, ed., Quantitative International Politics: Insights and Evidence (New York: Free Press, 1968).

conditions of the crisis with certain outcomes, for ultimately we would like to know why one party prevails or why stalemate is reached.

The Missile Crisis

The Cuban crisis ended in a negotiated settlement, the terms of which included withdrawal of the offensive missiles and bombers the Soviets had introduced into Cuba and an American pledge not to invade Cuba. We face two interesting questions here: why the crisis ended in a negotiated settlement, and why that settlement was on these terms. We would expect a crisis to end when or after each party to it had concluded that termination was in its interests. Such calculations may be particularly complicated, for while the decision to begin a crisis may require only expectation of gains over the immediate issue, the decision to end one may entail considerations of prestige and influence involving a nation's relations with many other countries. We have already been impressed by the possibility that crises arise when a nation seeks to increase that influence and overcome recent setbacks abroad. If these conditions are present a nation is unlikely to settle on termination if that will cost it further in influence.

Thus we would expect a nation to decide to terminate a crisis if it has attained its objective or has lost so substantially that it must cut its losses. But termination requires two parties to agree in some sense: one to accept victory and the other defeat, or both to accept negotiated settlement, deterioration, or war. We must remember that, in general, nations' interests are not entirely opposed—that is, any gain for one is not necessarily a loss for the other. However, in a crisis, just because it is a quick confrontation in which prestige is at stake, important interests are likely to be opposed at points short of resort to war.

This is an important point, for in the missile crisis the obvious high risk was war. The Soviets were given the choice of relenting or facing at best conventional naval war in the Caribbean —which they were bound to lose because of the American naval supremacy in the area—or at worst general nuclear war, presumably initiated by the Soviets when they found they could not prevail in the conventional struggle at sea. The United States, on the other hand, also feared nuclear war and hence was prepared to settle for the immediate objective of restoring something approximating the status quo ante. If the United States had pressed for surrender rather than for settlement, she might have obtained it, but at a cost in cooperativeness of the Soviet Union, which would have placed the subsequent nuclear testban and *détente*, as well as the Allied position in Berlin in jeopardy.

On the basis of these considerations, we can attempt a statement of the conditions conducive to termination of a crisis by negotiated settlement. Thus: 'When the instigator of a crisis has failed to achieve his objective but the respondent has failed to achieve restoration of the status quo ante, and the military situation is unstable and therefore threatens escalation if force is resorted to, a crisis will tend to end in negotiated settlement.'

This proposition clearly encompasses the case of the missile crisis. There, the Soviets had failed to complete installation of their missiles because the United States had imposed its blockade, but the United States had failed by that blockade to force the Soviets to withdraw the missiles and bombers already in Cuba. And although the United States could resort to local conventional military action, the very inferiority of the Soviets in that arena would almost force them to resort to intercontinental warfare, which would be very likely to turn quickly into global nuclear war.

The Berlin Blockade

But will this proposition apply to the Berlin Blockade? Various reasons have been suggested for the Soviet agreement to end the blockade. American Ambassador Walter Bedell Smith argued, as have others, that the counterblockade began to hurt the East more than the blockade hurt the West. General Clay contended that the revival in West Germany was responsible. Trygve Lie, Secretary-General of the United Nations, believed that the triumphant airlift and the force of world public opinion brought about its removal. Western diplomats were inclined to believe that the Soviets desired to rejoin the "diplomatic club" and again exert some influence on Western actions. And others have cited the loss of prestige of Communist parties throughout Europe as a motivating factor. But these considerations, although quite likely elements in the Soviet decision, are somewhat superficial. It is more likely that, having completed consolidation of their position in East Berlin and having quite obviously failed in West

Berlin and West Germany, the only advantage the Soviets could expect from maintaining the blockade was its continuing drain on the West and its tying up of Western military air transport facilities. But the disadvantages of its continuation were substantial: it reinforced the new-found unity of the Western powers and of the West German states, and it prohibited the Soviets from interfering with the establishment and consolidation of NATO, the Marshall Plan, and the establishment of a West German government. It seems that the Soviet Union decided, instead, to promote neutralist sentiment in Europe, taking advantage of some hesitancy in France over the increasing strength of West Germany. Ascription of the removal of the blockade to such a broad shift in Soviet tactics rather than to specific causes or to Soviet designs is strengthened by the fact that the subsequent Council of Foreign Ministers meeting, which had been vehemently demanded by the Soviets, served only to point up the lack of a coherent public Soviet policy on Berlin. In short, the firm stand of the Western Allies, reinforced by the effectiveness of Allied resistance to Soviet incursions and of Allied countermeasures, seems to have forced a change in Soviet strategy, if not in Soviet aims.

It is clear, then, that the Soviets had failed to drive the West from Berlin, but also that the West had failed to restore the previous situation in which it had free ground access to Berlin. Militarily, the United States had a monopoly on the atom bomb at the time, but although the bomb could have done considerable damage, it could not have itself liberated Berlin; and the Soviets had massive ground superiority in Central Europe. Thus our proposition appears to apply to the negotiated termination of the Berlin Blockade.

Some Tentative Conclusions

We must realize, however, that the proposition does not tell us all we would like to know. In the first place, it does not give us much indication of how quickly a crisis will be so terminated. The Cuban crisis ended in several weeks, but the Berlin Blockade lasted about a year. The undesirability of prolonging the Berlin Blockade—that is, its failure to benefit either party—became obvious as soon as the Allies demonstrated an ability to manage the airlift throughout the winter. How, then, do we explain the fact that the blockade lasted until early May? The mis-

sile crisis ended rapidly in large part because the threat of escalation into major military conflict was posed immediately by the
rush of Soviet ships toward the American blockade. But the Berlin
Blockade could be stretched, or at least allowed to persist, without major immediate threats. This, then, allowed the Soviets to
feel out the West for terms and then to select a time that made
settlement look like less of a capitulation than it was. In other
words, face-saving is important in any such superpower confrontation—particularly for the instigator who eventually desires
a negotiated settlement—and it will be sought with greater commitment and persistence if the threat of major war is not imminent.

Our proposition is also limited in that it deals only with
negotiated settlement of crisis. We are also interested in crises
that simply deteriorate or degenerate or fade away, such as the
Berlin crisis of 1961 including Khrushchev's new ultimatum and
the building of the Berlin Wall; or the Quemoy crisis of 1958,
involving Communist Chinese shelling of the Nationalist Chinese
offshore island through the summer months, which eventuated
in a regularization of that shelling after the United States had
convoyed supplies to the island under Communist fire and thereby raised the possibility of an American war with mainland China.
And we are also interested in crises that terminate in war, such
as those opening World War I, World War II in Asia, World War
II in Europe, the Suez crisis of 1956, and the Middle East crisis
of 1967.

Study of these varieties of crisis along the lines of our study
of several crises terminating in settlement, as well as further
testing of our developed propositions about them, must be undertaken by students of international politics if we are to be able to
develop comprehensive theories of crisis, and perhaps eventually
of international politics as a whole.

Before concluding, we should ask what contribution our
analysis of crises—brief and underdeveloped as it was—can
make to our study of international politics. Our first interest is
to be able to explain why individual instances happen as they
do in international politics. Our propositions have been statements of conditions found to precede the outbreak and the termination of crises. But those conditions have been chosen because
our general understanding of the nature and dynamics of international politics suggests that these conditions might be contributory factors. Our propositions are not incomprehensible—as

would be propositions that linked crises with the cycles of the moon and planets, or with the color of the clothing worn by national leaders. We will not be able to pass additional judgment on the usefulness of our propositions until we attempt to unify them with our knowledge (or the things we come to suspect) about other aspects of international politics, such as war and alliance and cooperative control. Later we shall also wish to compare our findings with those of other scholars who have written about aspects of international political action. And we shall wish to employ our propositions to improve our ability to anticipate or predict international political happenings, and perhaps even to increase the possibilities of controlling them. But these efforts must await further study—first in this book and then in our classrooms and research institutes. And now, having made this brief and somewhat tentative start, we move on to another major international political phenomenon, one that is sometimes the culmination of crisis: war.

chapter **10**
Studying War

An Approach to War

War has attracted more attention than any other aspect of international relations. There have been numerous studies of particular wars, many studies of war as a general phenomenon, many theories, partial theories, or pretheories of war. Obviously, we cannot analyze, or even mention, many of these studies. Indeed, in 1942 Quincy Wright, still one of the foremost students of war, produced a two-volume, 1552-page work called *A Study of War.* Since that time, several hundred more wars have erupted, and several thousand more books and articles on them have been published.

In our limited space, we must concentrate on questions most fundamental to the study of war, paying particular attention not so much to the actual nature and causes of wars as to the *ways* in which we can describe its nature and discover its causes.

We can then examine briefly some major theories of war, see whether they agree or conflict, ask whether they can be reconciled where they do conflict, and decide how they might be tested against actual instances of war. Eventually, we would like to establish a general theory of war strong enough to tell us when wars of various sorts will occur and, if possible, why they will occur under certain circumstances or conditions. We might approach such a theory in the way we began to approach a theory of crisis: by examining various categories of wars to discover their conditions. Or we might approach it by deducing statements about the conditions for the occurrence of wars from general theories of their causes, such as the theory that wars are caused by economic factors, or the theory that they are caused by insane leaders, or the theory that they are caused by the international system of sovereign states seeking to dominate one another.

The Nature of War

Since our ultimate objective is to develop a theory of war in general, rather than to explain the occurrence of any particular wars, we shall examine various explanations of war as an international political phenomenon. Depending on their comprehensiveness and state of development, these explanations may be theoretical frameworks, pretheories, or theories. A theory of any international political phenomenon, we have said, must first state the distinguishing characteristics that enable us to recognize a political event as being an instance that the theory should be able to explain. It must then indicate the requisite conditions for the occurrence of that phenomenon. The statement of conditions will probably be organized around the stages of the development of the phenomenon—such as the outbreak of war, its expansion, and its termination. Both the precipitant conditions and the underlying conditions must be included—both the immediate causes and the permissive conditions, as they are sometimes referred to. These are the basic requirements. They may not actually explain the occurrence of the phenomenon, but they should enable us to anticipate and recognize its occurrence, and they should at least provide a framework in which to ask the additional questions that may stem from our perplexity.

But to make such progress, we must first examine the nature of war. We arrive at the essential characteristics of war by asking, What do we wish to distinguish war from? Even to ask such a question, we must have in mind instances that qualify for inclusion. Our examples would probably include the First World War, the Second World War, the Korean War, the war that followed the Suez crisis, the war that followed the Middle East crisis of 1967, the war in Vietnam, and the border war between India and China. We wish to distinguish such wars from several other phenomena such as peace. In the postwar years it has often been difficult to view international relations as a condition of peace, for we generally view overt violence and continuing animosity as indicators of war rather than of peace, and these have characterized much of postwar international relations. Furthermore, we would wish to distinguish war from crisis in peacetime. The difference here seems to be largely the generally shortened time-span of crisis coupled with its unusually heightened tension. In addition, we would probably seek to distinguish war from the Cold War, which is characterized by continuing tension and suspicion without overt violence. We might also want to distinguish war from punishment, which is what results when one party uses overt force and violence against another that does not fight back.

In terms of these distinctions we could view war as reciprocal political conflict violently undertaken or prosecuted. More explicitly, war is *violent interaction* resulting in reciprocal destruction and pain or death. But we may wish to go farther, distinguishing civil war by adding "among states" to our definition, and perhaps even adding that it must be declared (and international law thereby involved). The latter addition would curtail our list of wars, for undeclared war has become the fashion nowadays. In any event, we shall probably wish to eliminate instances of terrorism and provocation (such as often occur in the Middle East when there is no war on) even though they are often characterized by instigation and reprisal of the sort that initiates war.

Instances that qualify as wars under our definition will differ in various ways: in the quantity of interaction per unit of time, in the nature of the destruction (especially the weaponry used and the strategy employed), in the degree of reciprocity (or how evenly matched the parties are), and in how many states are parties to the war. All these features could prove significant both as consequences of the manner in which the war is initiated and as determinants of its development and termination. Thus in examining and testing theories of war we may find it desirable or even essential to make distinctions among wars in terms of

Figure 10-1.

DESCRIPTIVE MODEL FOR THE STUDY OF WAR

OUTBREAK
1. The Initial Violent Exchange: Key Decisions and Resulting Actions
    a. Initiation: —movement or destruction across or outside own borders
       —based on belief that war is more promising than non-war (i.e., was decision rational?)
    b. Response: —within and/or beyond own borders
       —defensive or destructive
       —based on belief that success is possible and war acceptable (i.e., was decision rational?)

INTERACTION
1. Continuation
    a. focus on relative strengths and desires, as in study of outbreak
    b. intrinsic dynamics of war (inertia or momentum)
       —"national honor" considerations
       —difficulty of negotiating a settlement
       —ideological exaggeration on each side
2. Pattern (which will determine type of war)
    a. escalation/de-escalation (destruction, targets, allies involved, weaponry, etc.)
    b. causes of the type or nature of war

TERMINATION
1. Study of Decisions (which contain information about the pattern of the war)
    a. Why does one's competence or sense of conflict deteriorate or disappear?
2. Possible Types
    a. unconditional surrender
    b. conditional surrender
    c. settlement
    d. disintegration
    e. expansion into a new war

these variations. We shall also want to distinguish further among the stages of war—something done by developing a descriptive model like that in Figure 10-1.

A Descriptive Model of War When we examine precipitating conditions of war, we will again be interested in the decision processes within the countries that are parties to the war. The first decision to attract our attention will be that to launch an attack. Such movement or destruction outside a country's borders or across another's borders may be in response to grievous provocation or a deliberate unprovoked first strike. We would expect a nation to make this decision if it believed that war would be more promising than nonwar, or else that the adversary would not respond. If the attacked party does not respond (or capitulates) then in our terms what has occurred is simply punishment.

The decision by the attacked party to respond will be based, we would presume, on a belief that success of some specified sort would be possible and that war is acceptable. This response will be crucial because it will help to set the level of conflict. It may be defensive or destructive, or both; it may occur within the country's borders or beyond them, or both; and, most significantly, it may match the attack or it may escalate the conflict.

These two sequential decisions give us the first interaction of war. At this point our concentration shifts somewhat from the decision level to the interaction level, for we shall be concerned with the continuation or development of the war and its pattern. We would expect the continuation to be a product of the relative strengths and desires of the parties (including, perhaps, allies drawn into the conflict) and what might be called war's intrinsic dynamic, its inertia or momentum. This last factor is produced largely by the raising of considerations of national honor, by the difficulty of negotiating a settlement with an adversary, and by ideological exaggeration, all of which nearly always accompany war.

When we study the continuation or development of a war, we shall be particularly interested in its nature and pattern in terms of the variations proposed above. It may escalate or deescalate in extent and in stakes. Furthermore, the conflict may be even or uneven. In any event, the nature of the interaction coupled, perhaps, with changes in the considerations or even in the regimes of the participants will at some point bring about termination.

In studying the termination of war we shall again be particularly interested in the decision process. War may terminate in unconditional surrender, conditional surrender, negotiated settlement, or disintegration. Or it may end in expansion into a new and broader war involving a larger area and probably more parties. We would expect to find that war will terminate when the competence or sense of conflict of one or more of the parties deteriorates or disappears — or, put another way, when new considerations arising out of the pattern of the war (and its costs and benefits) or of a change of regime (which might itself be a consequence of the war) alter the interests of one or more of the parties.

It should already be clear, however, that this comprehensive examination of the conditions of the war itself is not completely satisfying since we began examining immediate precipitating conditions without examining long range ones. Indeed some of these are conditions that will always exist as long as international relations exist. Among them are the existence of states or other units capable of violence and the existence of conflict arising fundamentally out of the needs and wants of men organized into those units. Other causes are more specific, and may precede a war by months or years without resulting in violence. Although not visibly present, they encourage the conversion of immediate or novel conditions into war. They include such intangible factors as humiliation in a previous war (Germany after World War I), a corrosive and militaristic ideology (Nazism), and mentally unstable leaders (Hitler). We shall encounter many other possible long-range conditions in our study.

We have distinguished ongoing underlying requirements such as actors and situations of interaction generally involving some conflictual disposition. We have also identified permissive or encouraging conditions — often called underlying causes — as well as immediate or precipitating causes, which often take the form of instantaneous events such as assassination, border raid, or ultimatum. The lines between these are not always clear, nor need they be. But in examining statements about the causes of war we shall find it important to separate them in order to organize them for testing and application. The point is perhaps

clearest when we examine explanations of a specific war.
As Quincy Wright has written,

> Writers have declared the cause of World War I to have been the
> Russian or the German mobilization; the Austrian ultimatum; the
> Sarajevo assassination; the aims and ambitions of the Kaiser, Poin-
> caré, Izvolsky, Berchtold, or someone else; the desire of France to
> recover Alsace-Lorraine or of Austria to dominate the Balkans; the
> European system of alliances; the activities of the munition-makers,
> the international bankers, or the diplomats; the lack of an adequate
> European political order; armament rivalries; colonial rivalries;
> commercial policies; the sentiment of nationality; the concept of
> sovereignty; the struggle for existence; the tendency of nations to
> expand; the unequal distribution of population, of resources, or
> of planes of living; the law of diminishing returns; the value of war
> as an instrument of national solidarity or as an instrument of na-
> tional policy; ethnocentrism or group egotism; the failure of the
> human spirit; and many others.[1]

We shall find, if we examine similar literature on the causes of
war, that some general version of one or all of these particular
factors has been argued as a cause of war by some theorists. We
cannot examine even one of these general explanations in detail,
but by means of distinguishing among types of conditions we
shall at least be able to examine major theories.

Theories vary in their focus. Some concentrate on action,
some on interaction. We have already come to suspect that in an
analysis of the origins of war the most profitable focus will be
on action and the decision preceding it, whereas in an examination of the development and termination of war the best focus
will be on interaction. War itself is obviously an interaction phenomenon. But interaction is composed of actions. We examine
interaction for patterns where we do not expect individual decisions to vary much or to be of particular interest, but when we
do examine individual decisions, we find that they are products
of, or are heavily influenced by, the ongoing interaction of international relations.

We can be more precise by being more specific. In any situation, whether war or diplomatic negotiation, there is always continuous decisionmaking. In the model we employ, decision in-

---

[1] Quincy Wright, *A Study of War*, Vol. II (Chicago: University of Chicago Press,
1942), pp. 727–728.

volves calculation of the best course in view of the interests or objectives sought and the information the decisionmaker has. Further, there is always policy determination — or, in our terms, deliberate selection of the interests and objectives to be sought. This policy determination occurs in what we generally call a political process: those with particular interests and roles to play attempt to determine the policy by operating within the political process. Finally, there is always an environment, or a situation outside the unit making policy decisions. This environment will be perceived by the political actors and in various ways will influence policymaking and decision. Among the possible influences in the environment are internal nonactor elements (public opinion is one), national material factors (the economy and geography), and the systems of which the nation is a part (regional alliances and the global international system). Our interest will be in the perception of the environment, in the determination of objectives, and in the calculations designed to achieve those objectives in the given environment.

When studying war, we look at the decision to launch it and the decision to respond to it. We shall probably ask first whether the decision was rational — that is, sensible in view of the objectives and the environment. If we conclude that the decision was rational, we may be satisfied and stop our analysis there. But we may then go on to ask why the nation had the objectives and values it did. This is a question about the functioning of the political bureaucratic system within the country. And we may also ask why the environment was such as to present the nation with these particular alternatives. This is a question about the development of states and the systems of states over time — about the conditions in which or as a result of which the decisions made were rational, given the objectives. We might pursue either of these two types of questions — political system and environmental development — as far as we wish, but we are then concentrating more on national politics and political history rather than on international politics.

If we pursue the question of why the decision was made, we may conclude that it was a result of misinformation or of miscalculation. Thus some have argued that the American involvement in Vietnam resulted from misinformation about the nature of the threat — a mistaken belief that an international Communist movement stemming from Peking threatened all of Southeast

Asia—although others have disputed this. Some have suggested that the Japanese attack on Pearl Harbor, bringing the United States into World War II, resulted from a miscalculation of the American reaction, and many have argued that the North Korean attack on South Korea resulted from a similar miscalculation.

But there is another way to account for an apparently puzzling decision. It may be that other objectives and values, clandestine (for governments often keep secrets) or held by individuals who are not thought to be decisionmakers (such as lobbyists or graft-peddlers), are actually being sought, and that in terms of these objectives the action taken is rational. Thus perhaps in starting World War II Germany was not seeking her own national interests; rather, Hitler was seeking his own strange interests that might have combined the struggle for Aryanism with a kind of death wish. In any event, if we find that other undeclared values are being sought, the question is who sets them and why, and this again is a question about national politics.

To put it more compactly, our concerns here are two: Why do states want what they want? (or Who sets their goals?) and Why do they act as they do given these wants? This second question can be reduced to the possibilities of rational calculation or error and to the environment in which calculation is made. We may then be led to questions of what determines this calculation and what determines the environment.

How far we go in such studies will be determined by our interests and by the regularities we find. Our desire is to discover regularities that we can state and then compose into theories. We do not know how far and into what levels we shall have to go to find regularities. In part, our objectives of being able to predict and control may determine this. But in any case, explaining and understanding will require us to relate happenings to our beliefs about the ways in which decisions are made and actions taken and interactions developed. This large order demands that we become much more specific in examining the various possible levels for analysis and explanation of war.

Possible Causes of War   In Chapter 5, where we examined such levels in general, we grouped them in three categories: the individual, the group, and the set of groups. Our concern with the individual will be our concern with the decisionmaking in the government. Here we may examine conscious decisionmaking. Many analysts of international politics, and some analysts of war in particular, have suggested that analysis and theory ought to be focused on this level.

Conscious Decision

In 1941 Theodore Abel, in an article entitled "The Element of Decision in the Pattern of War," argued that we have unwisely neglected this level in seeking correlations of war with population pressure, the business cycle, mass psychosis, and other external occurrences. He examined twenty five major wars in history and concluded:

> The decision to fight, unless the opponent abandons resistance without a struggle, is not reached on the spur of the moment . . . . The rational, calculating decision is reached far in advance of the actual outbreak of hostilities . . . . the decision to wage war precedes by one to five years outbreak of hostilities.[2]

But this conclusion does not suggest studying the decision so much as examining the features of the world that may lead to such a decision, and which may also lead to postponement of hostilities. This is not to say that examination of decisions is not worthwhile; rather, it is to raise doubts about whether we could develop a theory that would satisfactorily explain war's cause in terms of decisions apart from the surrounding political milieu.

Focus on decisionmaking has recently developed from the efforts of Richard C. Snyder, H. W. Bruck, and Burton Sapin, who developed what they called an "approach" to the study of international politics. Their scheme emphasizes as basic determinants of state action three categories of factors, which they term spheres of competence, communication and information, and motivation. But each of these incorporates aspects of the external world in the same general way that our preceding analysis has. The crucial point is to develop statements that link particular qualities of such factors to particular decisions. The "decisionmaking approach" has been tested comprehensively against the American

---

[2]Theodore Abel, "The Element of Decision in the Pattern of War," *American Sociological Review*, 6 (1941) 853–859 at 855.

decision to resist aggression in Korea, but it has not generated specific propositions about either international politics in general or war in particular that would lead us to term it a theory rather than a conceptual scheme. Nor does it claim to offer such.[3]

This is the only general effort toward developing a theory that settles on the conscious mind of the decisionmaker as the determinant of international politics. It does categorize relevant aspects of decision and the factors that should be examined in such an effort, but it does not answer our questions. However, there are many studies of decisionmaking in organizations, and even several case-oriented studies of decisionmaking in state departments and foreign offices, but the propositions these have generated have not yet been extended far enough to meet our general needs. Rather, we must look briefly to other possible determinants of decision to go to war.

The Unconscious

There have been many studies attempting to demonstrate that wars result from such individual qualities as "selfishness" and "aggressiveness" as they are manifest in the population of a state and thereby influence policymaking. Similarly, some studies have sought to show that the selfishness or the aggressiveness of a decisionmaker is conducive to war. The chief school here is the psychoanalytical. Their studies of a decisionmaker like Woodrow Wilson[4] have suggested that aspects of an individual's psychological makeup—itself largely a product of his upbringing as well as his fundamental human nature—have played important roles in determining international politics. Similarly, it is a widely accepted belief that Hitler was mentally deranged and that this condition contributed significantly to his decisions to launch war in Europe.

In 1939 two psychologists summarized work on the biological and psychological aspects of personal aggressiveness and war. This is probably still an accurate summary of the thought of this school:

[3]See R. C. Snyder, H. W. Bruck, and B. Sapin, *Foreign Policy Decision-Making* (New York: Free Press, 1962), for the basic essay and the application to Korea.
[4]See Sigmund Freud and William Bullitt, *Thomas Woodrow Wilson* (Boston: Houghton Mifflin, 1966) and Alexander George and Juliette George, *Woodrow Wilson and Colonel House* (New York: Day, 1956).

In the absence of government—the organization of force to preserve the peace . . . it may very well be that an appreciation of the advantages of cooperation and an agreement to continue it will preserve the peace for some time. But underneath there is a powerful and "natural" tendency to resort to force in order to secure the possession of desired objects, or to overcome a sense of frustration, or to resist the encroachment of strangers, or to attack a scapegoat. Fighting and peaceful cooperation are equally "natural" forms of behavior, equally fundamental tendencies in human relations. Peaceful cooperation predominates—there is much more peace than war—but the willingness to fight is so widely distributed in space and time that it must be regarded as a basic pattern of human behavior. The cause of the transition from one to the other is simply when some change in the circumstances of the group alters the balance between the desire for cooperation and the conflicting desire to obtain self-regarding ends by force.[5]

If this account is accurate, it places these psychological attributes of members of a society (any society) as a general underlying prerequisite for war—a prerequisite that is always present. But we must still inquire into "the cause of the transition" from peace to war.

Whatever their specific impact, unconscious drives, if they are factors in the outbreak of war, will matter because they affect the perception or the valuation of policymakers or the publics that influence policymaking. If we find ourselves puzzled by the apparent calculations of policymakers, we may be inclined to ask whether there are grounds for belief that these men are influenced subconsciously in their perception of the world (perhaps they believe paranoically, for example, that all individuals or groups seek nothing but their destruction, and hence misinterpret the actions of other individuals or states), or in their valuation of various policies (perhaps they believe that war brings out the heroid in men and hence pursue more militant courses). To answer such questions we must study the behavior of individuals in a number of cases or decisions.

We may also wish to examine the possible impact of group psychosis or other collective unconscious effects on policymaking, in the suspicion that characteristics of the population that

[5]E. F. M. Durbin and John Bowlby, *Personal Aggressiveness and War* (New York: Columbia University Press, 1939), chap. 1, p. 25.

reside in the subconscious of each individual play important roles in determining public attitudes on issues of war and peace. The extent that public opinion affects policymaking is difficult to discover. We may come to conclude that, at least in an age of nuclear weapons and guerrilla wars, it does not markedly affect decisions to go to war, but it does affect decisions to make peace. Thus some have argued that democracies have a difficult time getting into and out of war because of the role of public opinion, which is slowly mobilized but even more slowly defused. These are, of course, possibilities that merit careful study.

The Governmental System: Bureaucracy

Another category from which to analyze war is the group: the state or various parts of it. The smallest of these is the governmental system, which includes the immediate decisionmakers (whom we discussed above) as well as the bureaucracy that is concerned with implementing decisions. Because it provides information and judgments to the decisionmakers, it is often important in influencing those decisions. This role of providing information was of great importance in the Bay of Pigs disaster. Intelligence officials assured President Kennedy that the invading forces were strong enough to prevail against the Castro forces — but they were defeated with ease by the Castro army. Similarly, we might suspect that intelligence sources informed North Korea that it would successfully defeat South Korea in 1950 without provoking intervention by the United States.

But the major importance of the bureaucracy is in taking measures once decision has been made, and in carrying on the functions of the government in the absence of new decisions. Thus the possibility that information will not be adequately conveyed — or will, in some sense, get lost in the bureaucracy — may help explain the continuation of war, as was the case with General Andrew Jackson in the War of 1812: unbeknownst to him, the war was over before he fought the Battle of New Orleans in 1814. Although we would not expect a bureaucracy to convey false orders for war (as in the movie *Dr. Strangelove*), we may find it useful to focus on the bureaucracy of government in explaining delay in carrying out the decisionmakers' orders.

The Governmental System: Legislature

Another part of the governmental system that may prove of some importance is the legislative branch or organ. There have been a number of studies of the role of the American Congress in foreign policy.[6] None of them suggests that Congress has been responsible for American decisions to go to war (although, according to the Constitution, Congress does declare war), nor has Congress been a major determinant of American decisions to make peace. Congress, however, does occasionally play important roles in foreign relations (particularly treaty-ratification, which must be performed by the Senate), and significant opposition in Congress may encourage or delay peacemaking. Legislative bodies in other states may have the same opportunities. Their roles will, of course, depend on the views of the incumbents and the structural and procedural roles these bodies play in the decision process. These in turn will depend at least in part on the political system within which the governmental system operates.

The Political System: Interest Groups

There have been very few arguments or theories suggesting that the advent of war and peace can be attributed directly to the governmental system. Rather, because that system is itself a part of the broader political system which includes interest groups and the population at large, arguments have tended to focus on the political system. These arguments may be placed in several categories. The first of these recognizes that decisions are determined in large part by what values the decisionmakers adopt. Consequently, politics may be viewed as an influence process. And political systems will differ in terms of how much access interests have to the political decisionmakers, and, further, by which interests are strong enough to take advantage of that access. The difference in access has generally been put in terms of the degree of democracy existing in states. The interests most

---

[6]See Bradford Westerfield, *Foreign Policy and Party Politics* (New Haven, Conn.: Yale University Press, 1956); James A. Robinson, *Congress and Foreign Policy Making*, rev. ed. (Homewood, Ill.: Dorsey, 1967); Holbert N. Carroll, *The House of Representatives and Foreign Affairs* (Pittsburgh: University of Pittsburgh Press, 1958); and other works.

suspect of using their access to promote war have been the military and the capitalist financiers and industrialists.

Following World War I there was considerable agreement on the contention that the big armaments dealers, particularly those who sold arms to both sides of a conflict, were the chief culprits in the outbreak of war. The famous Nye Committee reported to the American Senate in 1936, after investigating the activities of the munitions industry, that

> militarism meant the alliance of the military with powerful economic groups to secure appropriations on the one hand for a constantly increasing military and naval establishment, and, on the other hand, the constant threat of the use of that swollen military establishment in behalf of the economic interests at home and abroad of the industrialists supporting it. It meant the subjugation of the people of the various countries to the uniform, the self-interested identification of patriotism with commercialism, and the removal of the military from the control of civil law.

Thus, it concluded, World War I "was the logical outcome of militarism. . . . It seemed necessary to the prosperity of our people that their markets in Europe remain unimpaired."[7] Such arguments are still made, and perhaps with even greater force today. As he left office, President Eisenhower issued a warning against the increasing influence of the "military-industrial complex" over American governmental decisions.[8]

Such contentions have a long and colorful history. The arguments involved break down into several major types. One is that these economic interests, perhaps in league with the military, in one way or another influence nations to purchase arms, thereby stimulating arms races and increasing hostility and tension among nations, a process that eventuates in war once an appropriate occasion arrives. Furthermore, once war has broken out, the militarists are busy supplying arms to one or more parties and use

---

[7]*Munitions Industry, Report on Existing Legislation*, Senate Report No. 944, Part 5, 74th Congress, 2nd Session (Washington, D.C.: GPO, 1936), pp. 8–9. Quoted in Hans Morgenthau and Kenneth Thompson, eds., *Principles and Problems of International Politics* (New York: Knopf, 1950), pp. 62–63.

[8]For a useful analysis of the debate and examination of many of the relevant writings, see Marc Pilisuk and Thomas Hayden, "Is There a Military-Industrial Complex Which Prevents Peace?" in *Journal of Social Issues*, 21 (1965) 67–117.

their influence to expand the conflict wherever possible. A close relative of this argument is the contention that the military within a country needs or desires a war every so often to give its officers and recruits combat training and experience, and hence it may encourage a decision to go to war or attempt to prolong war until it has rotated enough troops in and out of the battle area.

The accuracy of such contentions has been the subject of much debate, but their attractiveness has lessened as the acceptability of war has lessened. We cannot here examine the evidence, but we can keep in mind the possibility that a permissive cause of war is possible pressure the financiers and industrialists, in collusion with the military, may make in order to maintain profits.

The Economic System and Its Politics

Somewhat further developed is the long-standing debate over the relation between imperialism and war. This is the argument that war in a sense is a consequence of economic development — a stage in the development of international relations which coincides with the existence of imperialism. The argument is generally associated with the socialists, who were most prominent around the turn of the century, and with Lenin, who wrote *Imperialism: The Highest Stage of Capitalism.*

The argument, briefly summarized, is that a capitalist economy will produce a surplus of both capital and goods, and that the businessmen will then desire markets for their surplus goods as well as places to invest their surplus capital. Thus they will turn to the government and encourage it to embark on imperialistic ventures that will provide such markets and opportunities. These imperialistic ventures will spark war both with the natives of the areas to be conquered and, even more importantly, with other imperialist nations also suffering from such surpluses.[9] These arguments have been concerned in a general way with the exercise of influence on a given administration in a given governmental system by interests outside that system. Much argu-

[9]For the classic statements of the argument, see J. A. Hobson, *Imperialism* (London: Allen & Unwin, 1902, rev. 1905); V. I. Lenin, *Imperialism: The Highest Stage of Capitalism* [many editions]; Harold J. Laski, "The Economic Foundations of Peace," pp. 499–547 in Leonard Woolf, ed., *The Intelligent Man's Way to Prevent War* (London: Gollancz, 1933).

ment has also centered on the effects of the nature of that system itself, particularly its dependence on popular support.

Thus, just as socialists have argued that a capitalist system produces war, democrats have argued that a dictatorial system produces war. Others have argued that a democratic system may be especially prone to war. These are arguments centering on political forms and the ideologies by which political systems are justified and supported. The argument about the causes of war is based on a belief that wars may be attributed to defects in the state rather than, as the psychologists argue, with defects in the individual. Thus some have argued that a democratic system will be more subject to the wills of its peoples. If those wills are peaceable, the system will be unlikely to go to war unless forced, whereas if those wills are warlike, the system will tend to go to war where the opportunity presents itself. Furthermore, the impact of internal propaganda designed to rally public support once the state is in a war will tend to prolong the war, according to this view, for such public enthusiasm is not easily turned off — particularly if the war is a modern, limited war in which the public does not experience something approximating total victory. In a sense, this is an argument not about political system but about public opinion. But when we face the question of what determines public opinion, we are increasingly impressed by the role of the state and its domination of much of mass communication and information.

It cannot be denied that certain businessmen made fortunes while Britain, France, and other imperial nations developed their empires, any more than it can be denied that many owners of stock in large industry in America today become increasingly wealthy as this industry produces weaponry and performs services for the government in certain areas when the country is at war. But this is not the point. The question is whether these industries or individuals influence national policy in ways that cause or contribute to war. Again, the debate has been lengthy and heated, with many scholars contesting the claims of the socialists and others. The conclusion to which one is impelled is that this possible influence could be important enough to deserve careful consideration in any study of specific wars, but that general theories of war cannot be based solely on imperialism since its nature has changed radically. Also, the influence of imperialist industrialists has changed, and there are many wars that clearly have nothing to do with imperialism.[10]

The argument which focuses on the nature of the political system was most popularly made, however, not about democratic systems but about totalitarian ones. The states that were believed to make wars were those not influenced by the people who would have to fight the wars. Authoritarian states ruled strictly by a small group of willful men with personal ambitions to rule greater empires were widely believed to be responsible for both world wars: the Kaiser's Germany for the first, and Hitler's Germany, Mussolini's Italy, and the Emperor's Japan for the second. Other political systems too, such as the ideologically fervent or the politically mobilized developing state now prominent in the "third world" merit attention as possible sources of pressures for war.

The plain fact seems to be that wars continue to occur periodically no matter what sort of political system exists. Nevertheless, we cannot simply dismiss the possibility that the nature of war and its termination, and perhaps even its outbreak, are affected to some extent by the nature of the political systems involved.

The Nature of the State: National Character

We have still another category of explanations of wars: the nature of the state itself. The aspects usually singled out for attention here are the populace and its national character, the physical environment (particularly its geography), and the nature of the state as an actor in international politics.

Arguments about national character are similar to those of a psychological nature that we examined above, except that they are used to refer to a particular people as in some way different from others. There is considerable controversy among scholars

[10]See John Strachey, *The End of Empire* (New York: Random House, 1960), for a review of the arguments and a consideration of the changing nature of imperialism. For the classic critics of the socialist argument, see Eugene Staley, *War and the Private Investor* (New York: Doubleday, 1935); Jacob Viner, *International Economics* (New York: Free Press, 1951), the essay "International Relations between State-Controlled National Economics" (1944), pp. 216–231; Joseph Schumpeter, *Imperialism and Social Classes* (New York: Meridian, 1955); and William L. Langer, "A Critique of Imperialism," reprinted in H. Ausubel, ed., *The Making of Modern Europe* (New York: Holt, Rinehart and Winston, 1951,) pp. 918–932.

as to whether or not the concept of national character is or could be accurate in such an application, but it is quite clear that such a factor, should it be relevant, could only be a permissive or underlying cause of a nation's going to war. We would still need particular situations or factors in our explanation, for the national character is consistent through time in its nature if not in its attitudes.

The Nature of the State: Geography

Many and various factors are suggested as possible determinants of national character. Some, such as the child-rearing practices of the culture, are well beyond the range of our consideration. But one that is not is the physical environment — particularly the geographic position of the state. It is sometimes argued that the climate, the available resources, and other geographical aspects exert considerable influence upon national behavior. That this is often true would be difficult to contest, for some nations are forced by their position to become maritime trading nations, whereas others are forced by the terrain and the climate to import food. The need for raw materials, for food, or for more living space are some of the realities of life that may motivate a nation to go to war.

A school of international political theorists developed out of this highly geographical approach. Called geopolitics, this approach emphasizes the use of the physical environment by the state in its international political activity. It cannot be disputed that the physical environment will influence a state's technology, culture, economy, political system, and, of course, its domestic and foreign policies. But for geography to determine the occurrence of war we shall need other features, such as particular national objectives, that can utilize geographic conditions or that are themselves partially determined by geographic factors. Thus, as a theory designed to explain war, geographical determinism is not sufficient.[11]

One way of supplementing geographical analysis is by the addition of our third category: intrinsic or inherent qualities of

[11]See Harold Sprout, "Geopolitical Hypotheses in Technological Perspective," in World Politics, 15 (1963) 187–212 and "Geography of Conflict," a special issue of Journal of Conflict Resolution, 4 (1960), for analysis of geographical theories. And for a broader view, see Harold and Margaret Sprout, The Ecological Perspective on Human Affairs (Princeton, N.J.: Princeton University Press, 1965).

the state. If we can assume, as most geopolitical analysts would, that a state is a sovereign entity seeking always to maintain its power to remain sovereign, it is but a short step, through assumption that these interests shared by each state will overlap and conflict, to the conclusion that nations are likely to engage in forcible efforts directed toward other nations. Thus a combination of geography and personification of the state as sovereign actor may indeed provide an intriguing explanation of war's occurrence. Furthermore, it is quite clear that geography will be a major determinant of the development and hence of the outcome of war. However, the trouble with theories which assume that the state seeks power to maintain its sovereignty in the face of a similar quest by other states is that it is just too simple to describe what actually takes place in world politics. We shall pursue this point further in Chapter 13 when we discuss efforts to theorize about international politics.

The International System

When we talk of the interaction of states, whatever their motives and whatever their actions, we are already verging on a systems analysis which falls into our third category of explanations of war: the set of groups. In a general sense, we may apply the term "system" to any collection of items or actors having some interrelation. Thus we could say that a class of students and a professor constitute a system; or we could say that the states of the Middle East, or the members of the North Atlantic Treaty Organization, constitute a system. We also, at the other international extreme, talk about the international system, or perhaps even the global system, which encompasses all the national actors in the world. Viewing the international system as the largest, most comprehensive system we have, we can then view other multinational systems, such as the United Nations, NATO, the Warsaw Treaty Organization, the British Commonwealth, the Organization of American States, and even pairs of states like the superpowers, as various subsystems of that all-encompassing international or global system.

But our use of the concept of system in this way is designed merely to organize our data. When we attempt to use the concept of system to explain why things happen as they do, we must tighten our definition or our specifications considerably. Thus

we specify that a system must be characterized not only by interaction but also by qualities of the system itself, such as a tendency
toward self-preservation. The basic concept here is *homeostasis,*
the principle whereby a system tends toward the reestablishment of an equilibrium when that "steady state" has been upset
by some new input or other change in the relations among the
components of the system. It is by this notion that systemic explanation of war may be attempted. The concept usually employed
—the balance of power—has been wildly used and misused by
analysts. Its explanation of war generally runs like this: the system is in equilibrium until one nation unites with another to
increase its dominance over others, or until one nation develops
so much internally (probably through industrialization) that its
power is great enough to threaten the others; at this point, the
system (in the form of the other states) acts to weaken this up-
start by waging war against it; when it has succeeded, equilibrium
or a steady state is reestablished and the system continues on
until it is again challenged by another such change. Now, if we
wish to view international politics in this mechanistic way, and
do not care to know the answers to such questions as why a state
suddenly develops so much power, or why the other states then
decide to unite to attack it, such a systemic explanation can be
quite satisfying. Of course it is easy to see how systemic theory
could explain alliance in terms of this same principle. We shall
perhaps inevitably find ourselves using such explanations—
although we must be careful to be explicit in our usage to avoid
the ambiguities and weaknesses of much balance-of-power analysis. But we shall also probably want to go farther in our explanation, and in doing so we shall have to move below the system into
its components.

Some Tentative   These, then, are the basic varieties of
Conclusions   explanation of war. We shall encounter
some of them again in more compre-
hensive form in Chapter 13, when we examine major theories
of international politics in their entireties and as presented by
scholars. As they stand, they are all somewhat underdeveloped
in terms of our objective of a comprehensive explanation of the
occurrence, development, and termination of war.

Nevertheless, it is still clear that we have here a great collection of possible explanations, most of which are at least plausible and therefore worth continued study and application. Some explanations fall into the category of inescapable conditions for war or any other international political relations—the decisionmaking explanation is the best example of those in this category. Others tend to serve as general, ongoing, permissive causes still in need of particular happenings or situations to trigger the violent outbreak of a conflict which has been manifest for some time in tendencies toward war shown by various nations. And some serve best as more immediate causes. However, for two reasons, we have not examined immediate causes in any detail: the enormous diversity of such specific instances, events, or conditions; and the difficulty of settling upon which event actually instigated a war. Thus World War I might be thought to begin with the assassination at Sarajevo, with various mobilizations, or with various declarations of war; World War II began with an invasion but was caused at least in part by previous annexations —we could similarly go on through the multitides of wars that have followed.

However, our purpose has not been to study the outbreaks or terminations of particular wars any more than it has been to examine each possible general explanation of war in full detail. Rather, it has been to uncover and consider the wide variety of explanations for war offered by scholars. We have found that the apparent variety and contradiction of these explanations can be condensed significantly by placing each explanation along the time scale from basic condition through permissive cause to specific cause. But we have also found that significant divergence continues even after we have done this.

Coping with Divergent Explanations

What, then, do we do when we encounter two (or more) different and apparently competing explanations of a given class of events (such as the outbreak of war)? First, we ask whether they can be in some way reduced to the same explanation—as some psychological and national character explanations can, for example. Second, we may test them against the facts of the case—examine the actual features of a variety of wars to see whether one or the other is obviously preferable. Third, if we find that they both seem to explain some instances but not others, we may attempt to view them as substitutable causes — saying, for example, that although wars require states with conflicting purposes, some of these break out for economic reasons and others for ideological reasons. A fourth possibility, if we are still not satisfied, is to compare our knowledge of and belief about other aspects of international politics. Thus we might find that all other happenings have economic explanations, and we might therefore be more impressed by an economic explanation of war. A fifth possible approach is to ask what else might follow from each of the two competing explanations, were it accurate, and to check these deduced consequences against other relevant cases. These are all strategies of theory-building and confirmation that we may employ in attempting to put together what we have been able to learn about the various phenomena of international politics.

Continuing Our Study

War and crisis may be related in several ways, for war is one possible outcome of crisis, and the factors we found in our study of crisis to be important precedent conditions to it are also among those offered as explanation of war. Similarly, we can see the role that alliance is apt to play in war, increasing the strength of combatant sides and perhaps even increasing the likelihood of war should one alliance threaten the stability of the system or decreasing that likelihood should alliances serve to stabilize relations among conflicting sides. In addition, our fourth major phenomenon, cooperative restraint or conflict control among adversaries, arises throughout a war and particularly in a negotiated settlement of war, and will therefore itself be an important aspect of the study of war and so may share some of the same determinants. Our further study of cooperative control will suggest some answers to this possibility.

Thus far in our study we should have been impressed with the diversity of possible explanations of war and perhaps dismayed about the possibility of ever settling on some single cause or single collection of determinants with which to explain all instances of war even narrowly defined. In a sense, this is an important feeling, for there can by now be no doubt that international politics is extremely complex and still well beyond our abilities to be definitive in our explanations. Nonetheless, it would be as mistaken to believe that we have made no progress in our efforts to understand and explain war as it would be to abandon our attempts to refine and generalize our explanations. For we have made progress. And if we pause to assess that progress by examining one notable effort to generalize on the basis of historical research similar to that which produced the several explanations we have examined, we shall see both the degree of that progress and the nature of what we still must learn.

On the basis of a study of the phenomenon of war in its many instances, Nicholas Timasheff, a sociologist long interested in war and revolution, developed a generalization about the movement from peace to war that has proved applicable to many if not most wars in the history of nation-states:

> Two or more states antagonistic to each other are likely to move from the state of peace to that of war if the following conditions are simultaneously present:
> 1. The antagonism must have reached the level of danger as specified, and be further reinforced by aggravating circumstances.
> 2. None of the parties to the conflict, especially the one likely to play the aggressive role, is dominated by exceptionally strong normative inhibitions to war.
> 3. One of the parties must have lost hope of achieving its goal short of war, after having tried other procedures or rejected them as inadequate.
> 4. Subjectively, according to the conclusions of responsible leaders, there is a fair chance of victory for each of the parties, while the problem of coast has not been raised or has resulted in a (subjectively) favorable answer.[12]

This statement, one of a number that could be developed, is general enough to be applicable to many cases. But because it is so general and so brief, it lacks much of the specification that some of our examined general explanations have. The crucial aspects seem to be the third point, in which one party loses hope of other means of succeeding, and the first point, in which antagonism is further reinforced by aggravating circumstances. It is in these two points that we might be able to insert a variety of alternative possibilities, any one or some combination of which would qualify as part of this generalization and would therefore

[12]Nicholas S. Timasheff, *War and Revolution* (New York: Sheed & Ward, 1965), pp. 96–97.

bring about war when the other conditions exist. Developing such additional elaborations upon this general schema is a task for both scholars in research institutes and students in classrooms studying the data out of which these same scholars attempt to advance the discipline. The efforts we have made thus far should give us grounds for strong suspicions about the conditions or causes of war, and further examination of cases of war should enable each student to contribute his formulation, which will eventually constitute part of a more general theory of international politics.

chapter 11
Studying Alliance

Alliances: Their Nature and Purpose

From time to time, nations will cooperate or agree to cooperate under certain conditions. This cooperation may take various forms. Friends may agree to cooperate in organizations designed to promote economic trade or aid such as the European Economic Community (Common Market) or the Communist counterpart, the Council of Mutual Economic Assistance (often called Comecon), or to promote technological development, as in the European Atomic Energy Community.

Nations that would otherwise term themselves adversaries will also agree to cooperate in activities of the United Nations, such as the Food and Agricultural Organization, or even occasionally in peace-keeping operations under the auspices of the General Assembly. Not only will adversaries at times engage in peaceful cooperative economic relations, but they may, if they operate under the principle of "collective security" on which the United Nations was founded, occasionally unite to defeat an aggressor.

The most prominent instance of cooperation among nations is that usually designated "alliance," a term generally applied to an organization or a commitment of a number of states to take certain cooperative actions against another state or states under specified conditions. By alliances we have in mind such agreements as the North Atlantic Treaty, the Warsaw Treaty, and the Southeast Asian Treaty. There are, however, instances of cooperation among several states directed basically at other states but not so formalized. Perhaps the best example of this kind is the long-standing Anglo-American "special relationship" (as it is often called), which has been characterized by many and varied moments of cooperation throughout most of the twentieth century. Usage varies, but cooperation not formalized by a specific treaty is often referred to as "alignment." Thus a developing nation that obtains most of its economic aid and political leadership or direction from a major power is said to be aligned with it rather than allied with it. On the other hand, a nation that openly refuses to tie itself to either side of such struggles as the Cold War or regional confrontations is generally termed "unaligned" or "nonaligned." Because strong alignments like the Anglo-American function like their more formal counterparts, we will find it desirable to consider both in our study of alliance.

But we wish to distinguish alliance from economic or other sorts of "nonsecurity" cooperation, as well as from collective security and from nonalignment; hence we shall use the term "alliance" to refer to a conditional commitment of a political or military sort exchanged by several states and directed at some specified (although not necessarily named) state. Such alliances usually establish organizations to oversee the keeping of the commitment and are generally formalized by the signing of a written agreement or treaty. It is primarily with alliances of this sort that we shall be concerned in this chapter.[1]

A Descriptive Model of Alliance

As always, we shall view alliance as the outcome of conscious policymaking. Therefore, the preceding conditions, the perception of the conditions, the believed interests

[1] For a more extensive discussion and a survey of the literature, see Edwin H. Fedder, "The Concept of Alliance" in *International Studies Quarterly*, 12 (1968) 65-86.

of each party to the alliance, the policy and action these factors determine, and the negotiation that results from such actions in the formation of an alliance will be of interest to us. Our question first will be, When and why do nations align?

Since negotiations terminate in the formalization of the alliance, we shall be interested in both the nature of the agreement — whether it is secret or open, written or verbal — and in the terms or provisions of the agreement. There are many distinctions to be made among categories and types of terms but a comprehensive collection has been offered by Hans Morgenthau:

> These interests, as well as the alliances expressing them and the policies serving them, can be distinguished in five different ways: according to their intrinsic nature and relationship, the distribution of benefits and power, their coverage in relation to the total interests of the nations concerned, their coverage in terms of time, and their effectiveness in terms of common policies and actions. In consequence, we can distinguish alliances serving identical, complementary, and ideological interests and policies. We can further distinguish mutual and one-sided, general and limited, temporary and permanent, operative and inoperative alliances.[2]

Our basic question here is, What determines the nature and form of alliance? We would expect one answer to be the specific features of the world situation and the interests of the parties to the alliance, but it is also possible that the way in which the treaty was formalized (negotiated or otherwise institutionalized) would have a significant effect on its nature and terms.

We would then be interested in the interaction that results from the alliance. We would want to examine both the regular interaction (which is similar to what happens among all nations whether or not they are allied) and the interaction that is a consequence of the alliance. In this category we would study both the routine interaction (such as periodic meetings of the appropriate military figures and of the political officials of the countries) and the responsive interaction that results from a crisis in which the alliance is a relevant factor (say, an attack of the sort foreseen by the alliance or the strong possibility of such an attack, which might lead to consultations or even to mobilization on the part of the allies). In examining these various types of

---

[2]"Alliances in Theory and Practice," in Arnold Wolfers, ed., *Alliance Policy in the Cold War* (Baltimore: Johns Hopkins Press, 1959), pp. 184–212, at p. 188.

interaction among allied parties we would be seeking to discover the morphology of these relations, that is, we would want to know whether or not there are recognizable patterns to such interaction, and, if so, whether or not we can explain them.

Our next concern will be the stages an alliance undergoes from inception through termination—its "life cycle." Here we might expect to find a period of expansion of the alliance following its establishment as it seeks to increase its strength and significance and as it attracts other parties because of its promise of increased security or territorial gains. Not all alliances will expand through acquisition of new members, but those that remain the same in number will probably expand by means of increases in the military forces of the parties, or at least improve their capabilities through more efficient cooperation. We would not be surprised to find that alliances will also tend to deteriorate before they formally terminate. Many observers have seen evidence of deterioration in both NATO and the Warsaw Treaty Organization in recent years, including virtual loss of members and lessening of committed military capabilities. We would want to consider both expansion and deterioration as major possible stages in the life cycle of an alliance.

We shall also be interested in examining the termination of alliances. Alliances may end in various ways, formally and informally. Chief among them are expiration, if a termination date was specified in the treaty, cancellation by one party or both, military destruction through defeat of one or more parties in a war, or unilateral abrogation or default by one party's refusing or failing to keep its commitment. The problem will be, What determines when and how alliances end? We may find termination to be a result of changes in the domestic policy of one or both parties, or a product of changes in international relations, or perhaps even a consequence of the previous life of the agreement. Because it is likely that termination will result from some combination of these or other factors, we would like to be able to be specific about which factors are crucial, and how they are.

Finally, we will be interested in the various stages of the alliances and in their effects on international politics and national policy—particularly whether or not alliances fulfill their purposes or achieve their objectives. This category of question will be of particular interest as we attempt to assess policy alternatives in an effort to influence the development of international politics.

Figure 11-1.

DESCRIPTIVE MODEL FOR THE STUDY OF ALLIANCE

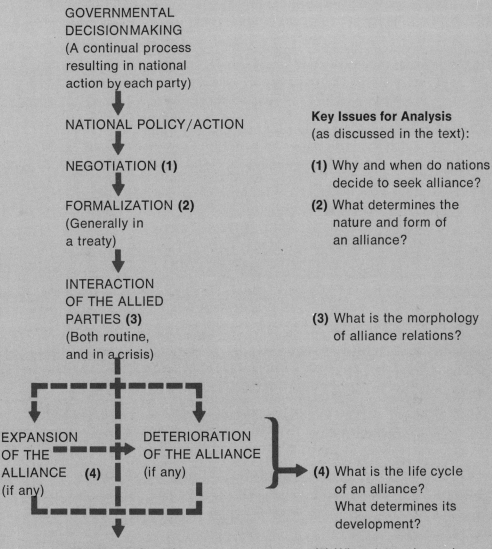

GOVERNMENTAL
DECISIONMAKING
(A continual process
resulting in national
action by each party)

NATIONAL POLICY/ACTION

Key Issues for Analysis
(as discussed in the text):

NEGOTIATION (1)

(1) Why and when do nations
decide to seek alliance?

FORMALIZATION (2)
(Generally in
a treaty)

(2) What determines the
nature and form of
an alliance?

INTERACTION
OF THE ALLIED
PARTIES (3)
(Both routine,
and in a crisis)

(3) What is the morphology
of alliance relations?

EXPANSION
OF THE
ALLIANCE   (4)
(if any)

DETERIORATION
OF THE ALLIANCE
(if any)

(4) What is the life cycle
of an alliance?
What determines its
development?

TERMINATION (5)
  1. Expiration
  2. Cancellation
  3. Military Destruction
  4. Unilateral Abrogation
  5. Default
  6. (other forms)

(5) What determines when
and how alliances
will end?

Our Approach   Once again, we have a multitude of interesting and significant questions about a major type of international political happening, as can be seen in the schematic, descriptive model of alliance in Figure 11–1. Since we cannot expect to deal adequately with all of them, we must find a way of coping with the plethora of issues in and instances of alliances to increase our ability to study and understand them as they have occurred in postwar international politics.

It often happens in our studies that we encounter a specific explanation of a particular happening and wish to judge its accuracy not just by examining its factual basis but also by testing the general principles it implies or assumes against other instances of the same general type. In this chapter we shall attempt to do just this in a brief but indicative way.

The Establishment of Alliances   We shall examine what scholars generally agree upon as the explanation for the establishment of the Warsaw Treaty Organization (the Warsaw Pact). Then, in order to test this against other instances, such as the creation of NATO, SEATO, the Sino-Soviet alliance, and the Anglo-American "special relationship," we shall attempt to derive from the specific explanation a general explanation of the creation of alliance and then see whether these other cases conform to it. If we find that the derived general explanation must be modified to apply to the other cases, we shall make the modifications that seem desirable and then reexamine the first case to see whether there remains something wrong with our general explanation. Then we shall briefly compare our conclusions with those of other scholars. Before we can be satisfied with our understanding of alliance we shall also consider several consequent topics of concern: the place of alliance in international politics and the work that remains to be done.

The Warsaw Treaty Organization

The "Treaty of Friendship, Cooperation and Mutual Assistance" signed in Warsaw by the Soviet Union and her seven East European allies (Albania, Bulgaria, Hungary, East Germany, Rumania, Poland, and Czechoslovakia) on May 14, 1955, followed

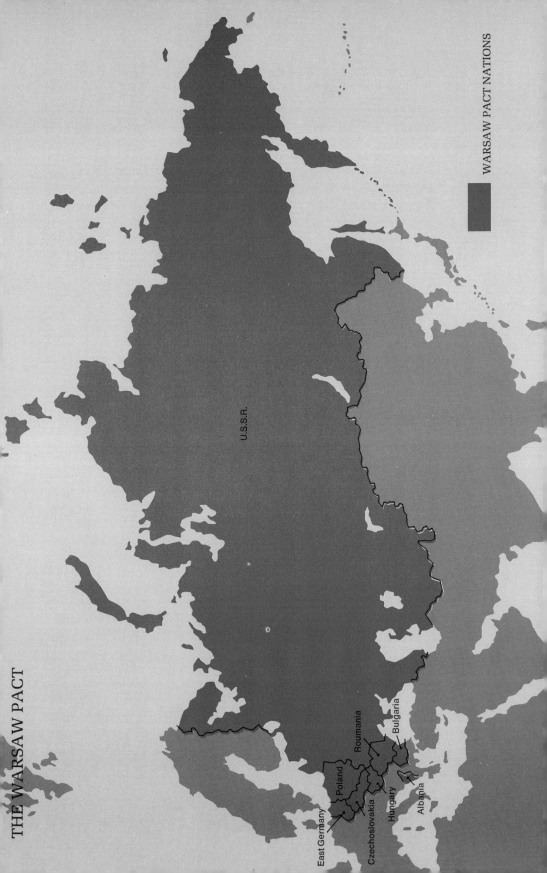

THE WARSAW PACT

U.S.S.R.

East Germany
Poland
Czechoslovakia
Hungary
Roumania
Bulgaria
Albania

WARSAW PACT NATIONS

by just nine days the ratification of the Western European Union that made West Germany a sovereign state and admitted her to NATO.

The North Atlantic Treaty had been signed six years earlier by the United States, Canada, Britain, France, Italy, Belgium, the Netherlands, Luxembourg, Denmark, Norway, Iceland, and Portugal, with Greece and Turkey joining in 1952. It provided that

> an armed attack against one or more of them in Europe or North America shall be considered an attack against them all, and consequently . . . each of them . . . will assist the Party or Parties so attacked by taking forthwith individually and in concert with the other Parties, such action as it deems necessary, including the use of armed force (Article 5).

It was to be in effect for at least twenty years. The Warsaw Treaty, also to be valid for twenty years, stated that

> in the event of armed attack in Europe on one or more of the Parties to the Treaty by any state or group of states, each of the Parties to the Treaty . . . shall immediately, either individually or in agreement with other Parties to the Treaty, come to the assistance of the state or states attacked with all such means as it deems necessary, including armed force (Article 4).

Thus the Warsaw Pact, at least in its formal statement, bore considerable resemblance to the North Atlantic Treaty. It could not have been a direct answer to NATO, for NATO had been created six years earlier, but it could have been a direct answer to the new NATO, which included West Germany. Indeed, after the Western powers had met in London, from September 28 to October 3, 1954, and then in Paris from October 19 to 23 and agreed to restore full sovereignty to West Germany and admit her to NATO (while Germany renounced the right to build atomic, chemical, or biological weapons and missiles and long-range bombers), the Soviets called a conference of European states and the United States for Moscow from November 29 to December 2, 1954. The announced purpose of this conference was to settle the German question and avoid splitting Europe into separate defense arrangements. But neither the United States nor any Western European states participated, and so the conference issued a warning that if the Western powers ratified the "Paris agreements" the Eastern European states would be forced to undertake their own collective defense arrangements to counterbalance the threat of revived German militarism. Thus the Warsaw Pact seems to have been a direct response to the resurgence of a militarily powerful and politically sovereign West Germany.

But was it militarily significant? The Soviet Union already had bilateral treaties with each of the nations involved, created in the years between 1943 and 1948. The Warsaw Treaty was distinguished from these bilateral treaties by the joint communiqué that accompanied the treaty and announced the establishment of a unified command for the military forces of the signatories. This joint command made possible immediate and coordinated implementation of the treaty's assistance provisions. By putting a Russian in over-all command of it, the Soviet Ministry of Defense had, in effect, control over the Eastern European armies — a position that could prove useful in the event of conflict should the armies of the East European states prove to be reliable.[3]

But the treaty was also an important consequence of other developments. The signing of it preceded by one day the signing of the Austrian State Treaty which legally ended the occupation of Austria by the Soviet Union as well as the Western powers. Soviet occupation of Austria had been the legal basis for the garrisoning of Soviet troops in Hungary and Rumania, and when the Austrian occupation ended there was no longer a justification for such troops. Similarly, the Warsaw Treaty legally integrated the German Democratic Republic (East Germany) into the socialist commonwealth and thereby called for a new justification for the continued presence of Soviet troops in East Germany. The Warsaw Treaty met both of these new conditions by establishing legal grounds for Soviet forces in all East European states.

But was this important to the Soviets? When Stalin had controlled the Soviet Union and its Eastern European allies, he had used informal political ties. After his death in March of 1953, his successors seem to have concluded that the increasing diversity in the bloc required that ties among the states be formalized. But because the "satellite" states could not be abolished and their territory simply absorbed into the Soviet Union, such formal arrangements as the Warsaw Pact seemed to offer the best

[3]For a detailed examination of the treaty's provisions as well as a consideration of the reasons for its creation, see Kazimierz Grzybowski, *The Socialist Commonwealth of Nations* (New Haven, Conn.: Yale University Press, 1964), chap. 5.

instrument for continued control over them. The pact was the single most important formal commitment binding these countries to the Soviet Union and limiting their freedom of action by prohibiting their joining other alliance systems as well as legalizing the continued presence of Soviet troops. In a sense, then, as more content accrued to the formal independence of the nations that had been simply satellites under Stalin, this increased independence was counterbalanced by provisions for joint consultation on all major issues and Soviet command of all troops.

These reasons for the treaty might give one the impression that it was wholly a product of Soviet minds and wholly in the interest of Soviet policy. But it must be remembered that most of the Eastern European members had fought several major wars against Germany in the previous forty years and hence were deeply fearful of Germany, especially after the Western decision to grant sovereignty and significant rearmament to West Germany. Thus all parties had a common interest in some form of military security arrangement.[4]

Deriving an Explanatory Proposition

These, then, are the conditions and factors that seem to explain the creation of the Warsaw Treaty Organization. If they actually do explain that happening, we ought to be able to generalize them and develop a proposition or collection of propositions explaining the creation of other alliances, one instance of which would be this creation of the Warsaw Pact. As we have seen in our study of crisis and war, just which factors we will select to incorporate into our general proposition will depend considerably upon our preconceptions about what factors tend to matter in international politics and upon our knowledge of the particular instance from which we are generalizing. But we must start somewhere, and have decided to start with the Warsaw Pact. Keeping this bias in mind, what then can we incorporate into a general proposition about the creation of alliance?

We have concluded, first, that the Warsaw Pact was a direct response to a similar action by the major adversary—in this case,

[4]See Zbigniew K. Brzezinski, *The Soviet Bloc* (New York: Praeger, 1961), chap. 8 and app. 1.

remilitarization of West Germany and inclusion of her in an existing alliance. Thus we might generalize that we would expect to find such a change in the military status quo precedent to the creation of an alliance by states fearful of such a change. This threat was all the greater in this case because of the concomitant creation of an independent Austria, which deprived the Soviets of their legal right to station troops in several states close to a newly threatening West German border and raised the prospect that other states might attempt to follow Austria's prescribed neutralist course, further weakening the Soviet military posture on Western borders. Thus the Warsaw Pact could be viewed as an effort to replace an undermined military position with a satisfactory alternative. We might expect such an innovation in circumstances where a change in the political and legal situation destroys the rationale for continued military presence.

But we have also examined conditions within the bloc and found that the continuation of Soviet control or influence, weakened since the death of Stalin and threatened further by the imminent termination of the authority to station troops in the bloc countries, depended on some new arrangement. Thus we might expect the creation of an alliance where the previous bases of political influence within the allies were weakening because of political changes, but where the increasingly independent states were not strong enough to resist the external adversary without assistance or to resist the decrease in political independence that would follow accession to the alliance.

Combining these factors into a general proposition, we might arrive at a formulation such as: "States will form an alliance when they confront a new and threatening change in the military situation." We know, however, that alliances do not occur every time such a situation exists. Thus we are inclined to add to the proposition something like this: "and the dominant power seeks ways to maintain its position of strength in confronting the adversary." We may, however, suspect that even this is not enough, and thus we may wish to include the intrabloc considerations we have raised: "and the basis of influence upon allies has weakened but could be strengthened by the provisions of the alliance." Integrating the three factors together, we might arrive at this: "States will form an alliance when they confront a new and threatening change in the military situation and the dominant power among them seeks new ways to maintain its position of strength in confronting the adversary and its position of influence over its allies in the face of tendencies toward the decline of each."

Testing At this point we have no way of know-
the General ing whether this proposition will prove
Explanation at all accurate in describing the con-
ditions under which major alliances have occurred in the postwar years — let alone whether it is true that an alliance will always be formed when such conditions occur. But the way of deciding whether or not the proposition is even useful, and whether our explanation of the occurrence of the Warsaw Pact makes some sense in terms of the nature of international politics, is to test it against other instances of post-war alliance.

North Atlantic Treaty Organization

The most obvious case with which to test this hypothesis is the North Atlantic Treaty, which the Warsaw Treaty so resembles, and which, too, was created by a bloc of nations in the same general area. Is the explanatory proposition developed from the case of the Warsaw Pact accurate when applied to NATO?

The first of our key factors — a new and threatening change in the military situation — does seem to apply to the creation of NATO. The treaty was signed during the Berlin Blockade, which had made painfully clear to the Allies their exposed and weak position in Central Europe and the increasing provocativeness if not aggressiveness of the Soviet Union. All the nations of Western Europe, as well as the United States, could and did feel a novel and more dangerous threat in the international politics of the time.

The second key element — the dominant power seeking new ways to maintain its position of strength in confronting the adversary — also seems applicable to the creation of NATO. After the Second World War the Western powers demobilized their forces, and as Eastern Europe fell under Communist sway their was little the West could do about it. Once it became clear that the West would have to reckon militarily with the East, it became important for the United States, predominant in wealth and in nuclear power, to be able to exercise its power on and near the

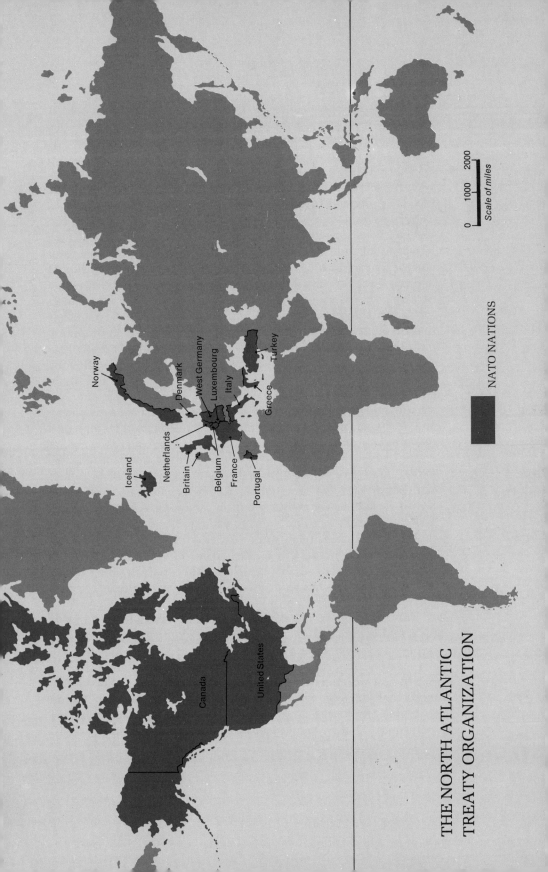

THE NORTH ATLANTIC
TREATY ORGANIZATION

NATO NATIONS

0   1000   2000
Scale of miles

Canada

United States

Iceland

Norway

Netherlands

Denmark

Britain

West Germany

Luxembourg

Belgium

Italy

France

Greece

Portugal

Turkey

borders of the Soviet domain. The best way of doing so was by stationing troops, not merely in Germany but also in other allied countries, and not as occupation forces but as allied protectors. An alliance like NATO offered such an opportunity.

Our third key factor—the dominant power seeking new ways to maintain its position of influence over its allies in the face of tendencies toward its decline—is more difficult to assess. The underlying fear of war in Central Europe was significant in almost all nations at the time NATO was conceived. There was, however, dispute over whether Stalin was aiming to absorb or conquer all of Europe or only the buffer states between Russia and the West. It seemed likely that the Soviets would be attracted by any political vacuum they found on the borders of their bloc, moreover, the armed forces of the West were at such low levels that many feared they would be unable to prevent a continuation of Soviet expansion. Like the Soviet Union among Warsaw Pact nations, the United States had a very dominant position among NATO nations largely because of her great industrial and financial strength which made possible the Marshall Plan and the atomic bomb. Many hoped that this would make possible an end to major war. The key question here is one of intent: Did the United States seek greater political influence over the member nations through the treaty? There can be little question that the United States for some years had considerable influence—in part also because of the Marshall Plan. There had been much anxiety in the United States over the strong showing of native Communist parties in France and Italy after the war, and over the wave of political strikes in those countries after 1948. However, by the time the treaty was signed, the danger of internal subversion seemed slight. Indeed, in explaining the treaty to the people, American officials tended to describe it as a natural consequence of fundamental affinity of mind and interest.

Thus, in order to make our proposed formulation applicable to NATO, we may be inclined to alter it slightly to eliminate the implication of conscious desire and replace it with a statement of the existing opportunity for the dominant power to maintain its position of influence over its allies. This factor may not be much more than an expression or consequence of the basic situation in which the parties to an alliance fear a recent change in the status quo. That is, there must be significant weakness in at least some of the participant nations, coupled with the possibility of overcoming that weakness by joining with one or more nations that can contribute greater strength. These two conditions in themselves make increased influence for the powerful most likely.

It would be possible to explain this difference by classifying the Warsaw Pact as something less than an alliance. Hans Morgenthau has written that "the alliances between the Soviet Union and the nations of Eastern Europe, codified in the Warsaw Pact of 1955, are in a class by themselves. They are not true alliances in that they do not transform a pre-existing community of interests into legal obligations. It is their distinctive quality that a community of interests is irrevelant for their existence and operation and that they are founded on nothing but unchallengeable superiority of power."[5] There is an important truth in this contention, owing to the predominance of the Soviet Union and its continuing influence over the internal regimes in the other member states. However, it underestimates the importance in the minds of East European states of the threatened remilitarization of West Germany—a consideration which Morgenthau recognizes only as a factor that might at some future point create common interests, but something that then seemed and still seems significant enough to have motivated alliance even among nations more independent than the states of Eastern Europe. Thus this consideration can be viewed as a basic common interest uniting the member states; hence we retain the condition that there be an opportunity for the dominant power to maintain a position of influence over its allies.

Southeast Asia Treaty Organization

We next turn to another alliance: the Southeast Asia Treaty Organization. Signed in Manila on September 8, 1954 by the United States, Britain, France, Pakistan, Thailand, the Philippines, Australia, and New Zealand (India, Burma, Indonesia, and Ceylon declined to join), the treaty states: "Each Party recognizes that aggression by means of armed attack in the treaty area against any of the Parties or against any State or territory which the Parties by unanimous agreement may hereafter designate, would en-

[5]Hans J. Morgenthau, "Alliances in Theory and Practice," in Arnold Wolfers, ed., *Alliance Policy in the Cold War* (Baltimore: John Hopkins Press, 1959), pp. 184–212 at p. 206. But see also the broader general view of George Liska, *Nations in Alliance* (Baltimore: Johns Hopkins Press, 1962), p. 3, who contends that "alliances merely formalize alignments based on interests or coercion . . . ."

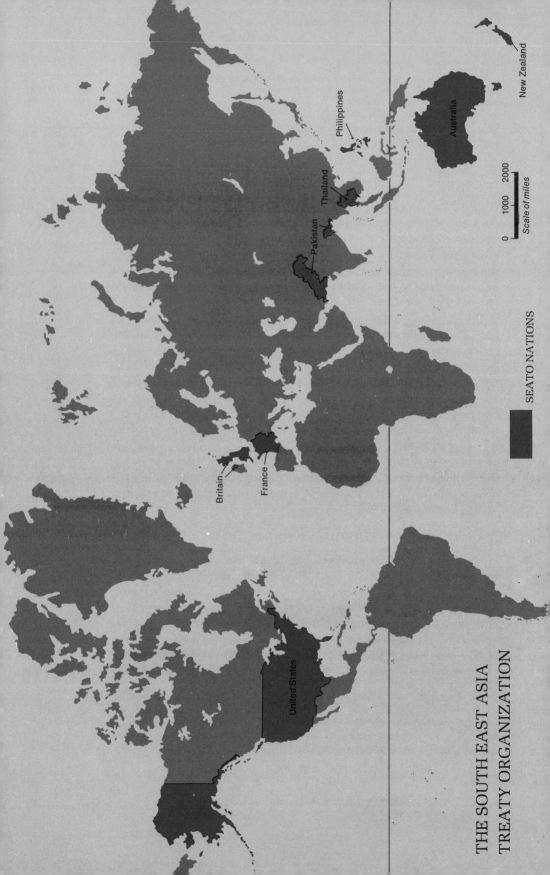

THE SOUTH EAST ASIA
TREATY ORGANIZATION

SEATO NATIONS

United States

Britain
France

Pakistan
Thailand

Philippines

Australia

New Zealand

0   1000   2000

Scale of miles

danger its own peace and safety, and agrees that it will in that event act to meet the common danger in accordance with its constitutional processes." Thus the treaty is simply consultative rather than binding in the way that NATO is. It is also different from NATO and the Warsaw Pact in that its membership spans most of the globe, from the United States through Britain to Pakistan and on to the Philippines. Indeed, only the Philippines and Thailand among the members are Southeast Asian states.[6]

Do our conditions apply to the establishment of SEATO? Our first—that the nations confront a new and threatening change in the military situation—does indeed apply. On February 18, 1954, as French positions in Indo-China deteriorated, the Western powers agreed at Berlin to call an international conference, with Communist China included, to meet at Geneva on April 26 to negotiate an armistice in Indo-China and a political settlement in Korea. The forces of the United Nations had managed to hold the line in Korea following some years of fighting, but the French forces in Indo-China were on the brink of defeat. Their stronghold in North Vietnam at Dien Bien Phu fell under siege, and when the SEATO allies could not agree to enter the war directly and by implication thus agreed to accept a defeat in the area, the search for a way of stabilizing a deteriorating position in Southeast Asia led to concentration on measures of "collective defense." The Geneva settlement which ensued on July 21 of that year partitioned Vietnam into North and South, but no agreement was reached on Korea. Secretary of State Dulles then called on "the free peoples of Southeast Asia" to join in collective arrangements for their security. The result was SEATO some six weeks later. It went into effect the following February 19, supplementing previous American treaties with the Philippines, Australia, New Zealand, Japan, South Korea, and Nationalist China. Since then SEATO's activities have consisted largely of cooperative planning and periodic consultation. It is clear that SEATO's creation came at a time of a perceived new and threatening change in the military situation: the collapse of the French position in Indo-China, which many feared would result in the fall of all of Southeast Asia to Communist forces.

Our second condition—that the dominant power in the alliance be seeking new ways to improve its position of strength in

[6]See George Modelski, ed., *SEATO: Six Studies* (Melbourne: Australian National University, 1962), for information on political and economic aspects of SEATO.

confronting the adversary—applies to a lesser degree. First of all, the American commitment was not one of troops but rather one of expressed concern. Second, it was not wholly clear just who the adversary was. Many viewed the Soviet Union as still the chief adversary, but Communist China was increasingly feared as a young and militant potential aggressor in Asia. None of the signatories had any common frontier with either nation. Furthermore, since troop commitments or other military development was not contemplated, the only improvement in the anti-Communist posture of the signatories was that of declared solidarity, but that solidarity was itself weakened by the strictly consultative nature of the treaty. Nonetheless, although the effectiveness of the treaty may be questioned—and it has been by scholars and statesmen alike—as the dominant power, the intention of the United States to improve its posture of opposition to China and the Soviet Union in the area cannot be questioned, and consequently our second condition applies to the situation.

Our third condition—that the dominant power seeks new ways to maintain its position of influence over its allies in the face of tendencies toward its decline—seems more relevant here than it did for NATO. The three Asian members are small states that stood to gain some security against Chinese and Soviet pressure while incurring increased internal and external hostility from parties and nations opposed to greater American, British, and French influence in that area. The general instability of political regimes in the area may well have encouraged American intervention through SEATO. Indeed, SEATO has occasionally proved a useful cover or justification for increased American military presence in the area—particularly in Thailand—as well as for increased American military and economic assistance to members and other states in the area. There can be little doubt that the United States sought increased influence over these states, even if it may have been sought just to increase the domestic opposition to pressures from the major Communist powers.[7]

---

[7]This point has been made by many students of American commitments. For example: "For the United States, alliances in the contemporary world are ways of organizing states under American leadership to defend a particular area against communist pressure. Their negative and restraining function, however, does not exhaust their usefulness. . . . Probably an alliance is most useful because it rationalizes and justifies the extension of American power and presence through commitments to a threatened area. . . ."—Charles O. Lerche, Jr., *Last Chance in Europe* (Chicago: Quadrangle, 1967), p. 78.

Thus far the alliances we have examined have been multi-lateral. There are several bilateral alliances worthy of examination both because they are or have been important factors in international politics and because we are interested more generally in the applicability of our proposition to bilateral as well as multilateral alliances. Two of these that we shall examine are the Sino-Soviet and the Anglo-American.

The Sino-Soviet Alliance

Just before the Communist victory in China in 1949, Mao Tse-tung, in proclaiming his celebrated "lean to one side" doctrine, said: "Internationally, we belong to the anti-imperalist front, headed by the U.S.S.R., and we can only look for genuine and friendly aid from that front and not from the imperalist front."[8] On February 14, 1950, the two nations signed a treaty of Friendship, Alliance, and Mutual Aid, pledging the Soviet Union to protect China from attack by Japan or any ally of Japan (which means the United States). The obligation is stated with unusual strength: in the event one is attacked, the other "will immediately render military and other assistance with all the means at its disposal." The Soviets also agreed to provide economic assistance, military advisers, and equipment.[9]

At the time the alliance was established, the Chinese had just triumphed after a civil war that had lasted off and on for decades, during which time the Soviets had in general supported the Chinese government rather than the Communist insurgents. Indigenous Communist insurrections in Burma, Malaya, the Philippines, and Vietnam suggested that these countries might be next in line. Historically, the Soviet Union and its Russian predecessor has tended to shift its attention to Asia when it has suffered a reversal in Europe, and vice versa. Thus the Soviet failures in Greece and Turkey, followed by the failure of the Berlin Blockade, seem to have coupled with the uprisings in Asia and the success of the Communists in China to draw Soviet attention back to Asia. In a sense, then, these conditions confirm the first two

[8]A. Doak Barnett, *Communist China and Asia* (New York: Harper & Row, 1960), p. 343.
[9]See Thomas W. Robinson, "A National Interest Analysis of Sino-Soviet Relations" in *International Studies Quarterly*, 11 (1967) 135–175. The text of the treaty is on p. 175. See also Raymond L. Garthoff, ed., *Sino-Soviet Military Relations*, (New York: Praeger, 1966) especially chaps. 5 and 6.

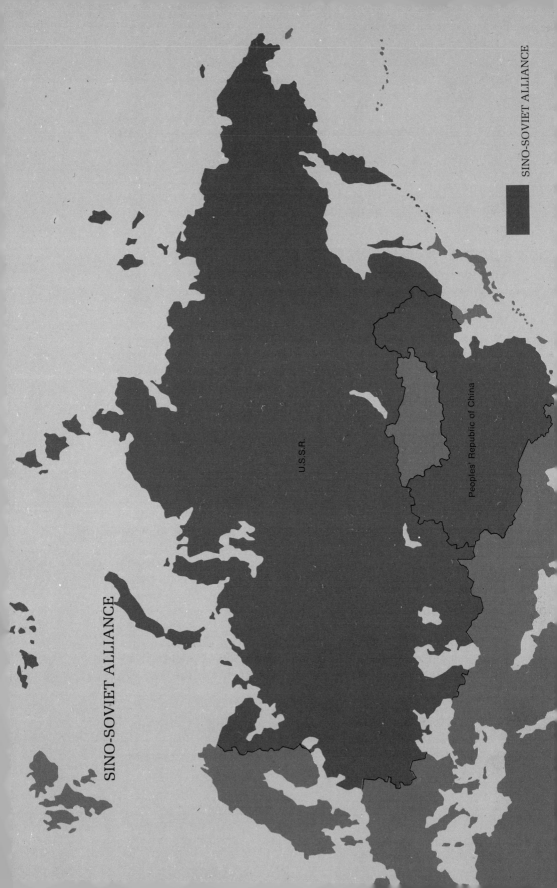

SINO-SOVIET ALLIANCE

U.S.S.R.

Peoples' Republic of China

SINO-SOVIET ALLIANCE

of our basic conditions. The new and threatening change in the military status quo was the failure in Berlin and the creation of NATO, which threatened to terminate the initiative the Soviets had possessed. The best way to confront NATO was in the Pacific, where the Western powers were involved, by weakening their hold on previous colonial dependencies and client states. Consequently, reinvolvement in Asia was expressed in the alliance and executed in the Korean conflict, which broke out four months later with Soviet and Chinese encouragement and assistance. Such reinvolvement served the dominant power as a new way of maintaining its position of strength in confronting its American adversary.

Furthermore, the alliance allowed the Soviets to regain significant influence in China of a sort which had previously been maintained through meddling in Manchuria and Mongolia. What appeared to be a Soviet offering of aid actually made the Chinese dependent upon the Soviets for economic and military assistance in a way that served to inhibit the growth of Chinese power and to circumscribe China's actions both in Asia and within the Soviet bloc. In view of the traditional hostility of China and Russia, manifest again much more clearly in subsequent years, it seems quite likely that such a reassertion of influence over China was a major interest of the Soviets in creating the alliance.[10]

The Anglo-American Alignment

The case of the Anglo-American alignment is somewhat less clear. The "special relationship" between the two nations, which extends back into the late nineteenth century, has had its ups and downs. Following World War II, the American restrictions on sharing information and assistance in the development of atomic energy strained the relationship, for the British expected such assistance in accordance with previous agreements. Cooperative arrangements were established, however, stimulated first by the Soviet explosion of a nuclear device in August 1949 and then by the outbreak of the Korean conflict so close upon the

[10]George Liska concludes, interestingly, that "in the Sino-Soviet bloc, to the extent that alliances have any autonomous effect, the Warsaw Pact has probably had on the whole a restraining impact on the Soviet Union, if only because of the domestic preoccupations of most of the member regimes; the dampening impact of the Sino-Soviet alliance on the more aggressive Chinese partner has been commonly assumed abroad."—*Nations in Alliance*, p. 40.

termination of the Berlin Blockade. There was a period of estrangement from 1954 to 1957, marked by differences on German rearmament, the war in Indo-China, and then the Suez crisis and
war (in which the United States strongly disapproved of the actions of Britain and France). But after 1957 the relationship was
strengthened and remained strong enough that the French were
able to block British membership in the Common Market at least
in part on the ground that she is not basically a European power.

It is difficult to settle upon a particular point within this ongoing alignment as the point when an alliance was established.
There is no special military treaty as there is in the other cases we
have examined. Yet there can be no dispute that there is in effect
a very strong alliance between the two powers. And it is significant
for our purposes partly because of its nonformalized nature and
partly for the conditions underlying its existence.[11]

It is quite clear that the relationship was reborn in the face
of the Soviet challenge to Western positions in Europe and the
Soviet development of nuclear weapons, hence our first condition — a new and threatening change in the military situation —
certainly applies to this relationship. "The offering of a new way
for the dominant power to maintain its position of strength against
its adversary," applies not because Britain herself fronted on
Communist territory but because the possessions and countries
in which the British retained strong influence while relinquish-
ing colonial control lay on the outskirts of both Soviet and Chinese
lands. Thus the alliance encouraged a cooperative effort to maintain Western positions of strength in the face of the developing
Sino-Soviet challenge.

The condition of the dominant power's desire to increase
its influence over the other power seems to have existed except
during certain periods in the time of estrangement from 1954 to
1957. Yet in the eyes of the British the justification for the continuation of the relationship has generally been that by joining
with the United States they could exercise influence over her
far beyond what their actual power would allow — in a sense, they
could employ their diplomatic skills and policy acumen, developed over centuries of Great Power status, to guide the United
States in exercising her preponderant power.

[11]See Bruce M. Russett, *Community and Contention* (Cambridge, Mass.: M. I. T.
Press, 1963), especially chap. 2 and p. 74.

But if the relevance of this third proposition is perhaps less strong than might be expected in terms of our previous findings, the same might be said about the applicability of the first two. One study of the relationship concluded:

> The U.S. — British accord should have been related directly to fear of the Soviet Union; in fact it had a largely autonomous momentum. The British did not decide to develop bombs for fear of the Soviets, and their offer in 1949 to rely on American-produced bombs was not confined to a period in which Russia would represent the main threat to peace. It represented an act of faith in long-range Anglo-American solidarity, difficult to understand in traditional power terms. The offer did not materially strengthen the U.S. effort as it might be directed against the Soviet Union; it did not add to the credibility of Anglo-American deterrence by creating a new center of nuclear might in the Western alliance. Neither country gained greatly from its provisions; only the Anglo-American alliance benefited.[12]

The same unusual features can be discerned in the Suez crisis and the subsequent persistence of the accord.

Some Conclusions

What, then, have we discovered in our effort to apply to other postwar alliances a general explanation of alliance derived from a particular explanation of the creation of the Warsaw Pact? We found three conditions that might be expected to be conducive to alliance: a precipitating threatening change in the military situation, a desire by the dominant power to increase its position of strength against the adversary, and a desire to increase its influence over its new allies when each of these was weakening or threatened. We found that they apply in varying degrees to all the alliances we examined, but that in Western alliances the feature of influence over one's allies is apparently more a consequence than an objective. This, plus the nature of the political relations and relative strengths of the nations in the Warsaw Pact, suggests that perhaps such influence or control is to some degree a feature applicable to alliances in which the dominant party is already particularly strong in its relations with

[12]Raymond Dawson and Richard Rosecrance, "Theory and Reality in the Anglo-American Alliance," World Politics, 19 (1966) 21–51 at 48–49.

its new allies. Or, from another point of view, it suggests that the Warsaw Pact is less an alliance and more an empire (or was so upon its inception) than alliances among nations of greater equality. Thus, although we have found the explanation of the Warsaw Pact to be generalizable, we have also had to reexamine it as an alliance, paying greater heed to the previously existing domination that characterized relations among the signatories even without the alliance. It remains true of this alliance as of others that its existence tends to increase the opportunity for the dominant power to influence the politics of its allies, and this is an important additional conclusion of our investigation.

Some Conclusions from the Scholarly Literature

We have proceeded this far in our investigation of alliance without much reference to the scholarly literature on the subject. Alliance has been a subject of long-standing interest to students of international politics, like war and international organization. Although differences exist among scholars, nonetheless there is what can be termed a "conventional wisdom" about alliances.

Alliances have generally been viewed as products of efforts to establish and strengthen nations' positions in relation to other nations and their alliances. More specifically, nations align in order to supplement each other's capability and thereby reduce the pressure with which antagonistic power can curtail their independence. In a sense, pressure is met with counterpressure directed at the adversary's weakest point or at his point of initiative. For alliance to occur, there must of course be some common interest. But this does not mean that all interests must be shared, or that each party must benefit equally from the alliance, any more than it requires that roles be similar and contributions equal.[13]

Our brief study tends to confirm these views, but places greater emphasis on the impact of alliance upon the freedom and policy of the member states. Furthermore, particularly in the instance of the Anglo-American alliance, it suggests that this conventional theory of alliance is too narrow in its statement of interests. As the study of alliance cited earlier concludes:

[13]For more comprehensive statement of this traditional alliance theory, see Liska, *Nations in Alliance,* chap. 1. esp. pp. 26–41. See also Hans Morgenthau, "Alliances in Theory and Practice" in Wolfers, *Alliance Policy in the Cold War,* pp. 184–212.

All of which goes to prove that between friends the balance of power does not mean very much. Neither the unilateral nor the bilateral possession of nuclear weapons has fragmented the alliance; neither has divided the policies of the two governments. History, tradition, affinity have been crucial to the alliance, rather than peripheral. The relationship is special in one notable sense: the theory of alliances does not explain it, but policy must take account of it.[14]

This conclusion was strengthened by a study of the development of the Anglo-American alliance in the postwar years. It seems doubtful that study of the other alliances we have examined would produce findings as divergent from traditional theory as this one did.

The Development of Alliances

Limitations of space do not permit us to examine the other stages in the life cycle of the alliances discussed above in the same empirical detail with which we examined their inception. But we may note some of the more interesting elements of these stages—elements that invite considerable additional research and theory development.

One key aspect of the development of alliance is its size. The assumption in political analysis has been that a political actor will seek to maximize his political support, and therefore will maximize the number of nations in his alliances. Some confirmation of this might be found in American alliance policy in the Eisenhower years which saw a proliferation of American alliances, both bilateral and multilateral, so great that it was commonly characterized as "pactomania." Yet a more instrumental view of coalition building would suggest that a nation would seek only "minimum winning coalitions" or alliances only as large as their creators believe will ensure winning a conflict or attaining whatever other objective the alliance is to serve, and no larger. Which of these propositions more closely describes reality can only be determined by further empirical study.[15]

[14]Dawson and Rosecrance, "Theory and Reality in the Anglo-American Alliance," p. 51. See also Russett, *Community and Contention*, esp. pp. 142 and 215.
[15]For various positions in this argument, see Anthony Downs, *An Economic Theory of Democracy* (New York: Harper & Row, 1957), p. 11; and William Riker, *The Theory of Political Coalitions* (New Haven, Conn.: Yale University Press, 1962), pp. 32–33.

Also, much more attention should be paid to realignments and dealignments characteristic of the development and deterioration of alliances.[16] If we were able to study the developments of alliances such as NATO, the Warsaw Treaty Organization, the Baghdad Pact and its successor, the Central Treaty Organization, in the Middle East, over the succeeding years, we would find considerable change in them—if not always in the formal membership, at least in the members' degree of commitment to and support of them. Of particular interest would be the roles of France in NATO and Communist China in the Soviet bloc as a whole.

We are also interested in the degree of integration achieved by the alliances. Political integration and its subdivision, military integration, are subjects very important for the future of both national and international politics, for they have resulted in significant changes in the size and independence of many international political actors in these postwar years. As we have seen before and shall see again, we cannot long divorce our analysis from political happenings within national borders, and integration (whether in the Common Market, in NATO, or in movements to consolidate states in Africa, Latin America, or Asia) is perhaps the clearest and most interesting reminder of this. It remains for the students of national and comparative politics and the students of international politics to cooperate in studying integration. Our understanding of the life cycles of alliances should be greatly improved by such study.

We are also very much interested in studying the effects of alliances. Our concern here is twofold. First, we know that alliances will have a significant effect on the practice of international politics simply because they are major creations and sources of major actions of the parties to international politics. In this study we are examining only the major types of international happenings. But if we also examined others, from the everyday interaction of normal diplomacy to more particular occurrences, such as arms races, we shall find that alliances will be of great importance in understanding these. Thus, for example, diplomatic relations among the North Atlantic allies are markedly altered by the existence of NATO, as, of course, are relations between those NATO allies and their adversaries of the Warsaw Pact. In addition, alliance provides in some ways an alternative to an

[16]See Liska, *Nations in Alliance*, esp. pp. 42–60.

arms race, for one motivation of an alliance is to increase one's capabilities without increasing one's arms. Furthermore, where alliances confront each other, increase in the capability of one side through aggregation is likely to stimulate either the same sort of aggregation on the other or else unilateral arms build-ups in the adversary, and thereby what might have been an arms race between nations in the absence of alliances is likely to turn into an arms race between alliances. Such an arms race, it is clear, could prove to be much more complex and unstable than an arms race between individual states because alliances are by their nature somewhat unstable and subject to diplomatic and military alteration. These matters, too, merit considerable attention.

One further interest in the effects of alliance arises from our more general concern with the applicability of our knowledge and our theories to practical problems of international politics. Our efforts to influence or control these happenings may be materially aided by the use of alliance, and to be more certain of this we must know not just what happens to alliance, but what effect alliance has on international relations.

If we were convinced that alliance contributes to the security of its parties, that would be of interest. But even this contention, which some would believe almost self-evident, is subject to debate. One analyst has written that "to the extent that military power is now less usable, because of either its more restricted legitimacy or the risk of escalation, alliances should be somewhat less valuable than they used to be," and has examined the attractiveness of alliance to great and small powers, nuclear and non-nuclear states, developed and underdeveloped countries.[17]

Another analyst has argued that:

"Far from increasing security, the military competition between the two groups, and the final bipolarization of the power structure, tends in a cumulative fashion to increase tensions and to make conflict more likely. . . . Alliances, far from relieving each member of an alliance from burdensome expenditure on armaments, create a competition between power blocs which imposes ever-increasing defense expenditure upon their members." . . .

Once an alliance is made with a country there is a strong interest in the continuity of the government of that country, and certainly in the prevention of any internal political change which would

[17]Klaus Knorr, *On the Uses of Military Power in the Nuclear Age* (Princeton, N.J.: Princeton University Press, 1966) pp. 152–163, at p. 153.

threaten the alliance. Thus the United States has been led to support repressive and unpopular governments rather than risk internal change. Inevitably also, economic and technical aid has developed on a discriminatory basis, determined by short-term considerations of strategy rather than long-term objectives of welfare.[18]

Problems   Although we may wish to quarrel with
for Further Study   these assessments we can do so only
on the basis of careful study of the effects of alliance. Not enough such study has been undertaken; at every turn we are confronted by the need for more. We may then rightly ask, How close are we to a theory of alliance? The answer seems to be that although we are closer to a theory of alliance than we are to a theory of crisis, we are less close than we are to a theory of war. The conceptual work of analyzing aspects, features, and stages of alliance has been done. Studies of particular alliances have existed for some time. But the linkage of these two types of work into related propositions about the causes, development, and effects of alliances under different international political conditions has not yet been completed. Moreover, even when we achieve such a coherent set of propositions about these aspects of alliance, we shall need to ask how close this is to a satisfactory explanation of alliance. If we accept a theory of alliance, we can explain any particular alliance by showing that it is a manifestation of the regularity described in our theory. But we could explain the regularity in our theory only in terms of other knowledge about the relations of nations and perhaps the coalition-behavior of other actors besides states.[19]

This does not mean that we do not in large measure understand alliances and coalition-behavior. We certainly have considerable understanding of the sort that enables us to look back on any given happening and not be grossly puzzled by its nature and development. On the other hand, we do not yet approach systematic knowledge of the sort that would make us confident in efforts to predict or control. There is considerable literature containing efforts to predict the future of alliances now in exist-

[18]John W. Burton, *International Relations* (New York: Cambridge University Press, 1965), pp. 78–79.
[19]See, for example, studies of coalition in small groups, such as those in J. David Singer, ed., *Human Behavior and International Politics* (Chicago: Rand McNally, 1965) and those appearing frequently in the *Journal of Conflict Resolution*.

ence, or even the likely future role of alliance in international politics.[20] But as students of alliance and other international political occurrences, we can contribute significantly to the improvement of that literature, and the bases on which it is developed, if we concentrate our efforts on generating and testing propositions about the various stages in the life cycles of alliances and then on linking those propositions into coherent theories that might in their turn be extended to cover alliances not only in the postwar years but also at other times. We should then find that the resulting theory of alliance will enable us to understand better the reasons why nations cooperate with their friends, and understand the problems that seem increasingly to arise in those relations. The result should make us better able to assess the policies of allied nations and to recommend more promising policies in cases where nations in alliance come to act more like enemies than friends. In addition, we may find that our theory of alliance, or cooperation among friends, can be linked to a theory of conflict control, or cooperation among adversaries, to an examination of which we now turn.

[20]Herbert S. Dinerstein, in "The Transformation of Alliance Systems," *American Political Science Review*, 59 (1965) 589- 601, concludes that, "it is hard to imagine Eastern Europe as anything but much altered ten years from now and Western Europe as remaining essentially the same. Paradoxically, it seems that the cohesion of the Communist Alliance system, once pressed into a rigid mold, will suffer much greater disintegration than the always loose non-Communist system. And the multiplication cf ideological variants of Communist probably will eventually attenuate the ideological force of Communism."

Burton, in *International Relations*, concludes that nonalignment will be the dominant feature of international politics in the future.

Riker, in *The Theory of Political Coalitions* (pp. 230–231), concludes that,

When the few remaining ambiguities of border territory have been clarified, the Age of Equalization will be over.

At that point the character of world politics will change rather abruptly. We will pass from the Age of Equalization to the Age of Maneuver. And there will then be an entirely different tone of world politics.

The main features of the Age of Maneuver will, I submit, be the following:

1. The price asked by neutrals or marginal members for their allegiance to one side or the other will rise steadily.

2. The tone of politics will become more intense in the sense that each decision will seem to involve the entire future of each coalition.

3. As a result of the previous effect, the danger of general warfare will increase.

4. Finally, as a result of all three previous effects, the two main opposing powers will exhaust their resources in maintaining their alliances and other nations will come to the fore as world leaders.

chapter 12

Studying
Cooperative Control

Instances **Although** most of our attention is
of Cooperation devoted to conflict in international
politics, most international political
happenings are in fact predominantly cooperative. This is clearly
true of most economic aid and trade and even more true of the
health, education, and welfare activities of the United Nations
and other transnational organizations. It is also true of the application of most international law to matters of diplomacy, commerce, navigation, and other so-called nonsecurity affairs. There
is also a high degree of cooperation in many instances of "security
affairs," including even war and arms races.[1] Among the most
prominent instances of cooperation in security affairs are arms
control measures, such as the nuclear testban treaty, peace-keeping
measures like the efforts of the United Nations in the Middle East

[1]The traditional distinction between "security" and "nonsecurity" affairs is somewhat misleading, for there is little doubt that national security is affected by economic activities, diplomatic practices, and other happenings that do not immediately involve questions of war and peace.

and the Congo, and the limitation of war that has taken place in Korea and Vietnam — all instances of cooperative control of conflict or of the preparations for resort to force and violence.

Our **We must examine cooperative control**
Approach **in some detail for two reasons: It plays**
an increasingly important role in inter-
national politics, and it is so often neglected or misunderstood. There are as yet few instances of multinational or international peace-keeping, but there are postwar measures of arms control and there is some prospect that nations will agree to additional measures. Consequently, although even arms control in large measure is still unprecedented (as are such diverse possibilities as space war and world government), we shall give it most of our attention in this chapter as a way of understanding cooperative control and, further, as a model for the study of other largely unprecedented international happenings.

We shall begin by examining the nature of the phenomenon of arms control and the few instances we have of it in the postwar years. Then we shall attempt to specify the conditions under which nations are likely to seek arms control measures. This we shall do by combining study of these few instances with our developing general understanding of international politics, in an investigation that is admittedly largely speculative. Such an effort must be followed by consideration of the likely life cycle of an arms control measure, beginning with the conditions under which we might expect various nations to succeed in establishing some measure of that control. This work would prepare us for speculation about the prospects for arms control by predicting the evolution and the interaction of the interests of states in arms control.

The preceding three chapters have been shaped by the desire to work through various approaches to the study of international politics directed toward the development of explanatory theory. In this chapter we shall offer an example of a more comprehensive and well-developed, if admittedly highly speculative, analysis of the sort we would like to develop in studying other phenomena such as crises, and wars, and alliances. Here, too, we shall find evidence that our discipline has recently made considerable progress, although it still has a long way to go. The tasks that remain before us should prove less difficult as our models of analysis gradually improve.

The Nature
of Arms Control

While usage has varied over the years, the term "arms control" is now generally defined so that it covers all multilateral measures designed to restrain or limit the military establishments of nations through the process of interaction. The term "disarmament," which preceeded "arms control" in popular usage, is now generally applied only to measures involving actual *reduction* of armaments. Thus disarmament is one type of arms control.

Arms Control in the Postwar Years

The instances in which limited disarmament or arms control has been achieved stand out not so much because they are significant as because they are so few. The period between the Rush-Bagot Agreement of 1817, which demilitarized the Great Lakes between the United States and Canada, and the Washington Naval Agreements of 1922, saw two Hague peace conferences (in 1899 and 1907) and a world war. During the period between these naval agreements (which were partially and ineffectually renewed in 1930) and Hiroshima, there were long-drawn-out League of Nations disarmament conferences and another world war.

Nonetheless, the postwar atomic anxiety encouraged other disarmament negotiations soon after the end of the war and the beginning of the United Nations.[3] From 1946 through 1948 dis-

---

[2]Much of this analysis derives from my study *Arms Control in International Politics* (New York: Holt, Rinehart and Winston, 1969).

[3]There is considerable historical literature on disarmament. Probably the most useful works are these: Merze Tate, *The Disarmament Illusion* (New York: Macmillan, 1942) and *The U.S. and Armaments* (Cambridge, Mass.: Harvard University Press, 1954); Philip Noel-Baker, *The Arms Race* (New York: Oceana, 1960); and Bernhard Bechhoefer, *Postwar Negotiations for Arms Control* (Washington, D.C.: Brookings, 1961). A bibliographical guide to postwar literature can be found in Bechhoefer, pp. 601–608. "Selected References" to interwar literature including bibliographies are to be found in pp. 1002–1026 of the Senate Foreign Relations Committee's *Disarmament and Security: A Collection of Documents 1919–1955* (Washington, D.C.: GPO, 1956).

cussion and negotiation concerned nuclear weapons, centering on the American Oppenheimer-Lilienthal-Baruch Plan and the Soviet alternative. The United States proposed internationalization of atomic energy, on which it had a monopoly, while the Soviet Union insisted on duplicating the American discovery itself, meanwhile relying on its immense superiority in conventional forces to counter American nuclear forces, which it sought to disarm. Most discussion in this period was general, and none of it linked Western nuclear forces with Eastern conventional forces as countervailing capabilities to be controlled concomitantly. As Cold War tensions mounted and political conflict in Eastern and Central Europe developed, debate over control (which the West sought) and inspection (which the Soviets opposed) failed to become realistic. The unlikelihood of compromise became clearer, and eventually negotiation deteriorated into minimal activity from the fall of 1948 to the fall of 1951. At the most, these negotiations, like others later, served to clarify somewhat the minimal conditions each side could be expected to insist upon.

Following its accession to the "nuclear club" in 1949, the Soviet Union became increasingly intransigent. As the Soviets narrowed the American nuclear advantage and the North Atlantic Treaty Organization narrowed the Eastern conventional superiority, the importance of assessing nuclear and conventional strength together, if not necessarily considering their disarmament, became clearer, and not surprisingly, each side continued to demand international reductions in the area in which it was inferior.

New proposals embodying concessions by each side, in the form of the first comprehensive plans for general disarmament, were produced occasionally from late 1954 to late 1957, although these plans emphasized the interrelation of nuclear and conventional forces, they also revealed the Western desire to prevent the Soviets from equaling Western nuclear stockpiles and the concomitant Soviet desire to retain its intelligence advantage over the West through preservation of its closed society. Positions could nonetheless be described as being closer in that the West began to recognize the importance to the Soviets of control limited strictly by veto power, and the Soviet Union, now a nuclear power, became willing to postpone the control of nuclear weapons to a late stage in the disarmament process.

What was happening, in the subsequent assessment of an American negotiator, was that "both the Soviet Union and the West, because of developments in military technology, were shifting their emphasis in the disarmament negotiations from 'comprehensive disarmament,' which became an ultimate objective rather than an immediate program, to 'partial measures.'"[4]

By December 1957, when the Soviets refused to participate in further negotiations, the parties had already discussed air and stationary ground inspection, zones of limited armament, and a ban on nuclear testing.

As each side improved its posture in weaponry in which the other had the advantage, the strategic balance was coming increasingly to hinge on means of delivering both nuclear weapons by airplane and rocket and conventional forces by ground transport and airlift. Following the first testing of a Soviet intercontinental ballistic missile and the launching of Sputnik I in the fall of 1957, negotiations on general disarmament ceased. In 1958 conferences on a nuclear test suspension and on measures to prevent surprise attack were held. The achievement of a moratorium on nuclear testing and the collapse in the autumn of the talks on surprise attack (which the Soviets considered political and the Americans treated as technical) bespoke the new and increasing emphasis on partial measures of arms control.

But partial successes were preceded by more failures on an expanding scale. At the United Nations General Assembly in September 1959 both the British and the Soviets produced proposals for "general and complete disarmament" in three stages, and the Americans followed with their proposal the next spring. But the Soviets walked out of the talks in mid-1960, and negotiation was suspended until March 1962, when an Eighteen Nation Disarmament Conference was constructed of five Western, five Eastern, and eight nonaligned nations. The talks were notable both for the agreement once again to allow possession of nuclear missiles into the later stages of disarmament and for the continued refusal of France, one of the eighteeen, to participate—a refusal that, coupled with the continued exclusion of Communist China, rendered the discussion of general and comprehensive disarmament unpromising.

However, progress in limited measures was subsequently

[4]Bechhoefer, *Postwar Negotiations for Arms Control*, p. 314.

achieved in smaller and generally less formal bodies. The demilitarization of the Antarctic region was agreed to by the twelve countries with claims in that area. The December 1959 treaty was significant for its elimination of the possibility of competitive armament there and for its allowance of untrammeled inspection by and of all parties in the Antarctic.

The limited nuclear testban treaty of July 1963 resulted from talks beginning in autumn 1958 under the moratorium and continuing sporadically until suddenly, in June 1963, the Soviets indicated a willingness to consider an American proposal of August 1962 for an agreement excluding underground tests, which the United States maintained were potentially undetectable. The Soviet turnabout is often explained in terms of the post-Cuban missile crisis quest for a *détente* and as an effort to embarrass the Chinese. Once political conditions encouraged such an agreement, it was easily reached. Clearly the limited nature of the treaty, which provided for no inspection and for withdrawal with warning, contributed to the ease of its attainment. The experience of five years of negotiations on nuclear test suspension was also significant.

The agreement of 1963 establishing a direct telegraphic link (or "hotline") between the United States and the Soviet Union was based on an idea that appears to have originated in the early 1960s with American strategic thinkers concerned over the possibility of a major war as a result of misinformation or miscalculation. But this agreement came after the development of invulnerable deterrent forces had already substantially reduced the danger of preemptive attack.

The danger of competitive militarization of space was met by a General Assembly resolution banning the orbiting of nuclear weapons. It was passed unanimously in October 1963 following some six years of occasional discussion. This was a case of an arms control agreement undertaken before a threat had materialized or had been substantially lessened by conditions. Although the agreement did not provide sanctions, it was one in which sanctions seemed less important than mutual assurances that neither side would undertake action that would be costly, provocative, and unlikely to be useful if duplicated.

The attainment of these four limited measures (Antarctic nonmilitarization, the limited testban, the hotline, and the nonmilitarization of space), which were accompanied by reciprocated reductions in both defense budgets and in the production of fissionable materials for nuclear weapons in 1963 and 1964, suggested that it might be possible for the powers to agree on such further partial measures as extension of the testban to underground explosions, a promising general ban on nuclear proliferation, mutual destruction of obsolescent bombers (the so-called "bomber bonfire" intended basically to prevent the gift of such weapons to developing nations), and the establishment of adversary control or observation posts in Central Europe (similar to those operating in East and West Germany as a result of the Potsdam Agreements).

The Objectives of Arms Control

Many possible national objectives might be served by arms control measures like these. Most long-range national objectives, generally stated in such general terms as welfare, justice, national liberty, personal freedom, and equality, could only be served indirectly by arms control measures. Peace, however, is one general goal that might benefit directly by arms control.

This objective is traditionally put as "reducing the risk of war." It might be elaborated to include, besides war, threatening crises and underlying international instability. But the very term "risk of war" conceals more than it reveals about the nature of the problem with which arms control measures are intended to cope. There appear to be four clearly distinguishable elements in the risk of war.

The first is the probability that war will happen by accident resulting from mechanical, informational, or judgmental errors. Coping with such a danger would require measures to improve technical systems (many or most of which are already undertaken unilaterally as they are developed) or communications and other information-gathering and analyzing devices and procedures (an example of which is the hotline).

The second aspect of the risk of war is its possibility in terms of the capabilities of participants to wage war. This suggests arms control measures that exclude military activity from environments such as space, the Antarctic, Africa, or Latin America. It suggests also measures designed to encourage or provide pauses or cooling-off periods between crisis and explosion—during which time reconsideration, negotiation, or rearmament might be undertaken.

The third aspect is the desirability of war, which concerns

purposive rather than accidental war. This is surely a major, although often neglected, part of the risk of war—all the more important if one nation has particularly good active and passive defense capabilities or a promising "first-strike" capability. The danger arising from the possession of such capabilities might be met or preempted by agreements constraining defense, such as those proposed to prohibit the frenetic development of antiballistic missiles or the frenzied construction of blast-and-fallout shelters, or by the development of invulnerable second-strike capabilities to overcome such defenses—in effect achieving deterrence by threat of punishment that would make war a less desirable national policy.

The final aspect of the risk of war is its acceptability—the extent to which a nation will be willing to accept war as a "necessary" cost of attaining national objectives. This is differentiated from the desirability of war because desirability implies or suggests initiation whereas acceptability suggests willingness to run the risk should the adversary opt for war, and includes possible moral objections to war. The measures that might undermine this acceptability of war are similar to those controverting its desirability.

The other widely recognized possible objective of arms control measures is reduction of the destructiveness of war should it come. Of course, "destructiveness" should be taken to denote many possible undesirabilities of war: extent, violence, nature, nonmilitary penetration, and "dirtiness." Among general approaches to such limitation are measures of passive defense (shelters, evacuation, and other efforts to protect people and civilian property), disarmament which limits nations' destructive capabilities, and understandings to control the escalation of limited war. It is possible that measures taken to reduce the destructiveness of war may inadvertently reduce the undesirability and unacceptability of war, thereby obstructing the attainment of the first fundamental objective of arms control. It is this consideration that underlies much of the continuing debate over the merits of civil defense, just as, in Allied military strategy, it underlies the dispute between Americans and Europeans over the relative merits of increased conventional strength in Germany and the rest of Western Europe as against continued reliance on nuclear deterrence.

An alternate and more general statement of many of these

objectives is "control of the arms race." If the term "arms" is taken in a broad sense to include all aspects of the military establishment, one aspect of such control is curtailing the scope, size, nature, costs, and risks of the military establishment. The other is controlling the "raciness" of the arms race—the speed of its escalation.

Then, too, there are other objectives toward the attainment of which arms control measures might contribute. One possibility—often overlooked, probably because concentration on adversaries characterizes military affairs—is how such measures will affect allies. The most "legitimate" arms control manifestation of such an objective is the prevention of "catalysis," in which an allied nation initiates a conflict and draws in an ally by deceit or by activating alliance commitments. But arms control measures might also be undertaken for more "purely" political objectives of rewarding and punishing allies. The nuclear testban treaty certainly had consequences of this type. The British, particularly the then governing Conservative party, were especially happy about the attainment of the treaty agreement, whereas the French and the Communist Chinese were explicitly opposed and resisted pressures to sign it—thereby presumably losing favor with their allies and prestige with the nonaligned. There is also the possibility that allies and others will be punished in the future for developing nuclear weapons capabilities, such as the way that some have advocated punishing China by destroying her test sites and reactors. Agreements to undertake or sanction such activities would be arms control measures of a particularly violent sort, and could increase the very violence they seek to reduce.

There may also be internal reasons for the advocacy or acceptance of arms control agreements, such as the political fear of a highly militarized state, the economic disapproval of the cost and economic dislocation that characterize arming, the social fear of the militarization of society, and the moral disapprobation of the production of all or some weapons or of the threat or use of force. In addition there may be objectives of affecting the nation's international standing by insincere proposals for the sake of propaganda, prestige, favor, or other gains—an insincerity that many believe has characterized all or most arms control negotiations since the invention of arms or the calling of conferences.

These, then, are the prominent objectives of a nation toward which arms control measures might contribute. We must now examine very briefly but more specifically the conditions under which nations would be likely to seek such arms control measures.

Determinants of Arms Control Policies

Of necessity, adoption of policy on arms control will depend in part on the nature of the arms control possibilities under consideration. Beyond this, we are particularly interested in the internal political and material conditions and the external political conditions which will tend to interest a nation in seeking arms control.

National Political Conditions

The national political conditions can be viewed in terms of four types of determinants: personal idiosyncrascies of public officials, the requirements imposed on public officials by their governmental roles, the structure and operation of the government, and nongovernmental aspects of society such as accepted values, public opinion, national unity, and industrialization.

First, a nation might be expected to seek arms control if the ideology of the policymakers and policy enactors encourages this attitude. Important features of the quest for arms control may be countermanded by attitudes sometimes held by public officials. Undertaking arms control measures will, by definition, require explicit limitation of the national military effort—an idea abhorrent to many military and some civilian officials. Accelerating technological development of military establishments has been accompanied by increasing appreciation of the ways in which military establishments interact whether they are actually employed or not. Deterrence is now better achieved and warfare can now be better limited not only because weapons are more effective and controllable, but also because there is deeper and more widespread understanding of the effects of one political-military establishment on another. Much arms control analysis and many proposals have developed since World War II out of this increasing appreciation of both interaction and the developing concept of control.[5] Arms control as a doctrinal offshoot of

---

[5]On the changing view of the military toward disarmament and arms control, see chap. 15 of Jack Raymond, *Power at the Pentagon* (New York: Harper & Row, 1964). See also William W. Kaufmann, *The McNamara Strategy* (New York: Harper & Row, 1964).

disarmament and military strategy is a recent development out of realistic understanding of international politics and appreciation of the mounting threat of major war. There are still those who do not appreciate the potential merit of such limitation of national military effort, and should they be in power, their ideological conceptions may constrict or prevent a national quest for arms control.

It is likely that the aversion to a limitation of military effort stems from a failure to appreciate the fact that any two nations will at times share the same objectives — ranging from interests in mutually beneficial trade through desires to avoid major nuclear war. Inadequate appreciation by policymakers of the potential desirability of limited cooperation with the adversary will also inhibit national quest for arms control.

Another possible inhibitor is an unwillingness by national leaders to take chances. Human nature or conditioning has led some men to gamble while others insure. The large elements of uncertainty and risk in international security agreements on alliance and arms control, as well as an inadequate understanding of the exact nature of these uncertainties and risks and a failure to compare them with those that would characterize relations in the absence of agreement, may further lessen a nation's efforts to obtain arms control agreements.[6] Similarly, an unwillingness to risk losing face, which seems to be particularly characteristic of some civilizations as well as of some individuals, may inhibit such a national quest.[7]

Role requirements will be important in several ways. The military and industrial desire for maximal defense efforts is understandable and indeed justifiable (so long as it is not grounded in fear of limitation of military effort as such, or in other of the personal idiosyncrasies discussed above), for to the military is assigned the task of preparing for any contingency as best it can convince the executive and Congress it should, and to industry the possibility of seeking expanded production and profits in a capitalist economy. But in the United States, neither the military nor industry is expected or asked to establish political-military

[6]See, for an analysis of uncertainty and risk, C. J. Hitch and R. N. McKean, *Economics of Defense in the Nuclear Age* (Cambridge, Mass.: Harvard University Press, 1961), chap. 10.
[7]See, for an analogical analysis of face, Erving Goffman, "On Face-Work" in *Psychiatry*, 18 (1955) 229 ff. and chap. 6 of his *Behavior in Public Places* (New York: Free Press, 1962) on "face engagements."

policy. Answers to the question whether limitations on the military establishment are desirable depend on answers to more fundamental questions: What threats and promises are to be met, and how? These questions are to be answered by the political officials in a nonmilitary government. Their role requirements may not encourage them to seek arms control, but they will most probably not interfere with such seeking. Indeed, the requirements faced by most public officials responsible for the allocation of scarce resources as well as for national security will probably make it hard for them to oppose arms control formally. This is one reason why multinational discussion of general and complete disarmament continues despite little prospect for success.

Finally, nongovernmental considerations would be expected to intervene in the form of public opinion exercising the anticipatory sanction of electoral or even violent dissent. Thus a government may be interested in arms control when its public fears the possible international consequences of armament, or because it regrets the developing militarization of society, or because of an objection to the rising cost of the military establishment. Public opinion is of course particularly important where political pressures may determine the fate of officials in an election.

National Material Conditions

The major material conditions of concern to us here include geography and economy, which determine the impact of technological development. These aspects of a state are likely to be important contributors to its international political plans and actions, and several will be of particular importance to its arms control interests. Until the technological developments of the mid-twentieth century, geographic position would have been itself an important determinant of attitudes toward arms control. One would still expect to find a nation hesitant to disarm voluntarily when it has a hostile contiguous neighbor—certainly more hesitant than one with a hostile but distant neighbor. But at least over a short time span and with continuing "permanent" patterns of alignment, a nation may be able to cope with geographical problems by employing technological devices, as both major powers did by developing ballistic missiles. Similarly, geography no longer offers the protection it once did. Thus geography and technology can frequently be viewed as a pair or set of determinants, and what role geographic position still plays in the quest for arms control can best be examined with technology.

Natural resources themselves may prove important. The quest for nuclear power, for instance, will depend either on the possession of natural resources adequate to the needs of development plus the requisite technical competence and economic strength or on the political ways of obtaining assistance. But again the problems tend to arise as political rather than material ones.

The economy may influence a nation's interest in arms control in two ways: it may at some point provide a limit to possible armament that will compel a nation to seek security through agreement with allies or with adversaries, and it will pose continuing questions of allocation. But if there is an inherent economic limit to possible defense spending, it does not appear to have been reached by any prominent nation. Continued high-level arms spending, particularly if accompanied by major active and passive defense programs, may uncover such national limits, at least for lesser powers. It seems more likely that the limit on arms spending is a point or range where other possible expenditures and their consequences are preferred to more spending for arms and its consequences. Both the quantitative threshold and the preference scale will differ among nations, but all nations will face a continuing question of allocation.

The arms control implications of such allocation dilemmas will probably be greatest for second-rank nuclear powers, such as Britain in the mid-1960s and France and perhaps Communist China in the 1970s. It may be expected, then, that new nuclear powers, disinterested in nuclear limitation while they are developing their capabilities and testing their economic capacities, may become interested in a nuclear disarmament that would tend to equalize all nuclear capabilities. Similarly, we would expect lesser conventional powers to seek agreements discouraging costly and reciprocally disadvantageous local arms races within their areas if they have confidence in the agreements that might be achieved and if they do not fear specific uncontrolled disturbances in areas.

Another national determinant of immense importance often overlooked is knowledge. Conceiving and developing promising measures of arms control is clearly a prerequisite for arms control agreement. Moreover, knowledge may be viewed as a primary constituent of forecasting as well as of the technology exploited in the production of armament.

External Political Conditions

Among external political considerations or conditions important in stimulating a nation's interest in arms control will be its perception of the characteristics of its adversaries — particularly their plans, means, and actions. Neutrals and allies as well as adversaries will be important. Their allegiance, their relative power and their attitude toward international order will be of interest to a nation, for these factors will tend to influence their attitudes toward arms control significantly.

The key external variables that will tend to determine a nation's interest in achieving arms control agreements with one or more other nations will be position, power, and role. Position, a product of geography and allegiance, will make some nations as allies, others as adversaries, and others as uncommitted. Generally, allies are alternatives to arms control, for they may serve to compound the military establishment, particularly where technology or economy has placed effective limits on internal development. Hence a nation will tend to be more interested in arms control where allies are less attainable or more costly, provided that its failure to obtain allies does not automatically consign them to the adversary. Thus as the "permanent" postwar alliances disintegrate we may expect that the superpowers will become increasingly interested in settlements or ententes in areas of previous major confrontation like central Europe, and in areas of potential major confrontation like south Asia.

The existence of uncommitted nations may itself encourage major nations to seek arms control agreements extending or strengthening that uncommittedness in order to deprive the adversary of their assistance and concomitantly remove some of the burdens and risks of competitive arming by the major powers. Thus the United States and the Soviet Union seem increasingly interested in preserving the uncommittedness of India not only to maintain the political configuration of south Asia but also to allocate aid to both sides. One might expect similar increasing interest in insulating Africa from the Cold War and perhaps, should it slip from American grasp, the same for Latin America. A nation will tend to choose arms control where its allies do not seriously object or, indeed, where they insist on it. But the cost of pursuing arms control in the face of allied opposition will depend on the importance of the allies to the country and on their power over the nation. This power is a strange commodity. The more power (or capacity to shape its fate) that a nation has over another, the more that dominated nation can determine the action of the powerful. The clearer cases of this phenomenon occur in the threat to "collapse into Communism" that rambunctious but weak allies frequently make to the United States. But where security considerations do not predominate, it will be the subtler and more bearable but nonetheless discomfiting threats to prestige and leadership that dissident allies can pose. This effect can be seen in the actions and attitudes of France toward the United States and of Communist China toward the Soviet Union in the mid-1960s. Even if these allies are not essential to the security of their bloc leaders, they can loosen or jeopardize the bonds of the blocs by succeeding in behaving insubordinately.

It is important to distinguish here between the superpowers, just examined, and the would-be great powers. Would-be great powers, like China and France at this time, are apt to be hostile to any arms control proposals that would not irrevocably reduce the margin between them and the superpowers, for they are in a "catch-up" position in which the development and production curves are much more favorable to them than to the more fully developed nations. As long as time and continued effort seem on their side, they are unlikely to be candidates for any arms control measures that might interest their superiors.

There is still another category of nation, the "former great power." Nations such as Britain, forced to cut back on military programs because of higher-priority demands on their limited economies, become very much interested not only in arms control measures that would allow decreases in defense maintenance but also in measures that would keep the perpetual weaklings subjugated. It is expected in many quarters that this will be the eventual status of France (barring technological assistance from Britain and economic assistance from West Germany) and perhaps even of Communist China, because of the massive leads in technology and economic capacity of the two super-powers. These declining nations will be particularly interested in arrangements that make their shrinking global military capabilities less obvious as well as less expensive.

The military spheres of the perpetually weak nations are generally local and their efforts and concerns will thus be directed at comparable neighbors. The subsystems these interests and activities create are a major international political problem, for they tend to be characterized by local arms races and conflicts. These races and conflicts would probably not be so dangerous beyond their borders were the major powers not so heavily involved in their affairs. Significantly, even if the local powers were not interested in arms control measures (such as arms embargoes and weapon-free zones), the major powers could themselves undertake such measures by ceasing to arm them—if the major powers could be satisfied by the reliability of agreements reached and could accept the local alignment consequences of their own inaction.

The second key characteristic of nations is power. This raises considerations of means, or, in our case, armament. This variable is itself one determinant of position in that it sets limits: the technological and applied armament capabilities and the economic strength underlying them determine whether a nation that was previously weak can become strong, or whether a major power can become a superpower. Realizing this, a superior nation will be more interested in achieving arms control measures that slow the development of less powerful but ascendant adversaries and, conversely, will be less inclined to accept arms control proposals from nations superior to it—unless in each case the gap between significant power-position levels are apparently unbreachable. This is approximately the case for the distinction between the two superpowers and the major powers.

But also related to the position and power variables is the role variable which determines the plans and actions of a nation. It may be misleading to view nations as revolutionary or conservative in their general objectives, since rare is the nation that would not be happier under some different circumstances and would be unwilling to pay some price for the desired change. But there are significant differences among nations, both regarding their satisfaction with the existing international configuration and their willingness to alter it by violent or internationally illegal means. Thus, in a world of largely revolutionary states one would expect considerable interest on the part of a conservative nation in arms control measures that would tend to impede change, particularly violent change. Similarly, one would not expect a revolutionary nation to be interested in arms control measures if it confronted a conservative array of powers.

Because the orientation of a nation will heavily influence its plans and actions, the nation assessing the external determinants of its policy will be particularly concerned to discriminate between allies and adversaries in tailoring its policies to national roles. In the case of an adversary, the nation's assessment will focus not so much on the interests of the other nation as on the measure itself. It might be thought that achievement of arms control measures among adversaries must prove impossible because of divergent national interests. But let us not forget such achievements as limitation in war, one type of cooperative control that has always characterized national interaction, and the achievement of the limited arms control measures already undertaken. How might that be explained in the face of strongly divergent interests? Sometimes, short-run objectives coincide while long-term objectives or national interests remain divergent. Just as both sides may wish to limit a war, both superpowers desire to avert general nuclear war. And just as the superpowers, the has-been great powers, and the weak powers agreed on a nuclear test ban, so these powers can also agree on a nonproliferation agreement. Such cooperation may result, not from common altruistic motives, but from different objectives or different assessments of likely consequences. Indeed, the only requisite for arms control or any other multinational agreement is coincidence of instrument — agreement to undertake a measure, regardless of different expectations about its consequences or of differing state objectives. Hence, when a nation is assessing these determinants of its behavior, it will be attentive to the interests of its allies and to the instruments of its adversaries — a transmutation accounted for by the substantial differences in objectives among adversaries and by the absence of a common adversary nation among the others.

International Systemic Conditions

A nation's attitude toward arms control will be a product, not only of its assessment of the variables already examined, but also of its consideration of international systemic determinants — that is, the structure of the system and the nature of the environment it provides.

The structure of the system can be viewed as the product of the geographical distribution or configuration and the political alignment of its constituents. It has been argued that a nation's prime arms control concern with adversaries will be the possible existence of interests or objectives shared or tradable, and that allies will probably be viewed as a hedge against failure of the peace or failure of the cooperative controlling relations entered into with adversaries. In this light, strong alliances would appear to be favorable to arms control among the major powers. And it does appear likely that a bipolar world will make more possible and more likely arms control agreements by superpowers or by lesser powers protected by alliances, or at least by nuclear umbrellas, or by stable local arms situations, or perhaps by entire blocs.

However, although degeneration of alliances will render expectations unclear it will also tend toward reestablishment of a situation in which nations might better afford or risk disarmament because they would find it increasingly possible to compensate for internal cutbacks and constraints through external assistance—as was characteristic of the "balance of power system" before "permanent" alliances curtailed it.

But while unaligned nations may thus serve as contributors to the security of the parties to substantial disarmament, their primary importance, in the eyes of a major power and bloc leader, will be as indicators of the future conditions of the international order. In them lies the promise of victory or threat of defeat in the long-range "struggle for the minds and hearts of men." In a world where material gain is rarely possible externally, nations have been forced to tailor their hopes and expectations to the immaterial world of similarity, compatibility, and occasionally allegiance in the developing states. It would be unwarranted to expect a superpower to undertake long-range disarmament commitments if it did not believe that over time the rest of the world would come its way. This is the symmetrical beauty (at least momentary) of the dominant liberal democratic and international communistic world views: each is unshakably convinced that time is on its side. And thus, by extension, if the detorioration of alliances should proceed more rapidly in the adversary's camp, a nation would probably be willing to run risks in arms control because of the increased assurance it would derive from its faithful allies. On the other hand the nation might be less interested in seeking arms control because it would be more optimistic about the unfolding developments and perhaps even somewhat more fearful of preventive political and military action that its slipping rival might undertake. Our uncertainty about such possible motivations suggests the desirability of examining the context in which nations are influenced by the international system.

The primary environmental determinants perceived by the policymaking state will be economic, technological, and military. Economically, a nation may be inclined to intensify an arms race to weaken an adversary more pressed, and similarly might expect adversaries and allies to be more interested in arms control (and hence perhaps willing to pay a higher price for such agreements) under those conditions. It is also possible that perception of opportunities for the international sale of weaponry might weaken a nation's interest in pursuing arms control that would curtail local arms races elsewhere. In general, however, it is to be doubted that perceptions of external economic conditions will substantially affect a nation's attitude toward arms control unless its adversaries are much stronger economically and so could outstrip possible allied efforts. That either of the superpowers should feel this so strongly as to make questions of allocation turn into questions of capability seems unlikely and hence unimportant as a possible determinant.

Technological considerations may prove even more significant. Developments in the capabilities of destruction, transportation, and communication have forced a shift from defense to deterrence and a reliance on indirect approaches of drift and erosion embodied in indirect strategies of posture and maneuver. This has clearly changed the functions of weaponry substantially in ways that may offer opportunities for arms control. First of all, it is possible that the attainment of a virtual technological plateau — characterized perhaps more by the difficulty of achieving new breakthroughs on active defense than by acceptance of the unlikelihood of novelty — may make quantitative arms control of greater possible significance. It often appears that the significance of a measure and its attainability vary inversely. If so, we might expect a nation perceiving a technological stalemate to intensify quantitative efforts to gain advantage but at the same time to pursue qualitative restraints that would tend to "institutionalize" or extend the plateau.

But considerations about arms control possibilities will probably continue to focus on the levels and nature of armament because of its potential consequences rather than because of its unprofitableness. It was suggested earlier that existing armaments of some kinds under some circumstances may contribute toward the outbreak of war by creating incentives to preempt, or may facilitate (if not necessarily cause) it by mischief, inadvertence, accident, or miscalculation. Similarly, the nature of military establishments and the perception of threats may combine to encourage arms races that under certain circumstances may trigger war. Arms races of types ranging from the development of hostility and hostile deployment, through quantitative armament, qualitative armament, and mobilization, to adverse expectations and escalation of military activity are examples. The interest of a nation in arms control will be affected not simply by its perceptions of these dangers, which constitute material national determinants, but by its perception of similar interests in adversaries and allies in averting such dangers.

If international law and limitation procedures, for example, are dominant and the international society is characterized by law observance in the participants and by stability as a system, the opportunities for arms control will be perceived to be greater both because arms control does tend to be a static remedy for frequently dynamic ills and because there will be more opportunity for legal rather than powerpolitical regulation of armament. Similarly, if the conventions supporting limitation of confrontation and violent interaction are strong, the opportunities for arms limitations through sophisticated perception and communication will be larger and hence will encourage a national search for arms control.

Conclusion   We have been examining the conditions—from national political and national material to international political—that seem likely to encourage nations to seek arms control agreements as a way of jointly controlling the likelihood or extent of international armed conflict. Because there are few recent instances of major arms control agreements, it is more difficult to develop in inductive fashion a theory of the approach to arms control similar to a theory of the outbreak of crisis or war. Nonetheless, coupling what we do know of arms control with what we know more generally of international politics, we have been able to examine in some detail the factors likely to encourage nations to seek arms control. What we arrived at was a series of tendency statements. We could continue this examination by extending it to analysis of the stages by which nations, once they decide on arms control, can go in approaching, attaining, implementing, and maintaining arms control arrangements.[8]

Ultimately, then, we could combine these analyses into a theory of arms control that would enable us to understand why nations do or do not engage in arms control. We could then do the same for other instances of cooperative control among adversaries, such as the peace-keeping operations occasionally undertaken by the United Nations.

It is clear that the range of cooperative activities undertaken by nations—both friends and enemies—is an extensive part of the international political phenomena with which we must concern ourselves if we are to be able to understand the cooperative—and even the predominantly conflictual—happenings of concern to us, whether we be citizens or policymakers. Our examination of arms control should indicate the possibility as well as the desirability of furthering our understanding of international cooperation among adversaries.

[8]I have done just this in *Arms Control in International Politics.*

chapter 13
Theorizing about
International Politics

The Practice of Theorizing   All social scientific study is based on a search for patterns—repetitions or recurrences that can be observed, described, and hopefully explained by concepts and propositions combined into explanatory or causal theory. We seek patterns because a sense of understanding depends on there being some discoverable regularity rather than complete randomness, whether our subject be international relations or our day-to-day lives.

Although some scholars have suggested that patterns in international politics are actually cyclical—the same happenings occur over and over again—what we know of international politics fails to confirm such a contention. Others have argued that we can perceive what might be termed a "life cycle" of civilizations or nations: that all of them are born, develop, confront other civilizations or nations, deteriorate, and die.[1] More scholars,

[1]The most prominent of such theorists is Arnold Toynbee. See his *The Study of History*, which is most accessible in D. C. Somervell's condensation (New York: Oxford University Press, Vol. 1, 1947; Vol. 2, 1957). Also see his brief book, *Civilization on Trial, and The World and the West* (New York: Meridian, 1964).

however, have sought patterns or regularities at lesser levels. Some have suggested that the foreign policies of nations follow patterns in which they are alternately aggressive and then consolidative or recuperative. Others have suggested that phenomena like wars recur in certain patterns—most often cyclically in the way the business cycle has sometimes been thought to recur. But still others have probed even deeper into the happenings of international politics to the lower levels of material conditions, such as technology, or to attitudes and the resultant cooperation and conflict interactions that constitute phenomena such as war and alliance and therefore actually make up international politics.

We might attempt to develop evolutionary or, perhaps more appropriately in our age, revolutionary theories of international politics at any of these levels of analysis. Each is clearly significant, and each is to be found both in the world we are describing and in the work of others who are also describing it. But the feature that primarily distinguishes many recent efforts from most earlier work on international politics is the effort to transcend the combination of descriptive, intuitionistic theorizing by making theory explicit, explanatory, and increasingly empirical in both its origins and its confirmation.

In our explanatory analytical work in the preceding chapters, we have tried to avoid committing ourselves irrevocably as to just what patterns will be found on each level (from single interactions to the life cycles of civilizations) and which of these patterns will ultimately prove to be most fruitful subjects for international political theory. At this stage in the development of the discipline, this crucial decision should be left to each scholar and student; over time it should fall to the progress of the discipline generally. The work thus far done strongly suggests that each level deserves careful and extensive attention before we decide to commit all our resources and attention to any one—if indeed we ever make such a massive decision.

Our work has been concentrated at a middle range, examining recurrent happenings in international politics for similarities in their nature, origin, development, and outcome—in short, in their life cycles. Such study should provide building blocks for various broader theories, whether they be at the one extreme of "microtheory", built of interaction patterns, at the other extreme of "macrotheory", built of evolutionary stages of international politics, or (what seems more likely) at some intermediate level. Phenomena like war and crisis clearly can be usefully studied by themselves as we have done, but in such study we must remain conscious that they are composed of interactions (the microlevel) and that they reside or occur in longer-term evolutionary changes in international politics (the macrolevel).

Which of the many possible routes to theorizing we decide to take should sensibly depend on the relative importance to us of the various possible objectives of theorizing which are understanding the past, understanding the present, predicting the future, developing an ability to influence or control developments, or (the more academic objectives) generating propositions, testing them, and then linking them as "laws" into more comprehensive theories of international politics.

We have argued above (and will do so more explicitly in the coming chapters on prediction and control) that all these objectives will be served eventually by pursuit of the more immediate academic objectives of theory building. Some of them (particularly prediction) may be more readily served at present by shortcut methods that emphasize correlational rather than explanatory studies and that deal with particular problems like war prevention and not the underlying dynamics and stages of war, crisis, and other aspects of international politics. But even our approach increasingly promises to allow us to engage in prediction and control activities while our theories are still in early stages of development. For although they will tend to be conditional rather than causal, they will be focused on the major phenomena we wish to predict and control, such as war, crisis, and alliance.

Induction and Deduction

Our study of various phenomena arising in international politics has been basically inductive. In inductive study, one examines individual cases until he detects a pattern in them and then he develops a principle of causal relation that is built with other such principles into an explanatory theory. Thus, for example, if we had studied war in the same way that we studied crisis, we might have discovered that wars are preceded by economic unrest within one or several nations. If this perceived correlation between economic unrest and war were high — that is, if economic unrest is always or almost always followed by war —

we might conclude that when there is economic unrest there will be war. This principle, often stated as a causal law to the effect that economic unrest causes war, might then be combined with other principles about the causes of crises and alliances and other international phenomena into a general theory of international politics. If all the principles were developed by the same careful study of individual cases, then we would have developed our theory inductively. If the principles about causation of these phenomena were all economic in nature (for example, if we concluded that peace was always preceded by economic welfare and harmony in all countries, and alliance was always preceded by economic weakness) then our theory would be an economic theory of international politics – an argument that economic factors determine what happens in international politics. We might then set about testing it by observing other instances of international politics that we had not examined in developing our propositions and seeing whether they, too, could be explained by our theory.

But we might have proceeded another way in developing our theory: From examining domestic politics and discovering that economic factors are the most significant determinants of it, we might have developed the idea that economic factors will determine international politics. Then we might have said, if economic factors do indeed determine international politics, we would expect to find war preceded by economic unrest, alliance preceded by economic weakness, and peace preceded by economic harmony and welfare. Thus we would *deduce* from our general principle these subordinate principles, and develop our theory in that way. And we would test each proposition by examining specific instances to see whether they could be explained and even anticipated by the propositions.

Actually, of course, we generally operate by combining inductive and deductive operations. But if our immediate concern is developing a comprehensive and coherent theory as we have defined the term (a collection of propositions about the conditions and causes of a set of happenings), we shall be forced to rely more heavily on deduction than we have in our empirical studies above. Deduction enables us to unify and test our theory or its particular propositions. It also enables a theorist to work without continuing close contact with data. Thus it is not surprising, as we shall see when we examine various traditional theories of international politics, that deduction has been the favorite approach of most theorists.

The Requirements of Theory

Though we describe the contentions of traditional theorists as theories, in terms of the rigorous characterization of theory we have adopted, there are no comprehensive theories of international politics. We require that a full-fledged theory of international politics offer significant information, or contention, for testing in three particular categories. First, statically, it must tell us the nature of the units involved and their relations in international politics. Thus it must indicate the particular phenomena worth study and must describe the structure or configuration of the units in their relations that constitute these phenomena.

Second, it must offer a dynamic or a collection of determinant factors that serve to give these relations the shape they have over time. This is usually what we have in mind when we ask how the theory explains international relations.

And, third, either it must describe an explicit and elaborate evolutionary tendency in history, or it must indicate what major determinants account for the transformation of one system into another over time. Put another way, it must tell us why the structure or configuration of relations among the units changes over years, decades, or centuries, as it so obviously does. The usual candidates for such explanations are factors like technology and ideology. This feature of a theory serves to tell us how long the theory is relevant, under what conditions it is relevant, or (if it is considerably more ambitious) how it manages to remain relevant in the face of such transformations by explaining changes in the nature of relations and offering a way of translating its dynamic explanations of relations in one period into dynamic explanations of relations in another. This is perhaps the most difficult requirement to make of a theory, for it demands the successful meeting of the previous two features plus a temporal comprehensiveness that few analysts can achieve. But in any case, the theory must at the very least tell us the period to which it is relevant and indicate characteristics by which we may determine when and whether the period has ended.[2]

We would also expect a comprehensive theory to offer an implicit if not an explicit indication of the preferred research methodology for extending and testing its contentions. Not all theories will require particular methods, but most theories will derive the greatest profit from certain approaches. Thus, for example, our phenomenon approach will be of particular use in coping with theories (partial theories, in our terms) of particular types of happenings, such as wars and alliances, even over long periods of time and changes in the system. Similarly, studies of the foreign policy process and its operation will be of particular importance in coping with theories that concentrate on the national determinants of foreign policy rather than on the interaction patterns in which that policy finds expression and because of which the policy tends to be modified. Students of foreign policy and action will need to know more about the politics of the nations concerned than will those who concentrate on multinational interaction; hence each will emphasize different materials and different methods for obtaining them and testing the propositions they suggest. And it is quite likely that the ways in which a theory tells us of the units and relations involved and of the dynamic of those relations and of their transformation over time will suggest strongly to us particular research orientations.

When we conclude that all our theories are actually more like pre-theories or conceptual schemes than the deductively organized propositions that constitute comprehensive and efficient theories of the sort we seek, we are not contending that the discipline has made no progress and that we must therefore start from the beginning. Rather, we are indicating what almost all theorists themselves constantly point out: that all our products so far are in need of further elaboration, tightening, and testing. As they stand they do not tell us enough about the patterns of international politics and their determinants. As they are elaborated they will be found to differ significantly. As they are tightened they will be found occasionally to be contradictory within

[2]For seminal remarks on explanation of system transformation, see George Liska's review of Richard Rosecrance's *Action and Reaction in World Politics* (Boston: Little, Brown, 1963) entitled "Continuity and Change in International Systems" in *World Politics*, 16 (1963) 118–136.

themselves. As they are tested they will be found to vary in their accuracy as well as in their usefulness. But we may still find that they offer us promising questions and tentative conclusions about the nature of international political patterns and the causes or determinants of this interaction. And thus we shall find it useful to examine briefly some of the major theories of international politics that have not yet figured extensively in our study.

Systems Theory

We have examined the major problems in, and some of the major efforts at, theorizing about the decision stage. They include both attempting to determine the values, information, and calculation that together produce a decision, and studying the decision produced as it becomes visible in commands, implementation, and action. We have observed that because it is much easier to observe and study behavior than it is to study the determinants of behavior, many theorists of international politics have attempted to ignore these sources of action in favor of concentrating on international political interaction. These theorists primarily concerned with diplomatic activity and the interaction it produces, might ignore this values-into-action sequence entirely by "black-boxing" it — that is, by observing only what comes out of the "black box" that is the nation — or in other words, by studying only the national behavior which is observable as an input into international politics.

Systems theorists, as they are called, believe this is the only defensible approach because they assume that national foreign policy is a consequence of, or is determined by, the nature of the international system. In other words, the actions of a nation can be explained strictly in terms of the types of relations existing among nations and the place of that nation within that complex of nations and their relations. Put another way, any nation — regardless of its particular leaders, its type of government, its economic system, or other idiosyncrasies — would act the same way if it were in the same international position, that is, in the same position in the same system.

This argument is popular among some because they believe we have overemphasized the differences among nations (perhaps because of an over-concentration on ideology and psychology) and have failed to see the many similarities of the international relations of modern nation-states over the previous century and a half. In these terms, the systems orientation may serve as a helpful corrective.

Others accept—or, more accurately, assume, in order to test its validity—a systems theory of international politics because they believe we may find that all human activity and indeed all organic activity can be explained in terms of the operation of systems which share the same basic features. These are the General Systems theorists.

General Systems Theory arose out of a theory of biological systems and has since been applied to social, political, international, and any and all other systems in the world. Its underlying principle is that systems are to be found everywhere, and that all systems operate in accordance with certain laws. Several of these alleged laws are particularly important for our study of international relations.

In General Systems Theory, a system is considered to be open, or subject to inputs from without, that will in some way upset it. It also has a tendency to maintain itself in a steady state condition. This is not a state of perfect equilibrium (which would require that it be closed, or not subject to any inputs), but a state in which its basic organization is preserved despite upsetting inputs. The mechanism by which this steady state is maintained is called "homeostasis"—the same term we apply to the human body's correction within itself for upsetting inputs such as disease, heat and cold, and injury. A further important principle is that of "equifinality," which holds that the same final state may be reached in various ways because final outcomes are determined not simply by initial conditions but by conditions of inflow and outflow over a period of time.[3]

How might systems theory be applied to international politics? We find considerable interaction and interdependence among states: any foreign action by one will affect the others. Thus we are led to view these relations among states as constituting the international system. If we viewed the international

---

[3]For an account of these features of general systems theory and some consideration of how they might be applied to international relations, see Charles A. McClelland, "Applications of General Systems Theory in International Relations," in *Main Currents in Modern Thought*, 12 (1955) pp. 27–34, reprinted in James N. Rosenau, ed., *International Politics and Foreign Policy* (New York: Free Press, 1961) pp. 412–420.

system as including all states and other acting units, such as the United Nations, the international system would be basically closed (at least until the earth began to be visited by extraplanetary vehicles). Nonetheless, it would be subject to certain influences or upsets from its environment — particularly what are often referred to as "acts of God," for example, hurricanes and other meteorological phenomena. In any event, we can establish boundaries to the international system and then seek to find ways in which it tends to maintain itself in a steady state despite upsetting inputs.

Thus we find close affinities between systems theory and traditional balance of power theory. The latter suggests that whenever one nation becomes powerful enough to threaten the survival of its neighbors (perhaps through internal industrialization or else through external alliance), the neighbors will unite to return it to an appropriately weaker status relative to its opponents. In these terms, we could view the Second World War as an effort by the Allies to return Germany and Japan to nonthreatening status in the international system following their military development and territorial expansion at the expense of weaker surrounding states. Balance of power theory views war as a device consciously chosen by states to restore a desired balance when it is upset. Systems theory views such war as the system's way of returning to a steady state following the disrupting input of military development and territorial expansion which altered the equilibrium and threatened the continuation of the system in its existing organizational form.

Similarly, the explanation of crisis in systems might invoke restoration of balance by an aggrieved initiator following another setback (one of our findings about the conditions preceding the decision to initiate crisis), and might view the outcome as the system's dictates about the importance of restoration of the balance for system preservation: if the system required such a change, the initiator would prevail (as the Russians did in establishing the Berlin Wall), but if the system did not require it, the initiator would be forced to back down (as the Russians did in the missile crisis).

On the face of it, the chief characteristic of such an interpretation or explanation of international politics is the removal of volition from the participants. But what systems theory actually does is merely to shift the level of analysis from the conscious policymaking of the units (which is still essential if we are to have wars, alliances, and other happenings) to the interaction at the systemic level, and to view the happening, whether war, alliance, or whatever, in terms of its *effect* on the system — a disturbance and then a homeostatic restoration to a steady state.

Systems theory does not necessarily argue that the system in our sense causes wars, crises, alliances, and the like to happen. Indeed, systems theory attempts to avoid using the notion of causation at all, both because of the ambiguities and uncertainties we have found in it and because when we view a collection of units as an integrated system we are interested in the function each unit plays in the whole (such as waging war when the system's preservation requires it) and in the function each happening (such as war) plays in maintaining or altering the nature of the system.

Thus when we engage in systemic explanation of international politics we are not necessarily contradicting the explanations of other theories. Rather, we are shifting our focus of attention to a functioning system of interacting state units and we are shifting our focus of explanation to the level of the system as a whole. The criterion by which we would decide whether to use such an explanation would be its usefulness in aiding our understanding and our ability to predict and control — just as it would be for assessing other theories. On the face of it, we might expect, on the one hand, systems theory to be particularly good at explanation and prediction because of the comprehensiveness and exactness of its formulated laws; and on the other hand, we might expect it to be of little help in increasing the degree of control over politics because it does not focus on the actions and policies of states but on the operation of the system. Whether or not this latter weakness proves to be significant remains to be determined by further research and subsequent efforts to use systems theory for control purposes.

We have already suggested that one useful service of systems theory is to direct our attention back to the possibility that the structure of the environment in which a nation makes decisions and policies has a significant if not the most significant effect upon what those policies will be. Systems analyses of international politics tend to focus over and over again on the nature of alignments and the patterns of relations among nations in alliance. Thus there continues a major debate on whether stability is more likely to result in a bipolar world in which the two superpowers can control their allies or in a multipolar world in which the nations can realign to remove the threat of war whenever it arises. The answer is not yet clear, and the debate rages on among scholars.[4]

Again, the main characteristic of systems theory is that in shifting the emphasis to structure rather than to the policies and actions of individual states, it assumes that any state in a given position in the international system would act the same way regardless of its regime or leader. The question then is, How the system came to be the way it is? The answer to this would seem to be that the system probably arose and exists at least partly as a function of the regime and the ruler in its constituent units. In other words, a study of subsystems of the international system —alliances or even the political systems we call states—is probably essential to an understanding of how the system came to be as it is and, further, of how and why it is maintained in its existing state. Strict general systems theorists will deny this, saying that alliance and other happenings are products of pure power and position factors of the units in the system that we have discussed. But they will probably have difficulty accounting for system transformations in this way.

System transformation requires further attention. We have already considered several times the apparent trend in international politics away from a bipolar system in which all or most states are grouped around the United States and the Soviet Union, and toward a multipolar system in which some states continue to be so grouped but others form around other states, such as France, a United Europe, or Communist China. Alternately, some have suggested that the near future will see massive dealignment, in which most states disaffiliate entirely and become nonaligned. In most conceptions, such major changes as these in the structure of the system—that is, in the patterns of interaction among its constituents—actually constitute a change in the system itself, from a bipolar to a multipolar system. But even if we are

[4]For leading statements of various positions in this debate see Kenneth N. Waltz, "The Stability of a Bipolar World" in *Daedalus* (Summer 1964) 881–909; Karl Deutsch and J. David Singer, "Multipolar Power Systems and International Stability" in *World Politics*, 16 (1964) 390–406; and Richard N. Rosecrance, "Bipolarity, Multipolarity, and the Future" in *Journal of Conflict Resolution*, 10 (1966) 314–327.

not impressed by the magnitude of this change, we might still argue that the advent of nuclear weapons, which changed the ways in which military power could be used and made the threat of major war permanent and unusable, changed the nature of the system. Or we might simply argue that World War II, in which the major powers Germany and Japan were destroyed, changed the system by changing the nature of its units, or that the outbreak of the Cold War changed the system by changing the alliance patterns from unity among the United States, Britain, and the Soviet Union to unity between the United States and Britain against the Soviet Union. Which of these possible transformations of the system we choose to consider as actual transformation will depend not only on our definition of system but also on whether we focus on alliance patterns, the stakes of conflict, the types of units, or the means available (types of weapons or threats, promises, and other instruments of effective action). And which of these we choose to regard as important will depend on what we are seeking to learn about international politics at the time. But in any event, whatever our selection, we will want to be able to account for the transformation from one international system with certain features to another international system with different features.

Transformation Theories

Thus a fully acceptable theory of international politics must not only tell us about the units and their relations (the structure or configuration of the system) and the factors that bring about interaction (the dynamic, whether it be human greed, the economic quest for markets, or the warlike character of dictatorships, to cite but several of the many we have considered); it must also tell us of the determinants of transformation.

Marxist-Leninist Theory

One of the ways in which some theories explain such system transformation is to incorporate a stated revolutionary or evolutionary tendency. Of these theories, which are often called "philosophies of history," the most notable is the Marxist-Leninist theory. Marx, as we have said, paid little attention to international relations as such, but believed that history was progressing in stages demarcated by changes in the nature of the class struggle.

Lenin applied this notion to international politics by viewing imperialism as the last stage of capitalism and the cause of international war in that stage. Marxist-Leninists—those theorists who have further developed the ideas advanced by Marx and Lenin—today generally expect the class struggle to result in national revolutions toward socialism and the onset of international wars to spread national revolutions to backward countries until capitalism has been eradicated. When this happens its product, imperialism, which is the cause of war, will also vanish. The world is then expected to develop from a socialistic to a communistic society; at that point international relations (if any nations survive the withering away of their states) should be characterized by perpetual peace and worldwide welfare.

We cannot easily assess such a grand theory in a study like this. For one thing, it is not stated in terms of propositions that are explicit and limited enough to be testable. Also, even though the Soviets still adhere to the theory, there is so much disparity today between the theory and much of what transpires in this world of continually changing international politics, that we are less interested in attempting such testing. Moreover, we may suspect that we are not likely to find developmental theories that were produced before the advent of twentieth-century technology and mid-twentieth-century modes of state organization and control to provide adequate accounts of the evolution of contemporary international relations.

Developmental Theories

But if Marx is no longer in favor among academicians or other analysts of international politics outside the Communist countries, there are, nonetheless, other theorists who seek to take his place as developmental theorists. Perhaps most in vogue these years are the theories of economic development that claim to see significant relations between patterns of international relations (in other words, the nature and operation of the international system) and the state of economic development or perhaps of economic and political development of the system's constituent states.

We would probably not be surprised to find high correlations between level of economic development and type of international political action for a state, if only because the strength and hence the role of a state prove to be heavily dependent on its military might, and that military capability is a product in large part of national wealth and technological ability. Thus we find certain sorts of relations between the superpowers of high economic development and other sorts of relations between the weak and underdeveloped states and still other sorts of relations between superpowers and weak states.

One such theory relating the nature of international relations to conditions of economic development has been offered by A. F. K. Organski.[5] Organski notes that at one time, when all nations were preindustrial, the power differences between them were relatively slight. But the Industrial Revolution has changed all this, occurring in some countries before others and allowing the best-endowed countries to increase their power enormously while the unindustrialized weak nations have not been able to compensate. The result has been the creation of superpowers and major powers, some of which have been satisfied with things as they are and others of which have not. The dissatisfied strong powers are those most likely to initiate war and are most likely to succeed. The past and likely patterns of relations among the various weak and strong, satisfied and dissatisfied states can be examined for the sources of war and the conditions of peace. But we can expect additional change as more nations become industrialized and come to challenge the dominance of the present powers, until eventually all states will be industrialized (or perhaps incorporated into states that have been) and the nature of international relations will again undergo a fundamental change.

The historian F. H. Hinsley has attempted to explain the relationship between such changes and the nature of international relations — particularly the incidence of war — more explicitly. He contends:

> Even while they were being faced with unusual temptations and dangers in conditions of unusual instability, men with power were being subjected to quite unprecedented restraints. The growth of the modern state, the revolution in scientific and technical knowledge and the instability that resulted from the uneven advance of these things were developments which each produced, by what was virtually a dialectical process, its own deterrents.

[5]A. F. K. Organski, *World Politics* (New York: Knopf, 1958), esp. pp. 300–333. See also his *Stages of Political Development* (New York: Knopf, 1966).

The growth of these deterrents is almost as important, as a key to an understanding of recent times, as the processes which produced them — as significant a characteristic of the years since 1918 as the growth of the modern state, the scientific revolution and the prevailing inequality of power.[6]

The greatest political restraint, he argues, was the emergence of public opinion, which came to be a serious check on governmental action. But this was joined with the intensification of the pattern of creation of counterweapons for each new weapon, which kept weapon development fluid and even hampered weapon production. Furthermore, the governments themselves became much more professional and competent in exercising their responsibilities than they had been, so that conflict was less likely to be the result of inadvertence or miscalculation.

Hinsley grants that these developing restraints or deterrents did not suffice to avert World War II. But, in his view,

When one realizes the great rapidity and the enormous extent of the increase in men's knowledge and organization of power during the first fifty years of this century, and when one realizes also the complications and opportunities thrown up by the circumstances in which those things grew, then the surprising thing is not that that there were such violent wars and tyrannies in that period. It is that the wars and tyrannies were not more frequent and more violent even than they were. The surprising thing is not that men's uses of power were so unrestrained, but that men did not become much worse and much less wise than they had previously been.[7]

These views lead Hinsley to conclude:

What the Great Powers should do to be sensible in this situation is almost too obvious to need mention. They should profit from the stability that has slowly enforced itself upon their own relations to make a concerted effort to mitigate the internal difficulties of the backward countries and to limit the extent and the bitterness of the struggles which will set those countries against each other and against themselves.[8]

[6]F. H. Hinsley, *Power and the Pursuit of Peace* (New York: Cambridge University Press, 1963), p. 284.
[7]Hinsley, *Power and the Pursuit of Peace*, p. 280.
[8]Hinsley, *Power and the Pursuit of Peace*, p. 366.

These views all cluster around economic and technological attributes of the state as the chief determinants of the shape of international relations. And because these attributes are inevitably always changing, and have changed in massively accelerated ways in the twentieth century, these theories offer hypotheses suggesting a developmental trend in international relations that is a consequence of the economic and technological development of the states, compounded by the transnational effects and particularly by stimuli or encouragements of these internal changes.

We can hope that more study of the changes undergone by these determinants and of the changes undergone by the states may soon be better related to the changes in the shape of international relations so that we may develop comprehensive relational propositions about the effects of these determinants upon such international political happenings as war and crisis and alliance, and then test these propositions as possible contributions toward a confirmed comprehensive theory of international relations.

Progress in Theorizing   Continuing development of general theory plus increasing evaluation of proposed theory will be signs that our discipline is progressing. Students of the history of science have found that, as a science develops, unconnected causal explanations of the kind we have been attempting to construct here tend to be replaced by more comprehensive deductive systems.[9] In the words of a student of the development of the physical sciences:

> When the individual scientist can take a paradigm for granted, he need no longer, in his major works, attempt to build his field anew, starting from first principles and justifying the use of each concept introduced. That can be left to the writer of textbooks. Given a textbook, however, the creative scientist can begin his research where it leaves off and thus concentrate exclusively upon the subtlest and most esoteric aspects of the natural phenomena

---

[9]See R. B. Braithwaite, *Scientific Explanation: A Study of the Function of Theory, Probability and Law in Science* (New York: Cambridge University Press, 1953), a fascinating if somewhat involved study of many of the philosophical issues with which we have been concerned.

that concern his group. And as he does this, his research communiqués will begin to change in ways whose evolution has been too little studied but whose modern end products are obvious to all and oppressive to many. No longer will his researches usually be embodied in books addressed, like Franklin's *Experiments . . . on Electricity* or Darwin's *Origin of Species*, to anyone who might be interested in the subject matter of the field. Instead they will usually appear as brief articles addressed only to professional colleagues, the men whose knowledge of a shared paradigm can be assumed and who prove to be the only ones able to read the papers addressed to them.[10]

The study of international politics, it is quite clear, does not yet have a paradigm, or body of theory and accepted practice, on which all work in the field can be based. What we have said about our methods throughout this book could be accepted by many of those studying and writing in the field today, but would be rejected as hopelessly optimistic and visionary by others. Even some among those who would accept our social scientific orientation, emphasizing as it does theory building and examination of data, might well differ on the best possible approach to such study, and it is time we addressed that possibility more explicitly.

As we have said, all students of international politics generally confront the same world and can share the same data, and all have the same fundamental objective of understanding that world (even though some of us go beyond this objective to attempt to develop theory and to predict the future). Several fundamentally different approaches can be taken to these data, however. All of us must develop concepts that help us to manage them. Most of us talk in terms of certain basic phenomena that recur in one form or another throughout history. In our study we have singled out war, crisis, alliance, and cooperative control for special attention, among many other phenomena, like negotiations, trade, arms races, foreign aid, and the Olympic Games. Our criteria for selection have been two: the importance of the phenomena in international politics, and the extent to which they reveal fundamental aspects of the conflict and cooperation that underlie all of international politics. Some scholars would

[10]Thomas S. Kuhn. *The Structure of Scientific Revolutions* (Chicago: University of Chicago Press, 1962), pp. 19–20.

prefer to concentrate upon these other phenomena, and a few believe that it is better to go to an even deeper level and to analyze basic types of interaction—conflictual and cooperative—apart from the phenomena they constitute. Otherwise, most could agree on the importance of studying these phenomena or recurrent happenings.

But some approach them in significantly different ways. There are basically two dimensions to all study of international politics—time, and the various phenomena that constitute international politics at any time. Some students of international politics have contended that we cannot learn any reliable lessons from the past; hence the only relevant time period to study is the present or the immediate past. This approach, disparagingly referred to as the "current events" approach, cannot tell us much beyond what is happening. If it attempts to explain why, it is forced to rely on ad hoc makeshift theories that are at best underdeveloped and not likely to be either accurate or satisfactory.

Another major school, increasingly favored by some, is generally referred to as "historical sociology." One of its advocates has characterized it thus: "It is not a general theory in the sense of a global explanation or of a set of global hypotheses. . . . It is a general approach based on the following ideas. The search for timeless propositions, and the deductive method, are, at present, disappointing. We must proceed inductively; before we reach any conclusions about general trends manifest throughout history, we should resort to systematic historical research . . . ."[11] This scholar has suggested several stages of study: first, analysis of various historical situations or systems; second, comparison of historical systems to develop meaningful generalizations about aspects common to many; and, finally, comparisons between domestic and international political systems.

Not only does this proposal sound interesting, it is clear from preceding chapters that it could prove useful for our purposes. But it is also difficult in that it would require massive quantities of human activity over long periods of time, during which we could not expect to make any real progress on the particular questions that intrigue us and plague policymakers. Furthermore, in its early stages it is the kind of work that historians could and probably should do. And finally, it presumes consider-

[11]Stanley H. Hoffmann, *Contemporary Theory in International Relations* (Englewood Cliffs, N.J.: Prentice-Hall, 1960), p. 174.

able sophistication. For if we begin by studying one system, we cannot say anything about it with any confidence unless we can base our statements on a comparison. This is a point often missed but easily understood. If we are trying to discover why our world today works as it does and we develop some propositions about conditions producing certain happenings, we cannot have any idea whether or not they actually do have such effects without comparative study of other circumstances or of other cases. Otherwise we might, as a hypothetical example, believe that the creation of a second American football league has significantly affected the nature of recent war. Only by noticing that war has also changed (at least in some ways) when we had but one — or even better, when we had none — can we begin to suspect that other factors are the important ones. This particular example reveals nothing about international politics, but it illustrates the necessity of comparative study from the outset — something that makes the historical sociological approach even harder to succeed at than at first appears. This is an argument partly about its possibility, but mostly about its likely promise in the near future. And the argument suggests that (although we shall welcome whatever discoveries may eventually emerge from it) it is not highly promising now. We recognize that our approach will not produce a comprehensive general deductive theory of international politics tomorrow either, but it should produce a greater immediate understanding of the ways of operating with data as well as of the nature and sources of major types of international political happenings. For as we develop our theories of phenomena we can see our progress, test our early conclusions, and reformulate our propositions and theories in ways that are apt to encourage further progress, while those engaged in historical sociology must in large measure continue their massive efforts without such reinforcement because progress will require extensive efforts before it becomes visible, and longer efforts before it becomes usable.

The Prospect   There seems, as we have said before,
for Theory   little prospect for the time being of
developing a microtheory of international politics which focuses on interaction as the unit of description and as the event to be explained. Interaction, we have said,

takes varied forms, depending on whether it involves threat/ response, promise/response, exchange, or other types. Our task in developing a theory of international politics at this level would require explaining the occurrence of each of these types of inter-action and their combination into the happenings with which we are familiar: negotiation, alliance, crisis, war, trade, aid, and so on. Ultimately, we may hope for such a detailed and compre-hensive theory, similar to that of particle physics, which is still being developed to replace or transcend Newtonian physics. We may well find that there are aspects of international politics which we cannot adequately handle without descending to such a micro-theoretical level — not just to know what goes on in war, for in-stance, but to understand why one party wins a war and another loses. Such a descent does not now appear necessary, but that may be because we are so far from even a theory of war — let alone a theory of international interaction — that we cannot know how incomprehensible some aspects of international politics may prove. But until we have made more progress at our middle-range or phenomenon level, we cannot find out what will con-tinue to puzzle us and perhaps force us either to the interaction unit level on the one hand, or to the systems level, perhaps via historical sociology, on the other. It is our chosen gamble to per-sist on the middle-range level of phenomena and attempt to make our progress there, at least until any major limitations it may force on us become much clearer.

But what do we now know? What have we come to believe and suspect through our studies at this level? We have, first, some general beliefs about the likely shape or form or general content of international political theory.

It is clear from both our own studies here and the literature reporting those of others that any satisfactory theory will have to be a multifactor theory. If there is a single factor that basically determines all international political happenings (such as, per-haps, economy or man's nature), it is so remote and indirect in its role or effects that it cannot be useful to us until we have de-veloped a comprehensive theory showing precisely what these indirect effects are and what routes they take. It seems quite clear that a variety of factors or conditions, such as the patterns of alignment, the capabilities of the parties, and their internal poli-tics, will contribute to the shaping of any particular happening. It may be that ultimately each of these can be traced to some fundamental principle. Perhaps they could be reduced to economy through the role of economic development in alignment, the impact of technology and resources on capability, and that of popular needs and desires for goods on national policy. Perhaps we shall be able to discern a developmental pattern in the place of economy in such determination so that we may deduce the nature and importance of each of these factors from knowledge of the state of international economic development and application of our general theory of economy. But until we do we shall be little helped by knowing that ultimately economic conditions determine the various factors which in their turn determine the occurrence of war and alliance.

The point of all this is severalfold. On the one hand, although such a single-factor approach may ultimately provide an organizing focus for a general theory of international politics, or even of all politics, it is clear that it will take much investigation to reach a point where we could even formulate such a theory. Also, the way to reach that point must be by either a haphazard deduction from a general assumption of some form of economic determinism (which has proved dangerous in the past to theorists as great as Marx and Lenin and Schumpeter) or piecemeal investigation of the sort we attempt. The effort to reduce politics to economics, like other efforts of reduction, such as that to reduce everything to psychological mind-states, or even to the neural bases of such mind-states, is an extremely difficult task as well as a hindrance to economy of effort. In other words, if there is such a basic factor, until we have mapped its effects, we may be able to discover regularities at higher levels of abstraction that will enable us to do the same things with our theory (such as apply it in explanation, prediction, and even control) without delving to the level of that basic factor about which we know so little.

This reminds us that our basic objective is uncovering regularities which can be used with confidence in explanation, prediction, and control. If such regularities are at macrocosmic levels, such as patterns of alignment, national capabilities, and internal politics, they will perhaps be more easily used, and perhaps even more easily understood.

We may *then* wish to inquire why such patterns do hold — why there are these certain relations between alignment, capability, and politics on the one hand, and wars and crises on the other. But we may be able to use our knowledge even before we can answer those additional questions, just as physicists were able to use complicated physical principles long before they could offer any final answers about why they were accurate. Ultimately, it is a question of allocation of intellectual resources, which can be resolved only by reference to our values or objectives. To be more certain about what will follow from given conditions, and therefore to be able to predict and control — we rate these higher on our priorities than to be able to reduce all factors ultimately to economics or psychology or neural brainstates or particle physics. Consequently, we are prepared to settle at this time for theories that deal in units at such high levels of abstraction as interaction; or alignment, capability, and politics; or even war, alliance, crisis, and cooperative control. We reserve to ourselves the right — indeed, the intellectual duty — not to be fully satisfied with what we find out in our studies, and to keep pressing on toward more advances. In doing so we shall need help from economists, psychologists, physiologists, and physicists, even though none of these has yet solved all the relevant problems to enable us to attempt to reduce so complex and macrocosmic a field as international politics to such fundamental factors.

On the face of it, this may seem grounds for unhappiness and discontent. Actually, it should be cause for relief, for it suggests that many of our worries about the unscientific and backward nature of a field like international politics miss the point; we are or should be working at higher levels of abstraction than are the natural scientists, even other social scientists. All social scientists, including us, are concerned with interaction; but international politics often encompasses the economic, national political, and other such types of phenomena with which these other social sciences are primarily concerned. This is one of the reasons why we may suspect our theories to be multifactor ones — at least at this stage. For international politics is made up of a great variety of happenings (war, alliance, and crisis, and so on), which in their turn are constituted by a great variety of national happenings (policies and actions on many matters undertaken by many states). Thus, we are interested in and may be helped in our research by other disciplines — particularly political science, economics, sociology, social psychology, individual psychology, and even anthropology.

In addition to the physical and social sciences, mathematics increasingly may help us in our study, as we further apply existing mathematical tools to our data. Our theories are not generally quantitative, and critics of social scientific theory often point out this disparity between the social and physical science, arguing that social science cannot be scientific unless it is quantified. But this point seems somewhat mistaken.

If our variables can be quantified and if we understand the ways in which they are related, we may be able to apply mathematical tools to their analysis and thereby develop implications which our limited human minds might not perceive alone; and we would in any event be able to do so much more quickly with mathematical tools than without. Much can be done in this direction, as work in the last decade has shown.[12] There is still considerable doubt in many minds as to whether those things that can be quantified at this time actually reveal anything significant when studied. For example, some have questioned whether the quantitative study of communications flows (letters, telegrams, telephone calls) really tells us anything interesting about international relations. Others have developed some propositions about these relations and have attempted to test them with such data.

Several things must be quite clear today to any observer of international studies — or of social science in general. First, there will be many more efforts and much greater success at quantification and mathematical analysis in the future — and thus we shall later be in a better position to judge their worth. And second, as Anatol Rapoport (a mathematical biologist very much interested in international relations) has reminded us more generally, "the range of logical disciplines now called 'mathematics' has enormously increased, both in techniques and in the variety of conceptualizations, so that any inadequacy of classical mathematics for dealing with problems of social science can by no means be taken as an indication of the inapplicability of mathematics in principle.[13]

Until we are better able to quantify our data and to express

---

[12]See the various works by K. W. Deutsch, B. M. Russett, R. J. Rummel, A. S. Banks and R. B. Textor, *et al.*, cited elsewhere in the text. And see J. David Singer, ed., *Quantitative International Politics* (New York: Free Press, 1967) for some specific short studies relying heavily on quantitative methods.

[13]Anatol Rapoport, "Various Meanings of 'Theory'," *American Political Science Review*, 52 (1958) 972-988 at 977.

our propositions in precise form, we shall be limited in the extent to which we can ask for assistance from mathematics, and we shall be limited in the accuracy and manipulability of our propositions themselves. We are presently confined largely to statements of what we call "tendency," taking the form "X will tend to occur under conditions a, b, c . . . ." If we can develop appropriate indices of the various factors we are particularly concerned with (hostility, concern, commitment, war potential, and intensity of interaction, for example) we may be able to quantify our data and then our propositions or hypotheses so that we can arrive at probabilistic statements of the form "X will occur in P percent of the cases under conditions a, b, c . . . ." Formulating our variables into quantitative entities to make our indices and propositions satisfactory may be useful in training us in the application of mathematics, as well as in heightening our interest in improving our ability to find opportunities for such use. However, it may mislead us into believing that we can be more accurate than in fact we can, for most of us probably share a tendency to believe that anything quantified is more accurate and more worthy of faith or confidence than something expressed verbally. We must thus at the same time be both wary of and eager for quantification.

Indeed, this intellectual approach is perhaps the most appropriate attitude for us to take not only about quantification but about the development of the field as a whole. We have seen that we can begin to make clear and useful progress only when we are willing to state trivialities as well as profundities, to venture guesses as well as certainties. But if we are to combine the pedestrian but necessary with the extravagant yet possible in developing propositions and in combining propositions into theories, we must always be on guard against taking any particular contention to be accurate until we have satisfactorily confirmed it. We do not expect, nor could we ever achieve, certainty. Thus we must always recognize—as does the physical scientist—the possibility that we may be wrong. In addition, we must always be open to and encourage further testing of our work in order to be more justifiably confident of our conclusions and the progress which they mark. Much of the previous work on international politics, although essentially at least as tentative as ours, has been expressed as certainty or stated in a form in which it is difficult to discern the grounds on which it is to be believed. It is far better to have statements that are explicitly tentative, subject to constant revision and improvement if not absolute confirmation or dis-confirmation, than it is to have statements that contain implicit inaccuracies stated as if they were certain. We must be willing to venture educated guesses as well as to make continuing efforts to test and improve those guesses if we are to be able to move from suspicion toward knowledge as individual scholars and as a discipline.

As is clear from our previous work, we are best at "rational policy" analysis—that is, attempting to find reasons for a ra-tional state to act as it has, or suggesting rational action for a state in need of advice. But we know that empirical knowledge, our analytical abilities, and our understanding of the dynamics of international politics are still so underdeveloped that these efforts may be both misleading and inaccurate. This leads us to attempt our type of analysis focused on the conditions under which the major phenomena of international politics occur and those under which the policy decisions that bring them about are made.

In four previous chapters we examined war, crisis, alliance, and cooperative control. We did not consider the other major happenings: arms races, subversion (including assassination, terrorism, and sabotage), threats, espionage, and ideological, economic, athletic, and cultural competition; nor did we consider diplomatic relations, negotiation, trade, aid, cultural exchange, travel, collective security, and peace-keeping. While the former group is primarily competitive and the latter collaborative, each element in these two categories contains conflictual and coopera-tive aspects. The competitive includes cooperation basically because ultimately the very existence of the parties is at stake, and the collaborative includes competition because there are various differing states in action and scarce resources at issue.

We could and should go on to develop partial theories of each of these fundamental types of happening—just as we should continue the efforts only begun here to advance our theoretical knowledge of the four phenomena we have examined in more detail. We took varying approaches to that examination in order to indicate the several states of our knowledge about the four types and to suggest various ways of coping with differing states of knowledge and available evidence. Thus, we took crisis, which is still largely unstudied, and began the task of developing propo-sitions about its occurrence and termination. Then we took war, which has, if anything, been overstudied, and examined briefly a great variety of theories about its occurrence. When we studied alliance we began with an explanation of one instance and then attempted to generalize it and then test it against a variety of other instances. And when we studied cooperative control we took a phenomenon, arms control, which is largely unprecedented, and attempted to speculate, on the basis of its requirements and what else we know of international politics, about the conditions that would be likely to induce nations to seek it.

Although in each of these cases we made significant, if varying, progress, in none were we able to develop or find a full-bodied theory of the particular phenomenon. In each we endeavored to point to possible ways of formulating such theories and to suggest ways of increasing the likelihood of success in such ventures whatever the approach. We cannot claim to have made substantial contributions toward the development of a satisfactory international political theory. But that is not an appropriate task for a book like this one. We have succeeded in uncovering and examining the problems that are inherent in developing a satisfactory theory of international politics and the problems that need not encumber such study. It is but a relatively short step, of the sort which any student can take through further study of these phenomena along the lines suggested, to the development of interesting and promising partial theories of these phenomena. It then requires care and imagination to combine these into an interesting and promising theory of international politics. No single effort will complete the task even for those wholly in sympathy with our approach. But then, no such effort can yet complete the task even in the more advanced physical sciences either. Any such effort can make a significant contribution to the advancement of the discipline, whether it is made by the lifetime scholar in a research institute or university, or by an imaginative and diligent student in a university or college. One of the exciting and fascinating features of the study of international politics is that anyone can quite rapidly reach the frontier and understand and contribute to the work being done there to advance the discipline. In this field more than in most others, the student and the teacher are engaged in the same activity and can assist each other as collaborators; the chief difference between them is the somewhat greater factual knowledge and the heightened consciousness and more fully developed skill of the teacher. This book, like the teacher, has endeavored to present those requisite skills in a way that makes them easily transferable to the student so that he may begin to employ them to his own satisfaction and hopefully to the advancement of the field of international politics.

But his opportunities do not stop there, for when he has discovered the contributions of others and perhaps even made some himself, he may attempt to apply the relevant theories to the problems that offer the greatest challenge to us as scholars and as citizens — predicting events and attempting to contribute to our ability to influence their outcomes. Thus, as we conclude our examination of international political analysis we shall consider briefly what problems arise and what opportunities exist in prediction and control.

PART V

APPLICATIONS

chapter 14
Prediction

The Need to Control Events   When American policymakers were informed that the Soviet Union was placing missiles and bombers in Cuba, they had to determine what effects the action was likely to have and what the United States should do in response. They had to predict the likely effects of the action by employing their knowledge of the situation and their theory of international politics. And in order to select a response by the same general process they had to predict the likely effects of the various alternatives they could imagine. The object of all this prediction—beyond merely satisfying their curiosity and perhaps removing some of the vague fears engendered by the unknown and unexpected— was control: using knowledge to affect the course of future events. But the possibility of control is heavily dependent on the ability to predict. Prediction and control are the two major applications of our knowledge and understanding of international politics.

Prediction   Like most human activities, prediction
in Everyday Life   is always done but rarely done well.
Anyone can predict, but few can pre-
dict accurately. Yet, even accuracy in prediction is not enough:
we need prediction that is also *credible* — that can be believed or
accepted either because it seems likely to prove accurate or because the predictor is believed to be good at his task of predicting. The most accurate prediction in the world will be of little
use if we do not have enough confidence in it to act on it.

Almost everyone claims that men cannot forecast events,
or at least cannot forecast accurately. Nonetheless, we do predict, implicitly or explicitly. There should be little need to sub-
stantiate this fact. One publicist has written that "most men
probably make no attempt to predict even the immediate future.
But in order to live, men must at least implicitly predict the future. This sort of implicit prediction, made every day by nearly
everybody, shows itself most plainly in policy, individual or
group."[1]

"All our dealings with our fellow-men are based on some
kind of prediction of their actions," Robert MacIver, the famed
sociologist, has written. "We can go further and say that all knowledge is, in so far, predictive, since we know things and persons
not as momentary apparitions but through time."[2] In other words,
when we say that something *is* true, we are actually predicting
that something which was true when we observed or learned it
will *remain* true into the present in which we talk about it, and
perhaps into the future. And so, in the words of economist Simon
Kuznets, "The choice is not between making and not making an
extrapolation into the future; it is between making the projections
in overt and sometimes quantitative terms, and proceeding by feel
and by faith. Even inaction implies some picture of the future."[3]

Even though, as Ernest Nagel, the philosopher of science,
has written, "nothing comparable to quantum mechanics is available in the social sciences upon which to rest the assumption

[1] Ferdinand Lundberg, *The Coming World Transformation* (Garden City: Doubleday, 1963), p. 40.
[2] Robert MacIver, *Social Causation* (Boston: Ginn, 1939), p. 239.
[3] Simon Kuznets, "Concepts and Assumptions in Long-Term Projections of National Product," in Simon Kuznets *et al.*, *Long Range Economic Projection* (Princeton, N.J.: Princeton University Press, 1954), p. 36.

that human events are theoretically unpredictable,"[4] it is correct to say that man cannot foretell all the future in minute detail nor can he even foretell everything about all of some narrow temporal segment of the future. But anyone who continues to declare unequivocally that one cannot predict the future is in fact doing just that. For the very statement that "one cannot predict the future" contains an ill-concealed prediction that there will be a future, and that the future will be found to be such that one cannot say anything accurate about it in advance. So the important questions are neither, Can we predict? (which we must answer with a qualified Yes) nor even, What can we predict? (which we cannot yet answer), but rather, How do we predict? and How might we improve our prediction?

Obstacles   If we had an accurate, comprehensive
to Prediction   general theory of international politics,
prediction would pose little difficulty.
We would describe our present world and then apply the propositions of the theory to it and thereby project pictures of international relations as far forward as we desire. Of course, such comprehensive prediction is impossible now, and may well always prove to be so. One obstacle to it — the massiveness of the data and the difficulty of their manipulation — could probably be removed by a computer. But the other problem, developing the general theory of international politics, cannot be so easily resolved with or without a computer.

Indeed, our efforts thus far should have indicated several obstacles to such theory development. We can say significant things about various aspects of international politics — statements generally couched in propositions, perhaps loosely linked with one another in a suggestive if not rigorous general theoretical framework. But we are very far indeed from anything resembling a general theory of international politics that is deductively organized and that is comprehensive enough to enable us to predict most or all of those international political happenings we are interested in. This is not reason to abandon our quest. Just the

[4]Ernest Nagel, *The Structure of Science* (New York: Harcourt, Brace & World, 1961), p. 598.

reverse. For it should be clear by now that we can make a number of interesting and valuable statements about international relations, and at the same time make progress toward more comprehensive theory.

The Recalcitrance of the Subject

The underdeveloped state of our theory may not be the only obstacle to satisfactory or promising prediction. It is often argued that there are features of the materials that we are predicting and that actors themselves are employing that make prediction particularly difficult, and we must consider this possibility.

Among the materials of international politics are "agents" or "actors" and "tools" or "resources." The agents include individuals, groups, the population, deciders and leaders, states, and groups of states (alliances, supersovereignties, and condominia). It is sometimes argued that we can concentrate our predictive and policymaking attentions on only one category of these agents, the deciders and leaders. This reduces prediction to reliance on psychological data, and forces the predictor to be concerned with expectations and intentions. This sort of prediction may prove easier than any other single-cause prediction, and will quite likely prove easier than most possible, multiple-cause predictive schemata. But it may prove quite dangerous if, as would be expected from studies in other disciplines such as business administration, expectations and intentions derive primarily from objective conditions; thus this single-cause approach is based on an inversion of the primary causal sequence. The danger lies, of course, in prediction that is to be used in policymaking, for causal sequence (especially when it is to be altered and interrupted or otherwise influenced) is of great importance there. Other single-cause or multiple-cause predictive approaches have been suggested, of course, each based on the hope and presumption that at the international level of human intercourse it will prove possible to abstract from some of the complexity which hampers accurate and extensive prediction at lower levels.

Among the materials with which nations may act are geography, natural resources, population, technology, arms, and economies — the milieu or environment in which men conduct their international relations.[5] In general, changes in these elements over time are relatively easy to predict by extrapolation (a method we shall examine below). Herman Kahn, the civilian military strategist who has spent much of his life studying these, has remarked that "some kinds of trends you really can understand. You really do have a good idea of what the population will be 20 or 30 years from now. You have a reasonably good idea of what technology will be like 5, 10, 15 years from now. You have a very good idea of what a lot of gross national products will be like 5, 10, 15 years from now. You have very little idea of what the political situation will be but you have some idea of some of the possibilities."[6]

But such material predictions assume a relatively stable political situation, for the future will be made of situations and decisions as well as agents and resources. Situations generally call for decisions. And if it is difficult to project agents and resources and to foresee situations, how much more difficult it is to predict decisions without this information. Theodore Sorensen, President Kennedy's assistant, in his brief account of *Decision-Making in the White House*, suggested the magnitude of these problems. "In these last two years, for example, the President has had to judge whether this nation's resumption of nuclear tests would increase or diminish the prospects for a nuclear test ban treaty, whether new military assistance to the Congo would assure its pacification or bring it back into the Cold War, whether our quarantine around the island of Cuba would lead to Soviet submarine warfare, to a Berlin blockade, or to Soviet ships turning back."[7] And if the problem is this great for a man making the decision with all the intelligence resources of the United States government at his command, how much more difficult will it be for a predictor without access to all that information?

Perhaps less difficult than one might at first expect. It is

[5]A useful study of these, which even examines the problems of prediction, is Harold and Margaret Sprout, *The Ecological Perspective on Human Affairs, with Special Reference to International Politics* (Princeton, N.J.: Princeton University Press, 1966).

[6]Interview with Herman Kahn by Richard Hudson, *War/Peace Report* (March 1963) p. 3–7.

[7]Theodore Sorensen, *Decision-Making in the White House* (New York: Columbia University Press, 1963), p. 40.

both difficult and dangerous to generalize about the ease of prediction. It may vary in time span, detail demanded, and accuracy
required, in addition to the obvious differences in the nature and
scope of their subject matter. There are three basic types of predictions: the career or life cycle (birth, life, death) of something;
the characteristics of something at some time; and the doing of
something at some time or by some time. In general, it is probably
accurate to say that the prediction of each of these is more difficult than the prediction of the one preceding it.

The Particular Problems of Predicting International Politics

But it is the difficulty attendant to all prediction, or are there
things about international relations which differentiate them as
subjects of prediction from other familiar subjects like national
politics, economic development, and business? To answer this
conclusively would require comparative study of international
society, national politics, economic development, and business,
both as discrete aspects of life and as subjects of prediction. But
the enormity of this task has not deterred numerous scholars
from agreeing with Quincy Wright, one of the fathers of and leading figures in the study of international politics in the twentieth
century:

> The number of statesmen controlling the behavior of states has
> always been small and in the modern world has tended to become
> smaller with the result of diminishing the reliability of predictions
> based on a statistical analysis of their behavior. But on the other
> hand, the instability of the equilibrium, considering the high degree
> of freedom of states from external conditions and the imperfect
> organization of governments to manipulate such equilibria based
> on knowledge of the policies of governments. In fact, the internal
> stability of most states and their external independence has been
> diminished by the shrinking of the world with the consequence
> that predictions based on political knowledge have become pro-
> gressively less reliable.[8]

But are international relations so much more difficult to
predict because the actors are so much freer than are corre-
sponding actors in other fields? There are grounds for reasonable

[8]Quincy Wright, *The Study of International Relations* (New York: Appleton-
Century-Crofts, 1955), p. 115.

and substantial doubt. It is generally true that foreign policy is left to the discretion of officials not responsible directly to national political machinery. But this prima-facie independence seems to be severely limited by a number of factors that tend toward persistence or consistency over time. These factors may be divided for convenience into four classes.[9] The first includes what sociologists often refer to as "institutionalized conduct" (such as the great likelihood that the United States will elect a president every four years).[10] The second class is what is often termed the "operational code" (the habitual conduct that characterizes the Soviet Politburo and "the game of politics" in France, for example)[11] and which the French call la réglé du jeu ("the rules of the game"). The third group might be termed the "operational system" and includes the underlying source of real and permanent power (such as social class in the view of the Marxists). And the fourth is often spoken of as the "necessary structure" of any government — the essential machinery that permits the government to function effectively.

These four classes of perceived regularities assume unchanging basic realities in any society, including international society. Thus they will be more useful in the prediction of day-to-day developments than in the prediction of longer-run futures. But if such basic continuities do persist, they will permit much more detailed prediction by allowing greater concentration on lesser-scale data.

These factors would seem most applicable to analysis and prediction of governmental operation, and, as we have seen, much of our interest as students of international politics is in such governmental operation. The question, then, is whether or not there are general assumptions concerning international continuity (especially in dealings with highly-traditionalized nations, such as Britain, France, Germany, and, increasingly, the Soviet Union) that gave birth to rules of diplomatic practices and that might be called "rules for cohabitation" (especially in our nuclear age),

[9]This classification is offered by the American sociologist Daniel Bell in "Twelve Modes of Prediction," *Daedalus* (Summer 1964) 845–880.
[10]Bertrand de Jouvenel, the French political and social theorist, terms these "structural certainties." See his *The Art of Conjecture* (New York: Basic Books, 1967).
[11]See the two studies by Nathan Leites, *The Operational Code of the Politburo* New York: McGraw Hill, 1951) and *The Game of Politics in France* (Stanford, Calif.: Stanford University Press, 1959).

possibly including recognition of spheres of influence and appreciation of international stability, and that thereby severely
limit the freedom of choice of policymakers. Such persistent
regularities provide an important corrective to the view that decisionmakers are free of constraint.[12] Indeed, there seem to be
further constraints within most if not all nations that produce
very conservative attitudes toward "national interests" and thereby constrain international "adventurism" and "wheeling and
dealing."

The important point for the moment is that there is considerable reason to question the hasty assertion by many observers
of international relations that they are so much more difficult to
predict than other fields of social scientific inquiry. This is not
to deny that they are very hard to predict accurately, or even
that in some ways (particularly because they involve so many
differing participants) they may be more difficult. But the task
is probably not nearly so hopeless as some have suggested.

Our problems in predicting international politics have not
been limited to the nature of these materials with which we are
dealing. Another problem has been the inadequate availability
of data to be used in prediction, however we may do it. The greatly
increasing research on international politics and foreign policy
promises more data, and the increasing exploitation of technological advances in data storage and retrieval (through the use
of computers and linkages to centralized data banks somewhat
like central libraries), promises to improve the accessibility of
data. But we are still left with the problem of methods and techniques of prediction.

Prediction without Comprehensive Theory

The obvious approach to prediction—
application of our general comprehensive theory of international politics
—will not be sufficient until such
theory has been further developed. In the meantime we must
make do with what we have and can do. What predictive weapons
do we have in our arsenal?

---

[12]For an extensive study of such constraints, both international and domestic, as
they confront the United States today, see Stanley H. Hoffmann, *Gulliver's Troubles, or The Setting of American Foreign Policy* (New York: McGraw-Hill, 1968).

Prophecy

Prophecy is the oldest, and perhaps still the most used, method of prediction—based either on transcendental revelation or on terrestrial inspiration.[13] It has been applied mainly in religion, artistic creation, and technical invention, rather than in social science. Its chief weakness from the policymaker's point of view is its noncredible grounding, and from our point of view, the fact that it cannot be replicated.

Chance

A second but also unpromising method is the employment of chance (in the form, say, of coin flipping). Resort to this method might be sensible if we discovered that we had no useful information on the prospects for the future or that the predictive methods we had been using were mistaken or incredible more than half the time. But even in such instances the use of chance is limited (and its outcome probably distorted) by the necessity of casting possibilities in terms of yes-or-no or equivalent possible outcomes —outcomes that must in some other way be forseen.

Intuition

A third, and still generally unsatisfactory, method of prediction is the use of intuition—some kind of guesswork or "feeling" that is presumably based on evidence and principles which the predictor is unable (or perhaps unwilling) to divulge or specify. Allowing for large variations in the degree of evidence involved, this is the kind of prediction that most individuals attempt, and many scholars and policymakers undertake too often. Of course, the relative usefulness of the method, as well as the susceptibility of both the evidence and fellow students to this approach, depends on the nature of the material. Thus, for instance, there continues to be considerable debate in psychology over the relative merits of this kind of clinical prediction versus what is often called statistical (or actuarial) prediction.[14]

[13]A history of prophecy and its practice can be found in Richard Lewinsohn, *Science, Prophecy, and Prediction* (New York: Harper & Row, 1961).
[14]See, for example, P. E. Meehl, *Clinical versus Statistical Prediction: A Theoretical Analysis and a Review of the Evidence* (Minneapolis: University of Minnesota Press, 1954).

Analogy

A fourth, and somewhat more promising, tool of prediction is analogy, the search in past and present precedent for comparable cases and conditions that will permit reasoning that what happened in one case will happen in another similar case. Historical analogies are the most frequent and clearest examples, but much prediction by sampling works on the same principle, seeking typical samples and extrapolating from them to what it is hoped are analogous individuals or cases. But, as we have seen, it is usually difficult to find historical instances that correspond satisfactorily to present instances; hence this pure analogy method of prediction is not often sufficiently helpful.

Correlation

A fifth (and teasing) method of prediction is correlation. We sometimes discover notable correlations between the occurrence or development of one thing and the occurrence or development of another, even though there is no apparent satisfactory explanation for this. (This is, clearly, a very much simplified instance of the kind of analysis we began with in our efforts to develop international political theoretical propositions.) Examples are not hard to find. Among the more intriguing are correlations between sunspots and the business cycle, and, generally somewhat more regular, those between the lunar cycle and the female menstrual cycle. The absence of acceptable and convincing explanation may lessen the credibility of predictions based on such correlates, but they may still be used to predict those phenomena with which they are correlated. Needless to say, we would hope to find more useful correlations than those just mentioned. Indeed, it is quite possible that there are such correlations, some of which may be quite unperiodic, which only remain undiscovered because of the prima-facie incredibility of predictions based upon such apparently inexplicable coincidences.

Projection

Perhaps the most widely used and varied type of prediction is projection of the present, generally into one possible or expected future. Man is, sensibly, inclined to see the future as, if not like the present, only a distortion of it. One can arbitrarily divide the factors that compose the present into categories by their rate of change as well as the direction and magnitude of change. In effect this focuses attention on the crucial variables that can be expected to determine the extent to which the future will be different from the present.

Most such efforts involve the application of *models*—that is, partial representations of conditions on the basis of certain stated assumptions. A model for prediction will be a collection of believed relevant factors and relations, based on the assumption that they and they alone are needed to project an accurate picture of the future. Thus a model for prediction is in effect a collection of conditional hypotheses such that if the stated conditions hold (that is, if the abstracted variables and their linkages are in fact determinant and the data added about the present and past are accurate) then the projected future should come to pass. Of course, the data about the past and present that are fed into the model can be either unique facts or statistical aggregates (which can accomodate divergences), depending on the desires of the model and the nature of the information available.

For analytical purposes, we might distinguish three varying types of projective models. The first is built to extrapolate persistence or consistency. It will assume those factors that will persist over time, such as the structural certainties, operational codes, operational system, and necessary structures examined earlier. This sort of model will be more useful in predicting day-to-day developments, for it assumes these realities to be unchanging and permits us to concentrate on lower-level data that will vary over even such shorter time periods.

A second type of model extrapolates trends. Such models are used for studies of technology, population, voting, and economic development, among other topics. They have the advantage of being relatively easy to employ. All that is required is selection of the relevant constituents, plotting of recent data, and extrapolation of whatever trends are to be found in the data. The model can be sophisticated through the decomposition of the present into groups of factors with relatively similar rates of change, such as those factors with intrinsic stability that can be treated as short-term constants (like climate, topography, language, cultural tradition, and bureaucracy); those factors susceptible to linear evolution up or down (for example, population, communication, education, skilled labor, and capital); those factors that are somewhat cyclical (like, perhaps, the formation of political elites, the strength of the government, and war); and those factors that for our purposes and with our available knowledge seem to be completely fortuitous and unforeseeable (short-term objectives of political entrepreneurs, foreign pressures, and natural calamities, and so on).[15] This sort of model can also handle sophisticated realities in which some factors are known to change more rapidly than others. But it has one basic limitation: it assumes continuity in the trends it projects and it assumes a closed system. It is therefore unable to anticipate and deal with disturbance of the trends from outside, any more than it can cope with those factors it considers to be completely fortuitous and unforeseeable. The only variation it might allow would be variation around the trend lines, and how we would project that is not clear unless we found the variation to be itself regular.

This important weakness suggests the third basic type of trend projection model, which includes major foreseen changes in projected trends (and may therefore be forced to project several possible futures should there be several possible changes foreseen). To the extent that major changes are indeed foreseeable when the basic approach is extrapolation of trends, this model should be preferable to the other two. But it would be optimistic to expect to discover, recognize, and correctly handle such external changes when employing such a model.

It is because the weaknesses of these trend models are so clear that we hope to be able to develop theories that would enable prediction of a more complex and reliable sort. Even without general theory, we might be able to find and employ theories that are less complex in their substance and might therefore more easily (if also probably less reliably) be used for prediction. An example of this type, which tends to deal with fundamental problems, first causes, and other such single-minded theories of society, politics, and international relations, is the Marxist use of the "relations of production" to predict the social structure of a society. A second type of theory projects development by stages of a sort that are in some sense preordained and therefore previewable. In this category are the theory of inevitable progress and the theory that everything is cyclical.

---

[15]This type of model is discussed in Bell, "Twelve Modes of Prediction."

A third type of projection is accomplished by "acting out" the future in compressed time and abstracted reality by computer simulation or by "people gaming." These activities are not standard predictive endeavors. The problems of simulating people alone, to say nothing of people in international relations, have not been satisfactorily resolved. But such machine simulation does have the promise of permitting a systematic effort to combine different projections manipulatively to produce a variety of multifactor outcomes as well as to allow discovery of a variety of routes to the same outcome. Such an approach is still in its infancy, but may eventually make major contributions to our predictive abilities. The usefulness of political and military gaming—in which people play the roles of decisionmakers—seems generally to be in educating participants about the present and about procedural conduct, rather than in predicting the future. Nonetheless, both these devices can produce predictions, and we may hope that as they are perfected their predictions will prove more accurate.[16]

Invention

A significantly different approach to prediction, used widely but on a somewhat smaller scale by strategic analysts, might be termed "invention." The predictor here conceives of all possible futures (such as every conceivable type of first-strike attack the United States might be made to absorb by an adversary, or every conceivable surprise attack the United States might launch) and then attempts to assign probabilities to each possibility, generally through the application of the criteria of conceivability, consistency, comparison with other instances, and so on, and through the application of other predictive methods, such as intuition and projection, to each possibility. Clearly, especially in the practical application of this approach, there can be great similarities between the predictions fostered by this method and those by some other predictive efforts. But the emphasis is on the early stage of conceiving all possible futures, so that an unconventional or less likely possibility is not inadvertently overlooked. There are obvious practical limitations to such a predictive ap-

[16]On simulation and gaming see Harold Guetzkow *et al., Simulation in International Relations: Developments for Research and Teaching* (Englewood Cliffs, N.J.: Prentice-Hall, 1963), among many other sources.

proach. But the burden might be eased if typologies of possibilities were derived and examined in classes.

Negation

One type of possible prediction which is scarcely ever considered but often, if imperfectly, undertaken is prediction by negation. This approach entails predicting what cannot and will not happen and thereby eliminating the unlikely futures in order to narrow the range of possibilities (even if they are not actually formulated) to the most possible ones. If we begin with all possible futures the approach is comparable to the inventive approach just delineated, except that it does not require such scrupulous attention to so many possibilities; and of course we may not begin with a list at all, waiting, rather, until the range in which possibilities will be found is quite narrow to devote our effort to careful depiction of future possibilities.

Dialectic

The final basic type of prediction is the dialectic. This, we must recognize, is a sectarian approach that will be quite unacceptable to nondialectitians. It suggests that each happening or situation will in some (probably mysterious) way give birth to or stimulate the production of its antithesis. Because of its limited appeal and the lack of careful accounts of its possible employment, there is little point in our considering it here at length. But we should recognize that there are those who may use the principle of the dialectic to predict the future. We shall be interested to see whether it offers accurate and useful predictions; if it does, we shall have to give renewed consideration to it.

What Is to Be Done?

These, then, seem to be the fundamental methods or techniques of prediction in the absence of comprehensive general theory. As we have seen, there is some commonality among them, and occasionally our division is somewhat arbitrary. Furthermore, we could elaborate each almost without end through the use of actual predictions. We may hope that greater attention to such methods of prediction will contribute over time and effort to improvement of our techniques as well as our predictions. Ultimately, analysts of international politics and advisers to policymakers must reconsider each of these methods in terms of its particular usefulness in predicting foreign policy and international politics as a basis for decisions about what tools and techniques to develop further — those that will be appropriate to the subject matter of international political analysis and that will promise more comprehensive and accurate predictions.

We must remember that the demands on such predictive devices vary considerably with the question asked. For example, a little analysis will show the various demands raised by these four questions: What will the international situation be next year? What threat will Communist China pose to the United States next year? Will there be a nuclear war next year? What could the United States do to prevent nuclear war in the next year? Each of these questions asks for different sorts of prediction and hence will commend different methods or combinations of methods.

Policymakers will be particularly interested in having answers to these questions. For the efforts of the policymaker to control or influence the development of international politics and his country's future in the world are heavily dependent on such predictions. And those predictions must be and are made. As Theodore Sorensen reported in his study of decision making in Kennedy's White House, "Every decision a President makes involves uncertainty. Every decision involves risk. Almost every decision involves an element of prediction and at least latent disagreement with others . . . . The primary problem of presidential information, however, is usually not an abundance of reliable data but a shortage, especially in foreign affairs. The apparatus and operations of modern intelligence systems can obtain and assemble great quantities of heretofore unreachable facts, but they cannot predict the future. And it is the future which most often must be gauged."[17]

Thus not only is prediction a major application of international theory; it plays a large role in the other major application — control — which we shall examine next.

---

[17]Theodore Sorensen, *Decision-Making in the White House*, p. 11, 39–40.

chapter 15
Control

The Objective of Control Ultimately, whether we are policy-makers or concerned citizens or even scholars studying policy problems, the desire to improve our ability to influence or control international politics may be our ultimate motivation in undertaking our study. To succeed in such an effort we must develop both relevant theory and a precise understanding of the relation between theory and practice and of the problems of valuation that underlie action.[1]

[1]Various terms are used to characterize our interest, among them control, influence, manipulation, engineering theory, and praxeology. We need not linger over such common terms as control, influence, and manipulation, but the other two deserve brief attention. "Engineering theory" is a term that has been developed to characterize theoretical efforts which, instead of trying to explain why certain things happen (which is causal theory or explanatory theory), tells us what to do if we wish to obtain a certain objective or result—just as an engineer tells us how to construct a building conforming to specified objectives. The field of engineering theory has often been referred to as "policy science." See Daniel Lerner and Harold Lasswell, eds., The Policy Sciences (Stanford, Calif.: Stanford University Press, 1951). It has also been referred to as the science of relating ends and means efficiently. Raymond Aron, the French sociologist and scholar of international relations, has termed all the questions and topics in this area "praxeology," or the science of practice. See Raymond Aron, Peace and War (New York: Doubleday, 1967), Part IV, "Praxeology: The Antinomies of Diplomatic-Strategic Conduct," and his article, "What Is a Theory of International Relations?" in Journal of International Affairs, 21 (1967) 185–206, esp. 189n.

Policy Theory abstracts from the materials of
and Theory the world — both practice and circum-
stance or environment — in order to
bring some order to our view of it. This order is neither happenstance nor randomly selected; it is purposive, for it is intended
to enable us to understand what happens in the world at the very
least, and it may also be employed to enable us to predict happenings and then to alter likely happenings through our own
conscious action. Explanatory theory tells us why certain results
follow from particular happenings or actions, or at least that
certain results do indeed follow from particular happenings or
actions. We may then use this knowledge or belief in efforts to
influence outcomes by taking purposive action.

Whether or not we realize it, all human action not purely
random is based on theoretical notions. We are not generally
certain what will follow from any particular action we take, but
we do usually have suspicions. We get those suspicions by refer-
ring, in a sense, to what might be called our theory of the world,
or our theory of the part of the world with which we are then
concerned. We have, first of all, theoretical notions that tell us
to act as if "the sun will rise" tomorrow and life will continue.
We "know" these things only because our theories tell us. Often
such theories are very general, and usually they are quite unconscious. But we also have very specific theories about such
matters as obeying traffic laws and gambling. These theories we
may not follow. Thus we may speed on the highway because we
have a theory which tells us that a certain percentage of the time
(or, more likely, an uncertain percentage of the time) we will not
be caught. Similarly, we may bet irrationally because we want
to enjoy the thrill of betting on long odds even though it will
usually cost us greater losses.

All such action is based in fundamental ways on theory.
But that theory is itself based on such action — on our own action
sometimes, and on others' action most of the time. We learn at
home and in school and on the job what theories are believed
applicable or accurate about the actions and happenings that
concern us, and we then store these for retrieval when we need
them, and for modification when we encounter new data or better
theories. Thus theories are built out of action and particularly
careful thought about action, and they then serve to suggest,

guide, or determine action when we seek to attain specific objectives efficiently.[2]

The relation between theory and practice that holds for personal action or individual voting also holds for policymaking and action by states in international politics. Policy is made and action is taken because those responsible for doing so believe that this will efficiently achieve the ends they desire, and they have been brought to that conclusion by their own or their advisers' theories of what makes certain things happen in international politics and of what consequences will follow from certain state actions. But this makes policymaking sound much easier than it actually is, and we must consider now the ways in which states can and do use theory to inform their conduct, and the problems that arise when they attempt to do so.

Policy and Values All action has as its precondition a set of values that give the actor objectives to seek and that enable him to select among various possible means to achieving those objectives on the basis of the anticipated costs and benefits of each of these means. As we have said in previous chapters, the values a nation uses to establish foreign policy objectives are generally found in or derived from the political process. They may be the desires of the voting public, the wishes of effective interest groups, or the values of that set of leaders which one way or another keeps control of the government. More likely, they will be some combination of all three of these categories plus others, such as widespread beliefs about the nation's heritage and destiny, and views of major church leaders within the nation and perhaps even around the world.

These values also play a similar and related but distinguish-

[2]The effect of people's following such theories upon their action has been subject to considerable examination and dispute among sociologists and political scientists. In what is sometimes called the "Oedipus effect" or the "bandwagon effect," people are believed to alter their action to conform to predictions (and perhaps thereby to make predictions invalid unless the predictions have already taken this effect into account), and in the "underdog effect," people invalidate the prediction by acting to counteract it. For extended discussions of these matters and problems, see Robert Merton, *Social Theory and Social Structure* (New York: Free Press, rev. ed., 1957), chap. 11.

able role: They enable us to assess the moral or ethical rightness and wrongness of actions, policies, and even objectives. Throughout the history of thought on ethics, there have been two major schools disputing about the grounds for such moral judgment. One school has held that the rightness or wrongness of an act must be judged in terms of the act's effects. Thus national policy would be judged in terms of the good and bad results it brought to the nation, or perhaps to the world as a whole. The other school has argued that moral judgment should take into account intention rather than consequence, perhaps largely because we cannot be sure what the consequences of our acts will be, but we can always have good intentions. This dispute has not been resolved by philosophers over the thousands of years in which it has raged, and we can hardly expect to settle it here in several paragraphs. But we can note that, practically speaking, most of our moral judgment as a society is something of a cross between these two extreme positions. Thus we do not generally condemn someone whose action has bad consequences but was itself an accident, and we tend to praise a man for being good-willed. Nonetheless, most of our assessments turn heavily on the consequences of the deed, sometimes taking into account whether or not the person knew or even could have known those consequences when he undertook the act.

Policy and Knowledge

This kind of practical assessment indicates the great importance of knowledge about consequences, and the prediction we employ to get that knowledge. Presumably, the better our theories of international politics, the better will be our prediction of the likely effects of our policies and actions, and so the more successful will be our efforts and the more morally assessable will be those actions. We must understand the dynamics of international politics and the determinants that serve to make such politics change over time, if we are to develop theories of the world that will enable us better to predict the likely costs and benefits of various possible actions — and indeed even to predict what alternative actions will be likely to be open to us. When we are concerned with policy problems, our predictions will tend to concentrate on varying the points of possible impact — that is, those factors we can hope to change and thereby bring about a different outcome. And when we attempt to predict possible alternatives and their costs and benefits, we will have to build in various conditional statements. Thus we might say that in a certain situation if we do one of two things, and if the other side then does one thing our alternatives will be A and B, whereas, if it does another thing our alternatives will be P and Q. We may then assess these policies in terms of the costs and benefits to us (or to our attainment of the objectives we seek). And then, through rational calculation, we may select the policy course that seems likely to be most efficient.

When we select instruments to employ in our efforts to attain our objectives, we are not acting with perfect knowledge. Rather, we are making the best determinations we can in the face of ignorance and uncertainty. Some people will tend to gamble and others to insure. This seems to be a function of their psychological nature. But if they have principles or rules of thumb that tell them how likely various possibilities are (as prediction is supposed to) and if they have assessed the predicted consequences of each available alternative (as their values should enable them to do), they may then employ certain principles of decision in order to maximize their likely gain or minimize their likely loss in these particular circumstances.

Game Theory

The most prominent of the available approaches to the formulation of strategies of decision now occasionally employed is called "game theory."[3] Game theory is not really about games in the usual sense, nor is it a theory in our usual sense. The term "game" connotes interdependence among players' decisions. In other words, game theory is concerned with situations in which the best decision or strategy for one player depends on the de-

---

[3]Among the useful introductions to game theory are Thomas C. Schelling, "What Is Game Theory?" in James C. Charlesworth, ed., *Contemporary Political Analysis* (New York: Free Press, 1967), p. 212–238; Martin Shubik, ed., *Game Theory and Related Approaches to Social Behavior* (New York: Wiley, 1964), especially Shubik's introduction; R. Duncan Luce and Howard Raiffa, *Games and Decisions* (New York: Wiley, 1957), the definitive comprehensive survey. See also Schelling's applications in *The Strategy of Conflict* (Cambridge, Mass.: Harvard University Press, 1960); and Anatol Rapoport, *Fights, Games and Debates* (Ann Arbor: University of Michigan Press, 1960). All these have useful bibliographies that suggest other materials.

cisions or strategy adopted by other players — as is the case in what we usually call "games" as well as in love, war, business, and other social situations. Game theory is more a way of looking at and analyzing situations and the decisions that may be made in them than it is a theory. It does not describe the way people actually behave; rather, it recommends certain behavior as the most rational or efficient or promising, given a situation in which there is both interdependence among actors' decisions and uncertainty about how the other party or parties will act. In this sense, it is a policy theory, an engineering theory about how to make the most sensible decision given interdependence with ignorance and uncertainty. In a sense it is a theory of strategy and its chief application in the study of international politics has been to the analysis of strategic choices: how to behave in a crisis, or what sort of military weapons to buy and what sorts of threats to make about their possible use in deterring or punishing an adversary. Using game theory as a conceptual framework to emphasize the interdependence of decisions and to offer suggestions for sensible decision in such situations is not difficult, although it is involved. Both its usefulness and its actual importance in influencing the thinking of policymakers and their advisers will merit continuing attention.

Policy and Research

Policymaking and action are considerably less creative and innovative than they might be if they made greater use of the recent technical developments, such as decision theory and game theory, and of the continuing research findings of scholars in the fields of international politics and foreign policy. That greater use is not made is by no means solely attributable to the policymakers, who, generally welcome assistance from any quarter. Greatest use of such assistance thus far has been made by the military services and their civilian directors, rather than by the foreign ministries and state departments responsibile for integrating military policy into the broader foreign policy of a nation. One reason is that such analysis is often most clear and useful when it is quantitative, and military problems lend themselves more obviously (if sometimes misleadingly and dangerously) to quantification. The major research institutes that perform such tasks for the American government do most of their work for the

Department of Defense (for example, the Institute for Defense Analyses), or for one or another service (for example, the RAND Corporation for the Air Force and the Research Analysis Corporation for the Army). This research is generally done on the basis of contracts let by these branches to the institutes. Institutes that are somewhat similar in that they do policy research but concentrate on political and economic problems, such as the Washington Center of Foreign Policy Research, the Harvard University Center for International Affairs, and the Massachusetts Institute of Technology's Center for International Studies, do not generally have such close ties with governmental organizations. Those doing research that is more academic and less policy-oriented, such as the Princeton University Center of International Studies, have even fewer policy-encouraging ties. Thus what research is done on political and economic problems relevant to policy dilemmas may not be conducted or expressed in policy terms, and even if it is it may not find its way into the "policy machine."

It can still be argued whether or not much of what scholars are presently doing can contribute significantly to policy formulation. And because the discipline of international relations is still in such a state of flux and reformation, a strong case can be made in the negative. Nonetheless, even if this is true now, it will not continue to be so, for as scholars progress in the development of international political theory, that theory will be ripe for application to policy problems and those scholars will be increasingly able and ready to devote themselves to such work.

At this stage in the development of the discipline, most policy work relies on semiorganized information and on intuition. It can be argued that highly organized information and rigorous theory may tend to limit the flexibility of analysts and the diversity of possibilities considered, although this need not be so. But if it is argued that reliance on intuition promises considerably greater flexibility and creativity, the argument is almost certainly inaccurate. Intuition on matters of slight concern may be free and imaginative, but intuition on matters of grave concern, such as foreign policy, tends to be highly limited in its flexibility and imagination, relying instead on historical precedent and convention for both its raw materials and its solutions. Such appears to be the character of the foreign policies of most nations today as well as of the international activities of such organizations as the United Nations and the military alliances.

Creativity and Innovation   The major need now is for creative thought and innovation. Psychologists have recently undertaken many studies of creative thinking,[4] but their definitions of creativity vary somewhat,[5] and more is known of personality correlates of persons considered creative than is known of why a given person is creative.[6] There is general agreement, however, that the general pattern of creative thought entails analytical understanding of the problem (plus, of course, failure to solve it conventionally), relaxation of analytical constraints, achievement of what is called insight, and finally disciplined analytical testing of the creative insight. Psychologists will have to undertake much more study of thought processes before we will understand creative thinking satisfactorily, let alone encourage it efficiently. But with what is known now we should be able to examine the problem of coping intellectually with political matters and issues and reach conclusions with applications not simply to research in political science but also to problem-oriented study of policy relevance.[7]

We must remember, in undertaking such study, that creative thought about politics may be seriously constrained by limitations of language and concept. Often there are unpleasant facts to be faced, and, as Hans Morgenthau has written:

> A political science which is faithful to its moral commitment of telling the truth about the political world cannot help telling society things it does not want to hear. This cannot be otherwise in view of the fact that one of the main purposes of society is to conceal the truth about man and society from its members. That concealment, that elaborate and subtle and purposeful misunderstand-

---

[4]Among the notable are those published or presented in H. Anderson, ed., *Creativity and Its Cultivation* (New York: Harper & Row, 1959); Frank Barron, *Scientific Creativity* (New York: Wiley, 1963); Calvin Taylor, ed., *Creativity: Progress and Potential* (New York: McGraw-Hill, 1964); and Calvin Taylor, ed., *Widening Horizons in Creativity* (New York: Wiley, 1964).

[5]See, for the major variants, the essays in H. Gruber *et al.*, *Contemporary Approaches to Creative Thinking* (New York: Atherton, 1962).

[6]See, for example, the research summarized in Bernard Berelson and Gary Steiner, *Human Behavior* (New York: Harcourt, Brace & World, 1964), and in Morris Stein and Shirley Heinze, eds, *Creativity and the Individual* (New York: Free Press, 1960).

[7]For a preliminary general effort in this direction, see Harold Lasswell, *The Future of Political Science* (New York: Atherton, 1963), esp. chaps. 7 and 8, "The Cultivation of Creativity."

ing of the nature of man and of society, is one of the cornerstones upon which all societies are founded.[8]

Whether or not we agree with Morgenthau's assessment of human nature, we are quite likely to share his negative view of much of international relations at this time. But we must also remember that the future will be different from the past and hence will almost certainly require novel analysis and innovative changes in policy and action. And it is here that the staggering difficulties of international political analysis confront us. Walter Millis, the military historian, wrote:

> We do not have the language, the laws or the conceptual systems adequate to deal with the problems of international violence in the world created by the development of the thermonuclear arsenals . . . . There is no hope of advance toward the entirely practicable and realizable visions of a more peaceful and less bloody world order that are already before our eyes unless and until the underlying conceptual systems we bring to international politics are so modified as to make these visions attainable . . . each generation must rewrite the experiential evidence into language intelligible to itself and usable for its own purposes . . . . In every specific international crisis, no less than in the larger and more general issues, we should look as closely as possible for the realities behind the excited verbiage; all intelligent and vocal men should ask themselves constantly what the effective factors are, what the words really mean, where our old established concepts of international politics are in fact leading us.[9]

The challenge goes even deeper than this, for some traditional concepts are not only inaccurate but inadequate. Much of our way of thinking about international politics has been developed over a long period of time in which change was gradual enough that it could be incorporated into the discourse if perhaps not always into the language. But the increased tempo and pervasiveness of change has rendered such static descriptions of and prescriptions for dynamic reality both difficult and dangerous.

[8]Hans Morgenthau, "Power as a Political Concept," in Roland Young, ed., *Approaches to the Study of Politics* (Evanston, Ill.: Northwestern University Press, 1958), p. 72.

[9]Walter Millis, *An End to Arms* (New York: Atheneum, 1965), pp. 119–120.

Our problems, the obstacles to creative thought and innovative action, begin with our ignorance of the dynamics of international politics, our uncertainty about the other actors in international politics, and our unthoughtfulness about the great collection of objectives we seek. If we had better theories of international politics and foreign policy and more careful studies of our objectives and their relative importances, our imaginations could probably function much more efficiently in creating possible solutions to some of the problems that face any nation in today's and tomorrow's worlds.

From Idea to Innovation

But creative thought alone will not solve problems. A new idea must be employed. And to be employed in policymaking it must be institutionalized as innovation. There are two discrete stages to political innovation in a complex world. The first is acceptance of a new idea, a new option, or some other creation, by the bureaucracy and perhaps the nation at large. The second is the subsequent insertion of the resulting measure or policy action into the international system. At this point, we know very little about either stage, for our studies have not been directed to learning about organizational and systemic innovation in foreign policy and international politics.

The process by which innovation takes place within the policy machine, or the state as a political whole, may vary considerably. There appear to be three basically different possibilities. First, and perhaps most obvious in the area of foreign and specifically defense policy, innovation may be planned and its acceptance by the policy system determined in advance, almost as a matter of course. The prime examples of such occurrences are those of certain weapon systems (for example, long-range bombers or ballistic missiles). The RAND Corporation and other research institutes have developed the approach to successful achievement of this type of innovation.[10]

[10]See the pioneering study of C. J. Hitch and R. N. McKean, *The Economics of Defense in the Nuclear Age* (Cambridge, Mass.: Harvard University Press, 1961); see also the more recent collection of RAND lectures edited by E. Quade, *Analysis for Military Decisions* (Chicago: Rand McNally, 1965); and see the narrower collection of RAND studies edited by David Novick, *Program Budgeting* (Cambridge, Mass.: Harvard University Press, 1966).

A second possible type of bureaucratic innovation is what might be termed "entrepreneurship," in which one man or an office settles on an idea or program and shepherds it through the relevant political arenas. Such activity is generally most successfully engaged in by very powerful individuals such as Presidents (Kennedy and the nuclear testban) or ranking military officials (Admiral Rickover and the nuclear submarine program).

The third basic type of governmental innovation is that now often described in Charles Lindblom's term, "muddling through."[11] This may be of several varieties, as Lindblom has suggested. It may be conscious, as in most policy determination — particularly in foreign policy and national security policy and practice. There have been studies of this process in defense policy and budgetary affairs.[12] But the process may also be unconscious or, as Lindblom describes it in a recent book, "decisionmaking through mutual adjustment."[13]

Careful study of these processes, as is attempted by organization theorists and administrative behavior analysts, should produce useful insight about ways of encouraging innovation within national policy machinery. And in its turn this knowledge may contribute to national ability to insinuate national innovation into the international system. International systemic innovation so far has largely taken the form of creating new international organizations like the United Nations, but there should prove to be many lesser opportunities once nations better understand the processes of such innovation. Innovation always faces possible challenge by electoral sanction (in which the populace or the other political actors reject the proposed change) and then by international sanction (in which the system, or other nations

---

[11]See Lindblom's articles, "The Science of Muddling Through" in *Public Administration Review*, 19 (1959) 79–88 and "Policy Analysis" in *American Economic Review*, 48 (1958) 298–312. See also his book, *The Policy-Making Process* (Englewood Cliffs, N.J.: Prentice-Hall, 1968).

[12]See Samuel Huntington, *The Common Defense* (New York: Columbia University Press, 1961); Warner Schilling, Paul Hammond, and Glenn Snyder, *Strategy, Politics, and Defense Budgets* (New York: Columbia University Press, 1962); Aaron Wildavsky, *Politics of the Budgetary Process* (Boston: Little, Brown, 1964). See also Anthony Downs's two studies, *An Economic Theory of Democracy* (New York: Harper & Row, 1957) and *Inside Bureaucracy* (Boston: Little, Brown, 1967).

[13]See Charles Lindblom, *The Intelligence of Democracy* (New York: Free Press, 1964); see also Thomas Schelling, *Strategy of Conflict* (Cambridge, Mass.: Harvard University Press, 1960) for an analysis of "coordination" in activity.

constituting the system, refuses to accept the attempted alteration). But the likelihood of such rebuffs may be lessened by careful
preliminary study of the objectives to be sought and the obstacles
to their attainment.

Some Control Objectives

While any nation's foreign policy will seek innumerable
specific objectives, there are several that will be of particular
importance and general interest, and that raise problems to which
our previous studies are particularly relevant. Probably the foremost of these is war prevention: how can we, without sacrificing
all our other goals, avoid war in a world full of conflict? Another
objective is now often termed "war prevailance": How can we
survive a major war without surrendering (few still talk of victory
in a major war)? One objective that has become quite glamorous
in the postwar years is "crisis management": How can we conduct ourselves in a crisis in such a way as to attain our short-run
objectives without war? And another topic of concern to the major
powers is "alliance management": How can we maintain a co-
hesive alliance as the alliance's apparent success in preventing
or averting war increases the security and independence of our
allies? These are all major problems confronting the major nations
of the world. They press particularly on the superpowers because
these states have the greatest capabilities and the most extensive
responsibilities for the conduct of international relations. They
are the most consequential and probably the most interesting of
the "problem areas" challenging policymakers and creative analysts. But how can they be handled?

The Process of Policy Theorizing

Analytically, given the present situation and, in the absence
of a theory of international politics, our knowledge and beliefs
about the nature of international politics in the present age, we
attempt to determine what challenges to the particular objective
(such as preventing war) are likely to occur. We then consider
what alternative policies the nation might adopt to cope with the
challenge, and assess the likely consequences of each in terms of
their costs and benefits. On the basis of this information—or,
more accurately, informed and controlled speculation—we can

recommend a particular policy or a collection of policies into which we have built a number of options to allow for error or the discovery of new subsidiary objectives.

On the basis of analysis such as this, which is in turn based on our knowledge of the dynamics of international politics and the determinants of national foreign policy, it should be possible to work toward development of what might be called "engineering theories" or "policy theories" of such topics as war prevention and crisis management. These theories would in effect tell the policymaker (who should be well aware of the situation in which he finds his nation and its objectives) what to be on guard for, what alternative policies he might consider, what their likely effects would be (and hence, from the point of view of his national objectives and values, what their costs and benefits would be). In other words, such engineering theories could be major con-tributors to more efficient and conscious policymaking.

We do not yet have such policy-oriented theories, but we may be closer to them than we are to comprehensive, accurate theories of international politics and foreign policy. For our policy-oriented theories require attention to particular objectives and problems like war and its prevention but allow us to neglect or at least subordinate much of the rest of international politics. Thus our previous study of such key phenomena as crises and wars, if developed further, may enable us to construct useful policy or engineering theories at this time — theories that will require various and somewhat restricting assumptions but will nonetheless enable us to improve the quality of debate and ad-vice about policy questions because they concentrate on precisely what we need to know in order to resolve particular categories of problems. We would be negligent if we did not pursue this quest even in the present absence of comprehensive general theory. For it is obvious that everyone has ideas about how to avoid war, control crises, and maintain alliances, and it is equally obvious that some of these people merit more attention than others. The differences among them will be attributable to several factors: their knowledge of the situation, their ability to reason, and their theoretical knowledge of international politics. The better and more explicit (and hence more usable and more test-able and improvable) our relevant theoretical notions about inter-national politics, the better can be our theorizing about the best policy for a nation to adopt in seeking certain explicit objectives.

And if we do not continue to develop our theories of international politics and to attempt to apply them to policy problems, others with less understanding and more limited capabilities will do this anyway—perhaps to the detriment of the nation's security and even the destruction of world peace and welfare.

If we continue our investigations into explanatory theory and also consider questions about what a nation must therefore do to get a certain desired outcome and (in another form) what will be likely to eventuate if it does certain things, we may be able increasingly to apply our knowledge of international politics toward development of a "general theory of national control" that will increase a nation's control over its own fate by revealing what the determinant factors are, which ones are affectable, what effects various modifications have, and how a nation may go about affecting them. Then, by increasing our knowledge, keeping options open, and maintaining usable capabilities, we may be able to control our fates not only as nations but perhaps even, within limits, as a world society.

Scholarship and Responsibility

Whether this proves to be the case will depend heavily on the values and objectives of governments and their responsible citizenry. Knowledge of the sort we are seeking can be put to evil ends as well as good. The responsibility for seeing that it is the good ends that are sought and achieved lies with every individual. In extreme cases this responsibility may compel the scholar in us, as a seeker after truth wherever it may lead him, to give way to the humanity in us, as a seeker after peace and welfare and justice. In the past, scholars have sometimes found the demands of their vocation less powerful than the demands of their humanity. Like other scholars, the student of international politics may sometimes conclude that, rather than placing his discovered knowledge at the service of a government with which he is in conscientious disagreement, he must abandon that quest and suppress his findings. Let us all hope that we will not face such situations, whatever our countries. As individuals, we must always be aware that our responsibilities as human beings and our responsibilities as scholars may occasionally conflict. When they do, we may hope that our integrity as human beings will prevail.

PART VI
APPENDIXES

appendix I

Suggestions
for Further Study

Introduction The footnotes throughout the text of this book direct the reader to further discussion of particular points or of general topics that were mentioned briefly but necessarily slighted in the course of the book. The bibliographical notes here are not designed to duplicate those footnotes. Rather, they suggest major topics related to or following from those dealt with in each chapter that the student may wish to explore, and they cite relevant books and articles.

Chapter 1: International Politics The best way to increase one's general understanding of the nature of international politics is to read accounts of what actually happened in one or another instance of war, crisis, or some other type of happening.

In general, accounts of wars will tend to emphasize the interaction among several states and especially among their armed forces. There are, of course, many useful accounts of World Wars

I and II; their number continues to increase, and it should be no problem to find one or more both interesting and helpful. There are also a number of books on the Korean conflict—the most helpful probably being David Rees, *Korea: The Limited War* (New York: St. Martin's, 1964). But for these purposes the most useful war is probably the Vietnam conflict, which has the dual advantage of being contemporary as well as closely resembling much of the organized violence occurring in other areas and increasingly likely in the future. The literature on Vietnam is already voluminous, mounts continually, and becomes dated quickly as more sources become available. Any professor or librarian should be able to recommend here.

Accounts of wars seldom treat the other aspect of international politics of particular interest to us—the process by which policy is made by each party to the conflict, and, more precisely, why the state acted as it did. Increasingly we are finding the study of crises instructive here. For although, as we shall see later, policymaking in a crisis will differ from policymaking in a war, the crisis situation often offers clearer instances of the political and bureaucratic interplay that results in policy, precisely because in a crisis, decision tends to be made in a small group rather than throughout the entire bureaucracy.

By far the best instance we yet have of this is the Cuban missile crisis. The sources cited in Chapter 1—especially Elie Abel, *The Missile Crisis* (Philadelphia: Lippincott, 1966) and the memoirs of various officials involved in the decision, particularly Hilsman, Sorensen, and Schlesinger—are fascinating and quite revealing. Unfortunately, we lack (and always shall) the same detailed accounts of policymaking in the Soviet Union. But various speculative accounts of interest include Arnold L. Horelick and Myron Rush, *Strategic Power and Soviet Foreign Policy* (New York: Columbia University Press, 1965), especially Chapter 12, which attempts to construct reasoning that might have led to Soviet actions, and Carl A. Linden, *Khrushchev and the Soviet Leadership 1957–1964* (Baltimore: Johns Hopkins Press, 1966), especially the Introduction and Chapter 8, which attempts to untangle the political conflicts out of which Soviet policy flowed. Also interesting as a brief popular account of policymaking in a variety of crises is Edward Weintal and Charles Bartlett, *Facing the Brink* (New York: Scribner, 1967).

Such reading at the outset of a study increases awareness of what occurs in international politics. Later, after we have devel-

oped the analytical tools that are required, it will be possible
to examine this literature more critically to see what it may tell
us, not only about a particular occurrence, but about international
politics and foreign policy in general.

Chapter 2:   Much of the literature on social science
Social Science   concentrates either on the techniques,
particularly statistical and mathemat-
ical, that are increasingly employed or on the philosophical problems underlying any such study, particularly those of causality,
theory, and explanation.

Because quantitative approaches have been less prevalent
thus far in the study of international politics than in the study
of national politics, there is little point in our pursuing the subject here. The reader already well grounded in the requisite math
may be interested, however, in perusing J. David Singer, ed.,
Quantitative International Politics (New York: Free Press, 1968)
for indications of the sorts of work now being attempted by some.

The important philosophical issues underlying rigorous
study will concern us in detail in subsequent chapters. Somewhat more useful at this point would be consideration of the ways
scientists operate. Various works on the actual practice of physical scientists were cited in Chapter 2. Perhaps more relevant to
our concerns is a collection of essays by sociologists on how
they did their major research and what problems confronted
them: Phillip Hammond, *Sociologists at Work* (New York: Doubleday Anchor Edition, 1967).

Helpful in understanding the way science develops a consensus on the appropriate way of looking at the world and how
that consensus changes over time is the now widely appreciated
study by Thomas Kuhn, *The Structure of Scientific Revolutions*
(Chicago: University of Chicago Press, 1962).

The important problems connected with the use of the social
scientific method for studying international politics will be dealt
with in more detail in subsequent chapters.

Chapter 3:   This chapter is fundamentally an in-
Analysis   troduction to the methodological ap-
and Theory   proach of the rest of the book, and is
best followed by the reading of the
remaining chapters. A line of study both attractive and potentially

helpful at this point should be the articles by Hedley Bull and Morton Kaplan on the debate between traditionalists and modernists, articles cited in Chapter 2. They are interesting not only because they discuss a number of the key hopes and fears that differentiate the major approaches but also because they reveal something of the ways of thinking of their proponents.

A comprehensive account of various approaches to the study of international politics is Richard C. Snyder, "Some Recent Trends in International Relations Theory and Research," pp. 103–171 in Austin Ranney, ed., *Essays on the Behavioral Study of Politics* (Urbana: University of Illinois Press, 1962).

Further discussion of the problems and promise of theory can be found in Charles A. McClelland, "The Function of Theory in International Relations," *Journal of Conflict Resolution*, 4 (1960) 304–336; and in Stanley H. Hoffmann, "International Relations: The Long Road to Theory," in *World Politics*, 11 (1959) 349–354.

Chapter 4: *International Political Phenomena*	The text suggests further readings on the nature of war and of crisis; subsequent chapters will suggest sources for an extensive examination of these as well as alliance and cooperative control.

Perhaps the best supplement to these studies would be an examination of several other international political phenomena of varying significance. Thus one might consider the nature of foreign aid. Among the proliferating literature on this subject these books may prove helpful: John D. Montgomery, *Foreign Aid in International Politics* (Englewood Cliffs, N.J.: Prentice-Hall, 1967), which includes a comprehensive annotated bibliography; Andrew F. Westwood, *Foreign Aid in a Foreign Policy Framework* (Washington, D.C.: Brookings, 1966); Joan Nelson, *Aid, Influence, and Foreign Policy* (New York: Macmillan, 1968); J. Kaplan, *The Challenge of Foreign Aid* (New York: Praeger, 1967); Marshall Goldman, *Soviet Foreign Aid* (New York: Praeger, 1967).

Another topic worth investigation is negotiation. The best general studies of it are Arthur Lall, *Modern International Negotiation* (New York: Columbia University Press, 1966); and Fred C. Ikle, *How Nations Negotiate* (New York: Harper & Row, 1964). See also Thomas C. Schelling's *Arms and Influence* (New Haven,

Conn.: Yale University Press, 1966) for a rather different perspective.

It may also be interesting and instructive to examine a phenomenon like the Olympic Games — a "nonsecurity" happening that occasionally has striking political overtones, as the 1968 Olympic Games had because of the question of South African participation and the Black American boycott issue. Although there are no books examining the international politics of the Olympics, there is interesting reading in such periodicals as *Sports Illustrated* and in the news magazines.

Chapter 5: National Action and Its Sources A helpful conceptual introduction to the study of national action and the foreign policy underlying it, which will indicate what factors seem worth looking for, is James N. Rosenau's article, "Pre-theories and Theories of Foreign Policy," in R. Barry Farrell, ed., *Approaches to Comparative and International Politics* (Evanston, Ill.: Northwestern University Press, 1966), pp. 27–92, especially pp. 27–52.

Further discussion concentrating on the effect of type of government on foreign policy is Henry Kissinger's article, "Domestic Structure and Foreign Policy," in *Daedalus* (Spring 1966), pp. 503–529.

Examination of the objectives of states can be found in Chapter 5 of Arnold Wolfers, *Discord and Collaboration* (Baltimore: Johns Hopkins Press, 1962), "The Goals of Foreign Policy," and the article by Robert C. Angell, "Defense of What?" in *Journal of Conflict Resolution*, 6 (1962) 116–124.

A useful study of the ways nations decide how much of their resources to devote to foreign affairs is Paul Hammond's article, "The Political Order and the Burden of External Relations," in *World Politics*, 19 (1967) 443–464.

A greater understanding of the types of strategies nations may adopt may be achieved by examining recent literature on problems of military strategy today. A useful compendium is Henry Kissinger, ed., *Problems of National Strategy* (New York: Praeger, 1965). But perhaps more helpful as an introduction would be the article by Evan Luard, "Conciliation and Deterrence: A Comparison of Political Strategies in the Interwar and Postwar Years," in *World Politics*, 19 (1967) 167–189.

The best way to further one's understanding of national action more specifically is to study the foreign policymaking of several key states in some detail, searching particularly for information about the determinants of that policy or behavior.

We do not and cannot know much about Soviet foreign policymaking, but a recent historical study that stands out is Marshall Shulman's *Stalin's Foreign Policy Reappraised* (Cambridge, Mass.: Harvard University Press, 1963). See also, for more recent analysis, Jan Triska and David Finley, *Soviet Foreign Policy* (New York: Macmillan, 1968).

For an interesting comparison of British and American policymaking, see Kenneth N. Waltz's book, *Foreign Policy and Democratic Politics* (Boston: Little, Brown, 1967). The literature on American policymaking is monstrous, ranging from the very descriptive, such as Burton M. Sapin's *The Making of United States Foreign Policy* (New York: Praeger, 1966) through the memoirs of many public figures, including Presidents Truman and Eisenhower, to more academic studies, such as Stanley Hoffmann's *Gulliver's Troubles, or The Setting of American Foreign Policy* (New York: McGraw-Hill, 1968) and many critiques from various viewpoints.

Also of increasing interest are the foreign policies and world roles of France and Communist China. Unfortunately, the available literature on these countries tends to be more descriptive of policy rather than explanatory of its determinants, and to concentrate on the leaders, de Gaulle and Mao, rather than on their nations.

Chapter 6: The most exciting and stimulating
Interaction development in the examination of the
and Its Outcomes interaction of nations—the ways in
which the actions of each affect the
other and the patterns that may result—has derived from the application of insights from game theory and other theories of conflict behavior. Game theory is discussed briefly in Chapter 15, and reference is made there to the best introductory treatments of it. The leader of this approach is Thomas C. Schelling, whose early book, *The Strategy of Conflict* (New York: Oxford, Galaxy Edition, 1963), should not be missed. Schelling subsequently extended, applied, and modified his views in a study of military

strategy, *Arms and Influence* (New Haven, Conn.: Yale University Press, 1966). Closely related to much of Schelling's work but more concerned with integration and peace theory than with military strategy is that of another economist, Kenneth E. Boulding, whose book, *Conflict and Defense* (New York: Harper & Row, 1962), is both excellent and stimulating, if occasionally difficult, reading. Each has also written a number of articles, but perhaps the most interesting is Schelling's review of Boulding's book in "War without Pain, and Other Models," in *World Politics,* 15 (1963) 465–487.

Another student of game theory as well as international relations is Anatol Rapoport, whose books are cited in the discussion of game theory in Chapter 15. Rapoport is quite critical of most application of game theory to international relations, and his criticisms are best made in his book, *Strategy and Conscience* (New York: Harper & Row, 1964).

It is clear that there are many difficulties in the application of game theory—still a simple model of conflict behavior—to such a complex subject as international relations. But it is also clear that much insight into the processes of interaction and possible calculations about them can be achieved through its careful study.

The other important—and related—approach develops out of systems theory and might be termed "interaction theory." Schelling and Boulding have both contributed mightily. But see also the work of Charles McClelland, especially his article, "The Acute International Crisis," in *World Politics,* 14 (1961) 182–204, and these other articles: J. David Singer, "Inter-Nation Influence," in *American Political Science Review,* 57 (1963) 420–430; Steven J. Brams, "Transaction Flows in the International System," in *American Political Science Review,* 60 (1966) 880–898; and Maurice A. East and Phillip M. Gregg, "Factors Influencing Cooperation and Conflict in the International System," in *International Studies Quarterly,* 11 (1967) 244–269.

Chapter 7: From Analysis to Explanation   As this chapter indicates, explanation has many meanings to many men, but none is easily achieved to our satisfaction. For the philosophically inclined, the literature on the philosophy of science and the philosophy of history cited in Chapter 2 merits study.

For those more interested in immediate applications to political science, the opportunities for reading remain relatively sparse. A brief book by the sociologist George Homans, *The Nature of Social Science* (New York: Harcourt, Brace & World, 1967), which attempts to reduce sociology (and by implication political science) to psychology, should prove interesting.

Further, some will find helpful several books by political theorist Eugene Meehan: *The Theory and Method of Political Analysis* (Homewood, Ill.: Dorsey, 1965) and *Explanation in Social Science: A System Paradigm* (Homewood, Ill.: Dorsey, 1968).

But many will probably prefer to press on to coming chapters, where we shall confront actual instances of international politics and attempt to explain them.

Chapter 8: The issues and problems dealt with *From Explanation* in this chapter on theory-building may *to Theory* be further considered in the writings of the philosophers of science and historians of science cited previously. Perhaps the most helpful applied article is Harry Eckstein's study of internal war, "On the Etiology of Internal Wars," in *History and Theory,* 4 (1965) 133–163, which attempts to develop a preliminary theory of this phenomenon relevant to both national and international politics and which displays ways of coping with some of these problems.

But again, the best way to understand, and especially to cope with, these difficulties is to engage in some political theory-building.

Chapters There seems little point in taking up, *9, 10, 11, 12:* chapter by chapter, the topics of these *Theory-Building* four studies, for each examines the useful available literature as it suggests other topics and activities for consideration. The important points here are the desirability and possibility of international political theory-building and the demonstration of various aspects of this complex task. A revealing additional activity is examination of one or another study of some aspect of international politics to discover what theoretical explanatory contentions are indeed made — especially where they are made tacitly or by implication in an apparently descriptive work — and how they are tested by the scholar. It should be useful to ask of each work how this testing might have been improved by the author. And it would ultimately be very revealing to collect from various sources both theoretical propositions and evidence on a given topic and compare, attempting then to couple them into a prototheory of the phenomenon. Beyond those topics covered in these four chapters, possible topics would include foreign aid, negotiation, and the Olympic Games — some materials on which have been cited.

Chapter 13:   The footnotes to this chapter mention *Theorizing about* many of the most interesting or helpful *International* articles on the types of theory dis- *Politics* cussed. But a number of other articles and books merit mention and attention in any study of international political theory.

Neglected but helpful examinations of Freudian and Marxist-Leninist theories are Nathan Leites, "Psycho-Cultural Hypotheses about Political Acts," in *World Politics,* 1 (1948) 102–119; Morris Ginsberg, "The Causes of War," in *Sociological Review,* 35 (1939) 121–143; and William L. Langer, "A Critique of Imperialism," reprinted in H. Ausubel, ed., *Making of Modern Europe* (New York: Holt, Rinehart and Winston, 1951), pp. 918–932. The best work on geographical aspects is that of Harold and Margaret Sprout. See their book, *The Ecological Perspective* (Princeton, N.J.: Princeton University Press, 1966); and see Harold Sprout, "Geopolitical Hypotheses in Technological Perspective," in *World Politics,* 15 (1963) 187–212, and Harold and Margaret Sprout, "Geography and International Politics in an Era of Revolutionary Change," in *Journal of Conflict Resolution,* 4 (1960) 145–161. That entire issue of the *Journal of Conflict Resolution* was devoted to the geography of conflict.

The works of Hans Morgenthau are, of course, classics. They should, however, be read along with criticisms of balance-of-power theory. The most helpful of these are Ernst Haas's classic article, "The Balance of Power: Prescription, Concept, or Propaganda?" in *World Politics,* 5 (1950) 459–479; Inis Claude, *Power and International Relations* (New York: Random House, 1962), chaps. 2 and 3; Robert C. Good, "National Interest and

Moral Theory" in Roger Hilsman and Robert C. Good, eds., *Foreign Policy in the Sixties* (Baltimore: Johns Hopkins Press, 1965), chap. 15; Karl W. Deutsch, *Nerves of Government* (New York: Free Press, 1963), *passim;* and Alan James, "Power Politics," in *Political Studies,* 12 (1964) 307–326.

Among the more recent work employing or emphasizing various versions of systems theory, the following are particularly helpful:

Charles A. McClelland, "Applications of General Systems Theory in International Relations," in *Main Currents in Modern Thought,* 12 (1955), 27–34; Morton A. Kaplan, *System and Process in International Politics* (New York: Wiley, 1957) and "Some Problems of International Systems Research" in K. W. Deutsch *et al., International Political Communities* (Garden City, New York: Doubleday Anchor Edition, 1966), pp. 469–501.

Richard Rosecrance, *Action and Reaction in World Politics* (Boston: Little, Brown, 1963) and the review of this book by Geogre Liska, "Continuity and Change in International Systems," in *World Politics,* 16 (1963) 118–136.

And see also the "debate" over the stability of various types of systems among Kenneth Waltz, Karl Deutsch and David Singer, and Richard Rosecrance, in articles cited in the text.

Among the various recent efforts at progress toward an international political theory not cited before, the following stand out:

Arthur Lee Burns, "From Balance to Deterrence: A Theoretical Analysis," in *World Politics,* 9 (1957) 494–529; George Modelski, "Agraria and Industria. Two Models of the International System," in *World Politics,* 14 (1961) 118–143; Fred W. Riggs, "International Relations as a Prismatic System," in *World Politics,* 14 (1961) 144–181; Roger D. Masters, "World Politics as a Primitive Political System," in *World Politics,* 16 (1964) 595–619; Harold Guetzkow, "Isolation and Collaboration: A Partial Theory of Inter-Nation Relations," in *Journal of Conflict Resolution,* 1 (1957) 48–68; Bruce M. Russett, "Toward a Model of Competitive International Politics," in *Journal of Politics,* 25 (1963) 226–247; and Raymond Aron, *Peace and War* (New York: Doubleday, 1967).

Chapter 14:   Increasingly, prediction is receiving
Prediction   the attention of social scientists. Methodologically, we still have a very long way to go before we can have comprehensive, defensible ways

of predicting the various developments in which we are particularly interested. The early work of the Commission on the Year 2000 of the American Academy of Arts and Sciences shows much promise here. The first collection of papers from the commission was published as the summer 1967 issue of the academy's journal, *Daedalus,* and more are promised as the commission continues its work. Meanwhile, other groups join in the fray—or race.

Of course, prediction has always been with us. But in the past much—indeed, most—was either prophecy or, in the realm of international relations, strategic contingency planning work. What is most needed now are rather specific predictions based on explicit and defended notions (nascent theories) about world politics. Perhaps the best recent example—and certainly the most interesting—is the book by Herman Kahn and Anthony J. Weiner, *The Year 2000—A Framework for Speculation* (New York: Macmillan, 1967). A journal now exists to spread information about forecasting—*The Futurist* (published by the World Future Society, P.O. Box 19285, 20th Street Station, Washington, D.C. 20036). Bertrand de Jouvenel's *Futuribles* publications continue to be produced (largely in French) by the Société d'Etudes et de Documentation Economiques, Industrielles, et Sociales.

The best way to further our understanding of political theory and the predictive activity is to attempt to employ a theory predictively. Some of the theories or partial theories cited in Chapter 13 and in the preceding notes are detailed enough to allow such prediction; many others can be elaborated to make this possible. Of course, it is also possible to use Marxist theory, for example, in such prediction. What is essential to discover is the way in which theory can be so employed—and, as a consequence of the effort—the ways in which we can improve the development and formulation of our theories if we wish to improve their predictive capacity.

Chapter 15: Control

Control is perhaps the most fascinating and certainly the most immediately important use of theory. The chances are that no reader needs much encouragement to apply his theoretical insights or those of others to policy problems.

Perhaps the most interesting approach is to take the situation of a superpower and question how much opportunity it actually has to control or influence international politics. There is, of course, considerable literature on the alleged overcommitment of the United States abroad, especially on the American involvement in Vietnam and to a lesser degree elsewhere as a "global policeman." How can we tell what the limits of American power are? And then, how can we determine what the United States could do (if anything) to advance its interests more effectively in Vietnam? in Asia? or perhaps more significantly in the rest of the developing world?

The way we formulate these questions often not only reveals our predilections but distorts our calculations. It is crucial to the study of control and to the application of theory to practice that this not happen, but the challenge is great and the successful ways of meeting it are not yet clear because of the continuing deficiency of imaginative thought. The opportunities for progress are great, and the most profitable way to pursue the study of international politics following or accompanying the development of theory is to attempt to grapple with the excruciating policy problems. Such an approach will increase our understanding of the possibilities and difficulties of practice and broaden our understanding of international politics to incorporate more of the sources of national action.

It is important that we understand in detail the relation of facts, definitions, value statements, and reasoning in any study or proposal of policy. A useful discussion of these matters is Robert Levine's The Arms Debate (Cambridge, Mass.: Harvard University Press, 1963), chap. 2, "The Logical Structure of a Policy Position." Further useful discussion can be found in: Arnold Wolfers, "Statesmanship and Moral Choice," in World Politics, 1 (1949) 175–195, reprinted as chap. 4 of his Discord and Collaboration (Baltimore: Johns Hopkins Press, 1962); Henry Kissinger, "The Policymaker and the Intellectual," in The Reporter, 20 (Mar. 5, 1959) 30–35, reprinted as the last chapter of his book, The Necessity for Choice (New York: Harper & Row, 1961).

The increasing literature on policy problems is thus couched in more theoretical terms, much of it collected in the volume edited by Richard A. Falk and Saul H. Mendlovitz, Toward a Theory of War Prevention (New York: World Law Fund, 1966). Kenneth Boulding's writings have been relevant, including Chapter 15 of Conflict and Defense (New York: Harper & Row, 1961), "Conflict Resolution and Control" and his chapter "Toward a

Theory of Peace" in Roger Fisher, ed., *International Conflict and Behavioral Science* (New York: Basic Books, 1964), pp. 70–87. Also of interest is Amitai Etzioni's chapter, "Toward a Sociological Theory of Peace," pp. 267–293 in Llewellyn Gross, ed., *Sociological Theory: Inquiries and Paradigms* (New York: Harper and Row, 1967).

There is also a considerable literature of relevance to both the general problems of control and the specific problems, like peacemaking, peace-keeping, crisis management, and alliance management, in the journals devoted to international politics — particularly the *Journal of Conflict Resolution, World Politics*, and the *Journal of Peace Research*. More information about these and other helpful journals may be found in Appendix II.

Reading and Research
in International Politics

Introduction   Because the field of international re-
                 lations is changing and advancing
now with such rapidity, no textbook could possibly remain as
current and as accurate a reflection of the latest scholarly thought
as its author would desire. Furthermore, no textbook itself can adequately convey to the reader what the experience of doing his
own research would be, or even what varying forms the research
of others takes. For these reasons, the student should read the
discussions of the significant issues and the presentations of
research findings as they are published. Increasingly, these appear
as articles in the journals that serve the field, rather than as full-
length books.

   In the past, it was widely believed that students were neither
interested in nor able to understand the work of scholars in the
field; that privilege was reserved to other scholars who had undergone long training and often had done research and published
their findings. In recent years, the improved quality of education
at the high school and college levels, and a new seriousness of

purpose in students, have significantly increased the capabilities and the depth of interests of students. As a result, education at the college level is being reconstructed to include more student work in the literature of the disciplines and less in textbooks that merely rehash and simplify the basic content of the field.

This book may serve as a guide to the study of the literature and to the building of one's own theory through research. The theory-building can best be carried out through the organized study of the raw materials of the discipline—diplomatic archives, memoirs, scholarly reconstructions, and journalistic accounts.[1] The literature—especially that cited in the footnotes and in the preceding bibliographical notes—can most conveniently be studied in books of readings, or collections of articles and excerpts that bring together scholarly work now scattered. To facilitate this study, the companion volume to this text, *Readings in International Political Analysis* (New York: Holt, Rinehart and Winston, 1969) contains selections of major significance chosen and organized to accompany this book. Other collections with different orientations and emphases are also available, but by far the most useful is the comprehensive one edited by James N. Rosenau; *International Politics and Foreign Policy* (New York: Free Press, 1961; rev. ed., 1969). However, space limitations and time lags inevitable in book publishing make it impossible for collections of readings to be both comprehensive and current. Hence it is also desirable for the student of international relations to keep abreast of material in the significant journals in international relations and in related areas like comparative politics and foreign policy.

Indexes   One or more of the following indexes may be helpful in citing articles dealing with particular subjects in international politics:

1. The Universal Reference System (32 Nassau Street, Princeton, N.J.) publishes an annual annotated bibliography of international affairs, called Codex I (Codexes II through X cover other areas of political science), and quarterly supplements. These should be available at most academic libraries. And although they are

---

[1]The best available guide to these various materials is J. K. Zawodny, *Guide to the Study of International Relations* (San Francisco: Chandler, 1966), available in paperback.

somewhat difficult to get used to, because of the shortened form of citations and indexing necessitated by their use of computers, they can prove very useful in a search for articles and books.

2. *Social Sciences and Humanities Index* (New York: H. W. Wilson Co., 1913 — under various names) indexes approximately 200 periodicals in permanent volumes issued every three years, annual volumes, and quarterly supplements.

3. *The Readers' Guide to Periodical Literature* (New York: H. W. Wilson Co., 1900 —) indexes some scholarly journals and many popular magazines in biannual permanent volumes, annual volumes, and semimonthly supplements. Because of its concentration on popular periodicals, this index is less likely to be helpful than the *Social Sciences and Humanities Index.*

4. The Public Affairs Information Service issues weekly bulletins listing current books, government documents, periodical articles, pamphlets, and so on, cumulates these five times a year and in annual volumes as the *Bulletin* of the PAIS.

5. The United States State Department Library publishes *International Politics: A Selective Monthly*, including some articles and book-length monographic studies. This publication was begun in 1956 and is distributed to some libraries.

6. *International Political Science Abstracts* (London: Blackwell, 1952 —), prepared by the International Political Science Association in cooperation with the International Committee for Social Sciences Documentation with the support of UNESCO, is published quarterly and contains abstracts in English or French selected from various periodicals.

Periodicals   Hundreds of periodicals will occasionally carry articles of interest to the student of international politics. The following list names those periodicals most directly concerned with the subject and hence most likely to prove worth an occasional examination. I have tried to characterize the content or orientation of each very briefly, hoping that these comments will enable a reader to identify those most likely to be relevant to his particular research. Because some of these periodicals will not be available at all libraries and others will be found to be worth subscribing to, I have included information on subscription costs and procedures as of 1968 for the most useful journals.

1. *American Journal of International Law,* published quarterly since 1907 by the American Society of International Law, is devoted entirely to rather legalistic discussions of international legal questions and accounts of recent developments.

2. *American Political Science Review,* published quarterly since 1906 by the American Political Science Association, is devoted to articles and book reviews on all aspects of political science including international politics. Subscriptions, which include membership in the association, are $15/year, or $6 for graduate or undergraduate students, from the APSA, 1527 New Hampshire Avenue N.W., Washington, D. C. 20036.

3. *Behavioral Science,* published bimonthly since 1957 by the Mental Health Research Institute at the University of Michigan, Ann Arbor, includes articles on general theories of behavior and on empirical research specifically oriented toward such theories. Interdisciplinary in its approach, it occasionally carries articles directly relevant to international political theory.

4. *Bulletin of the Atomic Scientists: A Journal of Science and Public Affairs,* published monthly since 1945, includes many articles dealing with problems of international relations and national security. Subscriptions are $7/year from 935 East 60th St., Chicago 60637.

5. *Foreign Affairs,* published quarterly since 1922 by the Council on Foreign Relations, contains interesting articles on world affairs and foreign politics, many by major public figures. Subscriptions are $8/year from 58 East 68th St. New York 10021.

6. *International Affairs,* published quarterly since 1922 in London by the Royal Institute of International Affairs, is the British counterpart of *Foreign Affairs.*

7. *International Affairs: A Monthly Journal of Political Analysis,* published monthly since 1955 in Moscow, is interesting because it reveals the Soviet view of world affairs and even on Western books, which it reviews.

8. *International Conciliation,* published 5 times a year and since 1907 by the Carnegie Endowment for International Peace. Each issue consists of a pamphlet devoted to a study of some particular problem or country, except for the special issue each fall devoted to issues before the United Nations General Assembly. Subscriptions are $2.75/year from 345 East 46th St., New York 10017.

9. *International Journal,* published quarterly since 1946 by the Canadian Institute of International Affairs, is the Canadian counterpart of *Foreign Affairs.*

10. *International Organization,* published quarterly since 1946 by the World Peace Foundation, includes primarily articles about the UN, alliances, and other international organizations, plus extensive regular reports on the activities of all significant international organizations. Subscriptions are $6/year from 40 Mt. Vernon St., Boston 02108.

11. *International Studies Quarterly,* published quarterly since 1957 (called *Background* until 1967) by the International Studies Association, contains articles on all aspects of international affairs. Subscriptions, which include membership in ISA, are $8/year, student rate $5/year, from the Graduate School of International Studies, University of Denver, Denver 80210.

12. *Journal of Conflict Resolution: A Quarterly for Research Related to War and Peace,* published by the Center for Research on Conflict Resolution, is a major journal, publishing "systematic research and thinking on international processes, including the total international system, the interactions among governments and among nationals in different states, and the processes by which nations make and execute their foreign policies." It also publishes results of "gaming" (in which small groups are studied to develop and test hypotheses about behavior) and book reviews. Subscriptions are $7/year from the University of Michigan, Ann Arbor 48104.

13. *Journal of International Affairs,* published semi-annually since 1947 by the Columbia University School of International Affairs, generally devotes each issue to a special topic within the field. Subscriptions are $2.75/year from Columbia University, New York 10027.

14. *Journal of Peace Research,* published quarterly since 1964 by the International Peace Research Institute of Oslo, is an interdisciplinary and international journal of scientific reports of peace research and international politics. Subscriptions in the U.S. are $5.00/year from Universitetsforlaget, P.O. Box 142, Boston 02113.

15. *Journal of Politics,* published quarterly since 1939 by the Southern Political Science Association, includes occasional articles on international politics. Subscriptions, which include membership in the SPSA, are $6/year, or $3/year for students, from

the Department of Political Science, University of Florida, Gainsville 32601.

16. *Midwest Journal of Political Science,* published quarterly since 1957 by the Midwest Political Science Association, occasionally contains articles on international politics. Subscriptions are $6/year from Wayne State University Press, 5980 Cass Avenue, Detroit 48202.

17. *Orbis: A Quarterly Journal of World Affairs,* published since 1957 by the Foreign Policy Research Institute of the University of Pennsylvania, contains many relevant articles on military and political matters. Subscriptions are $6/year from 133 South 36th St., Room 102, Philadelphia 19104.

18. *Political Science Quarterly,* published since 1886 by the Academy of Political Science, contains occasional articles on international politics. Subscriptions, including membership in the academy, are $10/year, or $6/year for students, from Columbia University, 413 Fayerweather Hall, New York 10027.

19. *Problems of Communism,* published bimonthly since 1952 by the United States Information Agency, includes useful articles on developments in the Communist countries and in their foreign relations. Although one must remember that this is a government journal, students will find it useful. Subscriptions are $2.50/year from the Superintendent of Documents, Government Printing Office, Washington, D.C.

20. *Review of Politics,* published quarterly since 1939 by the University of Notre Dame, Notre Dame, Indiana, occasionally includes articles on international affairs.

21. *Revue Française de Science Politique,* published quarterly in Paris since 1951, is the French counterpart of the APSR and includes occasional useful articles on international affairs.

22. *Western Political Quarterly,* published quarterly since 1948 by the Institute of Government at the University of Utah, occasionally includes useful articles. Subscriptions are $6/year from University of Utah, Salt Lake City 84112.

23. *World Politics: A Quarterly Journal of International Relations,* published since 1948 by the Princeton University Center of International Studies, is one of the several major journals on international and comparative politics, and is indispensable for scholars in the field. Subscriptions are $7.50/year from Princeton University Press, Princeton, N.J. 08540.

24. *The World Today,* published monthly by the Royal Institute of International Affairs since 1944, contains many useful
summary and analytical articles about international developments.
Subscriptions are $5.30/year, or $4.80 for students, from Oxford
University Press, Press Road, Neasden, London NW 10.

This list does not exhaust the relevant and often helpful
periodical literature. A number of journals — particularly *Daedalus* and the *Journal of Social Issues* — will occasionally devote
an entire issue to a topic of major concern to students of international relations. Of course, many other journals include occasional articles of interest, but these listed here are the major
journals. A quick perusal of a handful of them — including especially *World Politics* and the *Journal of Conflict Resolution* —
is an excellent way to determine what questions most occupy
major scholars today; and these journals are the source of many
articles that will merit study in conjunction with the reading
of this book and others in the field.

Such reading of the article literature in the field — in a good
collection of readings by all means, and in various current periodicals if at all possible — should constitute an important extension of education about international politics and should deepen
one's understanding of the basic questions and findings of the
discipline.

INDEXES

Author Index

Abel, Elie
  The Missile Crisis, 3n, 55n, 141, 147n,
    320
Abel, Theodore
  "The Element of Decision in the
    Pattern of War," 188, 188n
Anderson, H.
  (ed.) *Creativity and its Cultivation*,
    310n
Angell, Robert
  "Defense of What?" 323
Aron, Raymond
  Peace and War, 303n, 328
  "What Is a Theory of International
    Relations?" 303n
Ausubel, H.
  (ed.) *The Making of Modern Europe*,
    196n, 327

Banks, Arthur, and Robert Textor

A Cross-Polity Survey, 16n
Barnett, A. Doak
  Communist China and Asia, 223n
Barron, Frank
  Scientific Creativity, 310n
Bartlett, Charles, and Edward Weintal
  Facing the Brink, 55n, 320
Bawly, Dan, and David Kimche
  The Sandstorm, 147n
Bechhoefer, Bernhard
  *Postwar Negotiations for Arms Con-
    trol*, 237n, 239n
Bell, Daniel
  "Twelve Modes of Prediction," 293n,
    298n
Bentham, Jeremy
  Principles of Legislation, 8n
Berelson, Bernard, and Gary Steiner
  Human Behavior, 310n
Beveridge, W. I. B.

343

Subject Index

Because these maps are Mercator projections,
areas are distorted and appear progressively larger
the further the distance from the equator.